African Histories and Modernities

Series Editors
Toyin Falola, The University of Texas at Austin
Austin, USA

Matthew M. Heaton, Virginia Tech
Blacksburg, USA

This book series serves as a scholarly forum on African contributions to and negotiations of diverse modernities over time and space, with a particular emphasis on historical developments. Specifically, it aims to refute the hegemonic conception of a singular modernity, Western in origin, spreading out to encompass the globe over the last several decades. Indeed, rather than reinforcing conceptual boundaries or parameters, the series instead looks to receive and respond to changing perspectives on an important but inherently nebulous idea, deliberately creating a space in which multiple modernities can interact, overlap, and conflict. While privileging works that emphasize historical change over time, the series will also feature scholarship that blurs the lines between the historical and the contemporary, recognizing the ways in which our changing understandings of modernity in the present have the capacity to affect the way we think about African and global histories.

Zainab Monisola Olaitan

Women's Representation in African Politics

Beyond Numbers

Zainab Monisola Olaitan
Institute for Pan-African Thought
and Conversation (IPATC)
University of Johannesburg
Johannesburg, Gauteng, South Africa

ISSN 2634-5773   ISSN 2634-5781   (electronic)
African Histories and Modernities
ISBN 978-3-031-76050-1   ISBN 978-3-031-76051-8   (eBook)
https://doi.org/10.1007/978-3-031-76051-8

This Palgrave Macmillan imprint is published by the registered company Springer Nature Switzerland AG
The registered company address is: Gewerbestrasse 11, 6330 Cham, Switzerland

If disposing of this product, please recycle the paper.

I dedicate this work to my family for providing me with the environment to grow, dream and thrive into the Scholar that I am today.

Foreword

Toyin Falola, Jacob and Frances Sanger Mossiker Chair in the Humanities and University Distinguished Teaching Professor, the University of Texas, Austin, Texas

African history has always been built around the strength and versatility of African women, as well as facts and discovered realities that lay credence to this truth. Unfortunately, the place of women in determining the affairs of the African situation has been diminishing compared to even the precolonial experience. Many individuals and scholars have examined and engaged this subject, proposing different solutions, discoveries, and blueprints to allow for the incorporation of women into the political scheme of African societies. However, the progress in this regard seems like a pyrrhic victory.

This book is a needed voice in the era of women's emancipation in African politics and the acute dismissal of their legitimate contribution to the continent's development. The author re-ignites the subject of the quota system in achieving women's participation in African politics and the approaches to affording them favorable ground for the representation of Africans in political structures. She notes the current continental efforts in embracing the quota system referring to political parties' adjustment of their philosophies and structures to allow some minimum number of women in the parties' decision-making processes and chances to contest political offices.

It is apparent that African nations have been mindful of the political emancipation of women and, as such, have been adjusting their constitutions, laws, and other rules that initially undermine the extent of the influence of women on African nations and societies. The author discusses how gender quotas could be an opportunity for power redistribution across the continent. She has made an insightful analysis of how this would be relevant to the development of every nation.

I find the direction of the discussions in the book intriguing and material to the general concept of the quota system for women's participation with her well-grounded discussions on descriptive and substantive representation. The author elucidates the differences in women's representation, highlighting the misconceptions of a quota system that arise from a lack of understanding of the distinction between the two. While the former tends to provide a numeric increment of women's representation in African politics, the latter aims to increase women's influential representation. In my mind, the message is that the focus of the quota system is to increase traffic, increase the number of people, and increase the influence of women. These two are sine qua, and the anticipated success of embracing the quota system cannot be achieved.

It is understood that while there could be a seeming effort to increase the descriptive representation of women in African politics by adjusting the structures and institutional permissibility, the continent still stands at a disadvantage point in expanding the extent of contemporary political influence of women, either because of the resisting political misconception of those in power or improper alignment of political purposes. Hence, on the two fronts, the continent might be failing.

The above suggests a critical problem that has erupted from an obvious prominent problem while trying to find a solution. This means that while trying to solve the issue of the emancipation of women in African politics by adopting a quota system, the supposed inadequacy of enforced quota systems became apparent. This implies that the continent has gotten it wrong with the existing quota arrangement or its enforcement; however, the author has suggested approaches to resolve the issues.

With the use of the combination of thematic and phenomenological analysis of data elicited directed from persons with first experience in political representation and women in African politics, as well as the engagement of the interpretivism paradigm, the author tries to balance the underlying problems facing the success of quota system in the continent. The author interrogates the value of quota, analyses the possible issues, and suggests commendable solutions to resolve the problem.

One of the most outstanding research qualities is the intentional consideration of quantitative, qualitative, and raw data analysis to support its discoveries and conclusions on different subjects fundamentally. More importantly, the author considered case studies from other countries, considering contexts and conceptual particularities to reach some conference problems that could attract conference solutions from the discourses.

From the different case studies and the engagement of extant and available data, it has been made evident in the book that there is a misdirection of effort in incorporating women's participation. The continent must put more effort into ensuring substantive representation of women by allowing their efforts to be felt and better appreciated.

Another critical aspect of the book that I find essential for readers is the ability of the author to link the prevalence of gender-based violence to the question of the quota system and substantive representation. She explains how gender-based violence would make every nation adopting a quota system take two steps backward because of the damning effect of the phenomenon. She has successfully provided approaches to solving these arrays of challenges to adopting the systems and made recommendations worth consideration by leaders, stakeholders, and policymakers across Africa.

Austin, TX, USA   Toyin Falola

PRAISE FOR *WOMEN'S REPRESENTATION IN AFRICAN POLITICS*

"This book provides a timely contribution to the growing literature on gender dynamics of inclusive development. In the book, Olaitan explores the current state of women's representation in politics, the adoption of gender quotas in different African countries, the value of quotas beyond numbers and whether quotas can be a means to foster the qualitative representation of African women. This book is a must-read for the most experienced political analysts and development practitioners, including policymakers, academics, public-private stakeholders, and civil societies, amongst many others. It offers a thoroughly researched and nuanced take on the assessment of the impact of gender quotas on women's representation in African politics beyond numbers to underscore its relevance in protecting women's interests."

—Professor Tinuade Adekunbi Ojo, *University of Johannesburg*, Johannesburg, South Africa

"This book is a needed voice in the era of women's emancipation in African politics and the acute dismissal of their legitimate contribution to the continent's development. The author re-ignites the subject of the quota system in achieving women's participation in African politics and the approaches to affording them favorable ground for the representation of Africans in political structures. Another critical aspect of the book that I find essential for readers is the ability of the author to link the prevalence of gender-based violence to the question of the quota system and substantive representation. She has successfully provided approaches to solving

these arrays of challenges to adopting the systems and made recommendations worth consideration by leaders, stakeholders, and policymakers
across Africa."
                —Professor Toyin Falola, Jacob and Frances Sanger Mossiker
            Chair in the Humanities and University Distinguished Teaching
                 Professor, the *University of Texas*, Austin, Texas

"The book offers a comprehensive understanding of how quotas aid wom-
en's representation in African politics. The analysis on women parliamentarians is very detailed and it helps us to understand the perception of
women parliamentarians and how they perform their duties in a system
that fundamentally excludes them. I highly recommend this book to anyone interested in quotas, women's representation in African politics and
why the participation of women in politics is important for protecting women."
                          —Yanga Malotana, Project Manager:
                   Future Democracies, Emerging Scholars Initiative,
                 University of Pretoria, Pretoria, South Africa

PREFACE

As a young woman, I have always pondered about how the presence of women in politics positively or negatively affects my life and that of other women. And how women's political participation can be an instrument towards the protection of women's rights and bridging the gender gap in our society.

This book is a modern take on an old debate concerning the relevance of gender quotas beyond numbers as many scholars consider the discourse around the relevance of gender quotas closed or old. However, can we really declare the debate old/closed when more than 50 countries are yet to institute measures to ensure that women are adequately represented in the political system? Moreso, the global average for women's representation in politics is not up to 40%, not to talk of the gender parity aspiration that international women's movements, feminist scholars and activists had. In Africa, the average for women's representation is 26%, still less than 30%, which is quite concerning. For instance, countries such as Nigeria, Ghana, Botswana, Sudan, Eritrea and many more have less than 20% of women in politics. Thereby consolidating the need to continually interrogate the adoption of quotas and how they are being used towards the protection of women's rights and interests. Also, necessitating the move beyond the theoretical debate on quotas to a practical and contextual discussion.

Furthermore, in engaging with the extensive theoretical debate on gender quotas, I noticed a significant gap in this discussion around how useful quotas are/have been in increasing the representation of women in African politics from the perspectives of women parliamentarians and women in general. This gap is one I set out to fill by engaging women parliamentarians, women working in civil society organisations on how they understand the necessity and usefulness of quotas in the current political climate of Africa. Hence, this book allows for the synergy between the debate on gender quotas and the relevance of quotas in the post 1990s/2000s period. It is a phenomenological work that centers the perceptions of women—who are often the subject and beneficiaries of gender quotas. By prioritising women parliamentarians who are beneficiaries of quotas and women working in civil society organisation as its research participants, the book shifts the framing of the debate from scholars to practitioners and women. It regards their voice and perspectives as central to the interrogation of the relevance of gender quotas beyond numbers.

In the course of my interviews with women parliamentarians in South Africa and Botswana, I had the opportunity to witness how they grappled with quotas within the broader system, how they perceive their influence on policies and legislations, and how they see themselves as agents of change towards the reduction of gender-based violence and femicide. Their responses to my questions allowed me to reframe my pre-conceived notion about the workings of the parliament and the impact of women parliamentarians.

I hope that by engaging with the book readers can understand women parliamentarians, their influence on gender-focused policies/legislations and the corresponding impact on women. And also that it can spark another conversation on the need to adopt a multi-intersectional approach towards the substantive representation of women rather than fixating on women politicians to address systemic discrimination against women within the African political system. The goal of fostering the substantive representation of women needs to include the dismantling of all oppressive systems of power that subjugate women at the intersection of race, class, gender, age and sexuality. By adopting a multi-intersectional approach towards the protection of women's rights and interests, we are able to foster a system that thrives on gender equality.

Johannesburg, South Africa   Zainab Monisola Olaitan

ACKNOWLEDGEMENTS

First, I appreciate the women parliamentarians and policymakers interviewed for this work. Your honest and insightful responses formed the foundation for this work's groundbreaking contribution to knowledge. I am also thankful to women working in different civil society organisations in Botswana and South Africa, as your invaluable contribution and responses consolidated the overall research.

I appreciate Prof. Toyin Falola for seeing potential in this work and also graciously agreeing to write the foreword for this book. Your contribution to the academic community is forever appreciated. I thank the editorial team at Springer for their invaluable effort in improving the book.

I am grateful to Prof. Christopher Isike whose guidance for the initial research that this book is based on helped culminate it into a good body of work.

I thank my family for being my constant drive for success and excellence. And to my friends with their unwavering belief in me and my abilities, I say thank you.

Finally, I thank myself for daring to dream, daring to achieve and personifying the saying that 'the sky is just the beginning'. Thank you and well done Zainab Monisola Olaitan.

CONTENTS

ABOUT THE AUTHOR

Zainab Monisola Olaitan is a Political Scientist working at the intersection of political philosophy, feminist thought and African politics with a focus on women's qualitative representation. She is a Research Fellow at the Institute for Pan-African Thought and Conversation, University of Johannesburg. She holds a PhD in Political Science from the University of Pretoria where she interrogated the impact of gender quotas on the substantive representation of African women. In 2022, she was awarded the Margaret McNamara Education Grant for her impactful research work on women and children. Dr. Zainab completed her MA degree in Political Science as a 2019 Mastercard Foundation Scholar at the University of Pretoria. She obtained her second degree in Philosophy, Politics and Economics Honors as a 2018 Mandela Rhodes Scholar at the University of Cape Town. In 2016, she completed her first degree in Political Science from the University of Lagos as the best graduating student in her department. Her research focuses on locating women across different sectors with a central question, how are women represented in Africa? She is deeply interested in understanding the impact of women's political participation on the qualitative well-being of African women. She has published widely in journals, book projects and policy briefs on themes bordering on feminist thought, gender and representation; African indigenous knowledge systems; and conflict and peace studies. She is a member of the African Association of Political Science (AAPS), the African Indigenous Knowledge Research Network (AIKRN) and the Lagos Studies Association (LSA).

Abbreviations and Acronyms

ACDP	African Christian Democratic Party
ANC	African National Congress
AU	African Union
BCP	Botswana Congress Party
BDP	Botswana Democratic Party
BNF	Botswana National Front
BPfA	Beijing Platform for Action
CEDAW	Convention on the Elimination of All Forms of Discrimination Against Women
CSO	Civil Society Organisations
DA	Democratic Alliance
ECOSOC	Economic and Social Council
EFF	Economic Freedom Fighters
FPTP	First-past-the-post
GBV	Gender-based violence
GBVF	Gender-based violence and femicide
IDEA	Institute for Democracy & Electoral Assistance
IFP	Inkatha Freedom Party
IPA	Interpretative phenomenological analysis
IPU	Inter-Parliamentary Union
MMP	Mixed Member Proportional
MP	Member of Parliament
NGO	Non-governmental organisations
PR	Proportional representation
SADC	Southern African Development Community
SONA	State of the Nation Address
UN	United Nations

LIST OF FIGURES

List of Tables

CHAPTER 1

Introduction

We are writing
for our mothers' mothers
and
their mothers
we are writing
for our daughters
and
the daughters of our daughters
we are writing
for our ancestors
and
generations to come.

−*Ijeoma Umebinyuo (2016)*

The book interrogates the impact of gender quotas on women's representation in African politics beyond numbers in order to underscore its relevance for protecting women's interests. I explore the current state of women's representation in politics, the adoption of gender quotas in different African countries, the value of quotas beyond numbers, and whether quotas can be a means to foster the qualitative representation of African women. The book also examines the limitations that can hinder the potential of quotas to increase women's representation in politics and protect women's interests with corresponding suggestions on how we can improve the political representation of African women. In addressing these issues, I argue that quotas are an important instrument for ensuring both the quantitative and qualitative representation of women in African politics. However, there has been too much focus on the numerical effect of quotas which creates an ignorance on the potential benefit that quotas can have for ensuring the substantive representation of women. I argue that countries that adopt gender quotas use it only as far as increasing women's numerical participation in politics rather than how quotas can help ensure the protection and representation of women's interests. I note that rather than see the numbers that quotas create as an end in themselves, they should be seen as a means to an end. The myopic use of quotas in African politics has yielded half-baked results for women's representation, while some countries are seeing increase in the number of women participating in politics, there is no correlative gain for the general women populace.

The book is centred around concepts such as women's representation in politics, gender quotas, impact, descriptive representation, and substantive representation. These concepts enable the book to interrogate the relationship between numbers and impact regarding women's representation in politics. Also, the book adopts gender-based violence and femicide (GBVF) as indices to operationalise what it means by impact of women's representation in politics. It uses GBVF to address the question of how we measure impact of women's participation in politics, specifically using legislations and policies that have been passed to address GBVF to guide the book's framing of impact or substantive representation of women. This operationalisation helps us to specify impact considering the contestation in literature on what constitutes women's interests. Hence, concepts on representation, quotas, numbers, and impact guide the book's interrogation into the numbers–impact dilemma.

This book primarily engages the assumption that women's increased participation in politics will automatically ensure the protection of women's interests. This assumption forms the basis for the analysis that this book embarks on, it problematises this claim using a tripartite method, it employs literature, theories, and data findings to investigate the validity of this assumption. The book uses South Africa and Botswana as cases to contextualise its interrogation into the value of quotas for women's representation in politics. These countries provide good background for the work, as they represent two sides of a coin; South Africa has a very high presence of women in its parliament at 45%[1] and Botswana has 11% of its legislative seats occupied by women, tilting towards low presence of women. Both countries have adopted some form of gender quotas to increase women's representation in politics; these create grounds for this book to base its examination on whether numbers are necessary to create impact.

Context

The widespread adoption of gender quotas to mainstream women into politics is one of the most significant "political developments of the modern era" (O'Brien and Rickne 2016: 112). This is because enhancing women's increased representation in politics is a top priority for governments and international feminist movements (Mansbridge 2005). Dahlerup (2006) notes that while political parties in some countries adopted gender quotas on their own, many countries embarked on constitutional amendments as well as the passing of new electoral laws that motivated for women to make up a specified proportion of candidates for election in the national parliament. Krook (2006: 113) attests that either as part of their mandate or in reaction to external pressure, political parties have enforced quotas to facilitate women's participation in their national parliament. Dahlerup and Freidenvall (2005) argue that this sudden and widespread implementation of gender quotas has been labelled the 'fast track' to balanced gender participation in politics. Schwindt-Bayer (2007: 289) adds that the adoption of gender quotas "raises both normative and empirical questions", such as whether quotas are needed, the rationale for their adoption, and their effectiveness around the world. Works have also been written on the effectiveness of gender quotas in facilitating women's parliamentary participation in the Global South. Indeed, quotas have been instrumental in mainstreaming women into politics globally, and Africa has not been left behind, even though the situation is not the same across the continent because some countries do not have a quota system in place (International Institute for Democracy and Electoral Assistance [IDEA]

---

[1] Although South Africa conducted an election in 2024 which established a new percentage for women in its national parliament at 45.04%, the scope of the book uses the 2019 election percentage of 46.5%. This is because the percentage of female MPs in the new parliament cannot be used to measure the effectiveness of quotas as it is yet to commence its parliamentary proceedings resulting in legislative and policy outcomes as at the writing of this book.

2021). This provides justifiable ground to state that in recent years, gender quotas have gained prominence as a widely accepted mechanism to correct the low participation of women in politics (Krook 2006: 110).

Gender quotas should, in theory, redistribute power and acknowledge that the underrepresentation of women is a concern for democracy. However, researchers and feminist movements have been critical of the implementation of quotas in Africa because all too often actual political strategies are condensed into a single demand for gender quotas. This stems from the misconception that a singular mechanism is required to substantiate the ability of women to influence national and political agendas on the continent. This misconception is responsible for the swift adoption of gender quotas in Africa, and as a result, there has been widespread adoption of different types of quotas on the continent. Dahlerup (2006) notes that South Africa, following its first democratic elections in 1994, is one of the first countries in Africa to adopt the voluntary party quotas. Although, Uganda implemented reserved seats as far back as 1986, which other countries such as Sudan, Djibouti, Somalia, and Eritrea have since adopted.

In exploring the effectiveness of quotas as a pathway to increasing women's presence in legislatures, scholars such as Paxton et al. (2010), Jones (2009), Krook (2009) note that there is an increasing interest in their broader consequences beyond ensuring descriptive women's representation. Mansbridge (2005: 622) argues that quotas guarantee women's descriptive representation because "descriptive representation is important and necessary for the protection of the interests of descriptively represented groups in the society". The focus on this relationship stems from the assumption that by virtue of gender quotas facilitating women's increased participation in politics, their inclusion in the political sphere will translate to better living conditions for women, which means that women's political participation is expected to result in putting women's issues on the decision-making table and change for the better (Childs and Krook 2009). These assumptions are a function of the equation that numbers equal impact. In this case, it means that descriptive women's representation necessarily leads to substantive women's representation. This is not to argue that quotas have not been helpful in ensuring some form of representation for women, but that there is a need to look beyond quantity to quality. There is a need to interrogate the relevance of quotas not just as a means to ensure women's descriptive representation in politics but also how it enables the substantive representation of women in Africa.

Gender quotas have been seen as the golden ticket to ensure women are represented in the political space, and more than 100 countries have already implemented them. Dahlerup (2006) substantiates this by asserting that the adoption of gender quotas represents a significant shift towards a precise strategy with ends and means. The potential for an increase in women's representation is heightened when quotas are used. With this strong faith in the efficiency of quotas to ensure women's political participation, the questions become to what extent can quotas ensure representation of women and whether it is only by increasing the number of women in politics or does it also foster a better quality of life for the general women populace. Schwindt-Bayer (2009) argues that while quotas effectively increase women's numeric representation, the longer impact of quotas, particularly if they influence the operations of institutions, are still up for debate.

The debates over the relevance of quotas have resulted in gender quotas being "perhaps the most radical and intensely debated reform in the area of gender equality" (Zetterberg 2009: 715). Some proponents argue that the general objective of quotas, which is to enhance women's political participation, has been achieved, and others contend that for quotas to be effective, they must transform institutionalised gender roles and guarantee that the interests of women are represented (Clayton and Zetterberg 2018; Nugent and Krook 2016). The reliance on gender quotas to facilitate descriptive women's representation often leads to studies overlooking the impact that the presence of women in politics has for women's substantive representation.

Hence, the discourse around the success of quotas needs to progress beyond how many women are in political office to how it benefits the lives of women. The assumption that once women get into politics, the lives of the general women populace will be better off is a slippery slope that needs to be addressed, not just to confirm or debunk it but also to avoid the easy way out for political leaders in addressing women-related issues. This need raises a fundamental challenge of how quotas help better the lives of women beyond ensuring women take up space in politics. While extensive studies have been carried out in different parts of the world to address this, Africa has not benefitted much from it, which is why it is important to interrogate the relevance of quotas specifically within the African context. Secondly, there is a dearth of studies that focus on legislative and policy issues to measure the effectiveness of quotas in engendering the substantive representation of women in politics.

Therefore, this book interrogates the utility of gender quotas to ensure the substantive representation of women in African politics. This gives rise to a few questions that must be answered. The first question is: what is the relationship between the numbers and impact in women's political representation in Africa? This question cast spotlight on the data about growing numbers of women in political institutions especially the parliament, forcing us to wonder if these numbers translate into impact in the form of stronger voice by women, inclusion of women's concerns, a change in the culture of politics to accommodate diversity in gender, etc. The second question is whether gender quotas have relevance beyond being a pathway for mainstreaming women into politics. This question examines if quotas can ensure the representation of women beyond numbers. The third question is how do gender quotas impact policy and legislative outcomes on GBVF in Botswana and South Africa? While the final question asks what alternative pathways are there to ensure the substantive political representation of women in Botswana, South Africa, and Africa in general? These questions guide the interrogation and analysis that this book embarks on in its bid to understand women's representation in African politics beyond numbers.

APPROACH

Using a qualitative approach of enquiry, this book combines a phenomenological analysis and a thematic analysis to gain insight into the opinions, perceptions, and experiences of participants on how they understand the impact of women's representation in African politics. The use of a qualitative approach is primarily justified by the recognition that truth, meanings, and knowledge are not only unique to the researcher but also are relative and socially created; hence, the book centres the perception of the participants in its quest to explore the relevance of gender quotas beyond numbers. The book succinctly captures the interpretivist paradigm as the perceptions and experiences of the participants are crucial to the interrogation it embarks on. More so, the construction of reality based on the experiences and opinions of the women in the parliament and women working in civil society organisations rest on the interpretation done by the researcher, thereby lending credence to the understanding of what the interpretivist paradigm is about. By conducting key informant interviews, the book focuses on how the participants understand their social reality, mostly their perception of impact of women's representation in politics further embodying an interpretivist paradigm. The interpretivist world-view is aware that each person's reality is created by the meaning they give to their experiences. Salkind (2012) asserts that research based on this paradigm collects information that can be used to define meaning in the participants' worlds through qualitative approaches like interviews.

The book adopts a multiple case study design, i.e., Botswana and South Africa to contextualise its interrogation into the numbers and impact argument. Ritchie and Lewis (2003) argues that a case study design enables the generalisation of numerous perspectives either through the collection of different data sets or the creation of multiple accounts from a single method (cited in Gray 2014). Yin (2015: 4) explains that "case study research is an empirical inquiry that investigates a contemporary phenomenon in depth and within its real-life context especially when the boundaries between the context are not clearly evident". The intended conclusion for a case study design can be either illustrative or confirmative, considering that this book intends to understand if there is indeed a relationship between numbers and impact, the adopted design allows it to either confirm or debunk the relationship. The selection of Botswana and South Africa as cases for the book is predicated on the need for nuanced and contrasting contexts to allow for understanding the book's central questions, the uniqueness of South Africa and Botswana with regard to women's representation, and finally the drive for a significant contribution to knowledge through the careful generalisation that a multiple case study provides.

The book's extensive source of data collection draws from semi-structured key informant interviews conducted in both Botswana and South Africa and legislative/policy outcomes on GBVF in both countries: 43 participants were interviewed in all; 36 female members of the parliament in South Africa, 3 female members of the parliament in Botswana and 4 women working in civil society organisation that focus on GBVF across the two cases. The interviews were conducted to understand the relevance of gender quotas in ensuring the protection of women's interests, i.e., reduction of GBVF. Specifically, the perspectives of female MPs, women in CSOs were gathered to understand how participants perceive impact and if quotas can be used for women's representation in politics beyond numbers. Also, different legislative and policy outcomes that have been passed on GBVF in Botswana and South Africa within a 12-year period (2010–2022) were collected. These legislations were used to trace the impact female MPs have on the legislative process by investigating how the number of women in the parliament translates to the number of gender-focused bills. It interrogated whether the presence of women in the parliament means there are more legislative and policy outcomes passed to address GBVF. The methods of analysis used in the book were interpretative phenomenological analysis (IPA) and thematic analysis. Firstly, IPA was used to analyse the findings from the interviews to allow for an in-depth and focused understanding of the research questions from the experience and opinions of the participants. IPA as a method of analysis enables in-depth examination into the lived experiences and perceptions of women who are in politics and those who are not to understand whether gender quotas impact the substantive representation of women. This method of analysis identified emergent themes from the responses of the participants and these emergent themes formed the sub-ordinate themes. The frequency of a particular emergent theme made it suitable to be a sub-ordinate theme and the closely related sub-ordinate themes were matched to the corresponding super-ordinate themes. The super-ordinate themes were used to frame the analysis of the interview data while the sub-ordinate themes served as the unit of responses. The researcher used quotes from the participants' responses to provide in-depth insight into specific super-ordinate theme under discussion. Thematic analysis was used to organise the different legislations that have been passed on GBVF. In generating themes from these legislations, the document review method was used to identify GBVF-targeted measures. The themes generated from the data set were used to provide an overview of the selected GBVF laws and policies in the two case studies in order to discuss the outcomes these legislations and policies on GBVF seek to achieve. This aspect of the analysis was important as it gave a holistic overview of how the presence of women in the parliaments translates to the passing of GBVF legislations and policies that protect women.

In theorising women's representation in politics, the book uses two theories, namely the theory of the politics of presence and the relational feminist theory to guide its analysis. The theory of politics of presence and relational feminism seek to explain the need for women's participation in the political system and the impact of women's representation in politics. The theory of politics of presence is an important democratic lens through which to understand the symbolism of women representing women in democracy, and relational feminism justifies the notion that only women can adequately represent women.

Different contexts were discussed in the book and it engaged the concept of representation based on the need to understand the role that representatives embody. The debate on the role that representatives embody is divided into delegates and trustees, the book delves into this debate to analyse the extent to which MPs can act or represent. It also examined the state of women's participation in politics with most countries having less than 30% women's representation in the political system. Based on this background, the book examines the concepts of descriptive representation and substantive representation to encapsulate the need to ensure women's representation both in numbers and in substance. The adoption of gender quotas and the different forms were engaged to trace the genesis of gender quotas a mainstreaming tool for women in politics. The book interrogates the value of quotas beyond numbers focusing on the debate between critical mass thesis and critical acts thesis as a means to foster substantive women's representation. It recognises that quotas enable women's representation in politics to reach a critical mass of 30% and beyond, this critical mass can be weaponised to foster the qualitative representation of women. The book combines both critical mass and critical acts focusing on the power of numbers and the intentionality of actions as a strategy to ensure the protection and representation of women's Africa. The book traces the implementation of gender quotas in Africa to spotlight African countries that have adopted some form of quotas to engender women's representation in politics. It situates the numbers and impact dilemma within the African context to understand how this phenomenon has been understood. The book analyses the impact of women's representation in African politics beyond numbers using data findings, literature sources, and theories. Finally, it recommends alternative pathways to improving women's representation in Africa focusing on how best to foster the qualitative representation of women.

STRUCTURE

The book has 9 chapters with each chapter contributing to the central aim. This first chapter introduces the book's rationale on interrogating women's representation in African politics beyond numbers and it lays the foundations and motivation for the book.

Chapter 2, Women's Political Representation and Its Different Forms, examines the discourse on representation, particularly the dichotomy between representatives as trustees or delegates. This dilemma needs to be unravelled to clarify the role that representatives play. It also identifies and explains the four different forms of representation: descriptive, substantive, symbolic, and formal representation. This chapter starts by establishing the current context on women's underrepresentation in politics. It examines the concept of representation and the different forms of representation to capture the means through which women's underrepresentation in politics can be addressed. Importantly, it delves into the debate on trustee-delegate, examining if representatives are mere delegates or trustees, i.e., do representatives just mirror the interests of their constituents or can they make decisions on behalf of their constituents? This debate is important to the book as it establishes the mandate of political representatives and the extent to which they can exercise that mandate. The essence of this chapter is to provide a background on the two forms of representation that the book focuses on, which are descriptive and substantive, and the relationship between them.

Chapter 3, Gender Quotas and Descriptive Women's Representation: Global and Continental Context, traces the adoption of gender quotas with an extensive understanding of gender quotas and its role in increasing women's descriptive representation. This chapter explains that the adoption of gender quotas has led to the increased participation of women in politics. It notes that the success of quotas depends on the type of electoral system coupled with the type of quota used within that system. It provides a continental context to the discourse on gender quotas and substantive representation of women. The chapter looks at the trend of quota adoption in Africa since the 1995 Beijing Platform for Action (BPfA) women's conference and the signing of the Convention on the Elimination of All forms of Discrimination Against Women (CEDAW), both of which tied increased participation of women to gender equality. This chapter also focuses on the issues and challenges surrounding quota adoption in Africa. It discusses women's political representation to highlight how the low participation of women in global politics created a shift that fostered increased attention on practical instruments to enhance their participation in Africa. This chapter situates the numbers and impact debate within the African context to lay a foundation for answering the first research question. The need to understand the relationship between numbers and impact provided impetus for this effort.

Chapter 4, Theorising the impact of women's political representation establishes the theoretical foundations for understanding the impact of women's representation in Africa. The theory of the politics of presence and relational feminism are critical lenses to understand how the presence of women in politics can foster the protection of women's interests. The first section of the chapter discusses the theory of the politics of presence in the form of a review of Anne Phillips's (1995) book *The Politics of Presence*, the justification for the theory and why it is relevant to the subject of women's representation in politics. The second section discusses relational feminism, its central tenets, justification for women's representation in politics. This section features a critique of the theory as relational feminism includes elements of homogenisation and essentialisation of women which are problematic for advancing gender equality. Finally, this chapter explains why both theories are relevant to the book and how they can be applied analysing women's representation in politics.

Chapter 5, Substantive Women's Representation in Africa: Issues and Debates, interrogates the discourse on substantive women's representation. This chapter examines the extent to which quotas can enable impact beyond the number of women participating in the political system. The chapter features an examination of the value of quotas beyond numbers to create an impact as well as the discourse on how best to ensure the substantive representation of women. This examination features a further discussion on the debate between critical mass and critical acts. It is important for this chapter to examine the ongoing discourse on substantive women's representation as well as the critical mass vs critical acts debate in a bid to assess the relevance of gender quotas beyond numbers. Specifically, it establishes the ground for analysing both the quantitative and qualitative impact that gender quotas has on substantive women's representation in African politics.

Chapter 6, Women's Political Representation in South Africa and Botswana, contextualises the subject of women's political representation within the two cases. It traces the adoption of quotas in both countries as well as general effort to increase women's participation in politics. The chapter embarks on country-specific discussion on women's representation in politics, adoption of quotas, efforts that were made to increase women's political participation, the types of quotas adopted and the current state of women's political representation in both countries.

Chapter 7, Understanding Gender-Based Violence in South Africa and Botswana, delves into the prevalence of gender-based violence and femicide in both cases as a precursor to operationalising it as indices to measure impact. The chapter starts by conceptualising gender-based violence due to its multiplex nature. The book adopts the 1993 definition of violence against women provided by the United Nations as it better captures the multiplex nature of the concept. This chapter highlights the drivers of gender-based violence and femicide to better understand its prevalence in Africa. Drawing from this, it establishes the extent to which GBVF has eaten deep into both cases showing relevant statistics. Secondly, this chapter identifies different legislations and policies on GBVF that have been passed in Botswana and South Africa. It also presents the aim of the identified legislations with an overview on what they sought to do and how they address GBVF. The overview on legislations/policies enables the book to confirm the data findings on whether the presence of women in the parliament translates to increased legislations/policies that address GBVF.

Chapter 8, The Impact of Gender Quotas on Substantive Women's Representation in Botswana and South Africa, is central to the book as it uses data findings to answer research questions and address the research aim. This chapter is divided into two parts: the first part analyses the responses of participants in line with the research objectives according to participant groups (female MPs in South Africa, female MPs in Botswana, and women working in CSOs). The section presents the research findings to address the objectives of the study; the objectives are to investigate whether there is a relationship between numbers and impact, to re-examine the relevance of quotas beyond being a pathway for mainstreaming women into politics, to measure the effectiveness of gender quotas in enabling women's substantive representation using GBVF, and to recommend alternative pathways to ensure substantive women's representation. The second part discusses and analyses the data findings to address the research questions. It examines how the research process has addressed the research questions with reference points to literature on women's representation in politics, and the data findings. The section answers the central questions. The questions are answered on a country basis for female MPs as their perspective is crucial to the research, and that of women in CSOs is done as a collective group. This highlights the responses of participants to allow for country-specific answering of the research questions. This section also uses the findings from the legislative and policy outcomes to confirm the impact female MPs have made on GBVF. A brief comparison between South Africa and Botswana is made to identify the differences and similarities in how gender quotas impact on policy and legislative outcomes on GBVF.

In Chap. 9, I present a general conclusion for the book, a perspective on findings and recommendations. The chapter revisits the rationale for the book and the guiding questions that underpin its analysis in order to establish whether the answers are adequate. The chapter identifies relevant recommendations on addressing the prevalence of GBVF and it also proposes further work that must be done to adequately respond to the gaps in public discourse and intellectual discussions that this book sought to plug.

SIGNIFICANCE

The significance of this book lies in its interrogation of women's representation in African politics beyond numbers into how they can be better represented. Its investigation on the impact of gender quotas on the substantive representation of women in African politics allows for readers to understand the relevance of women's participation in politics. Moreso, considering that the use of quotas in Africa has been limited to the numerical inclusion of women in politics without investigating the impact their inclusion has on the general African women populace, this book becomes a vital source. It is necessary that quotas are investigated beyond their primary task of ensuring numbers to see whether they are a means to engendering substantive representation. Also, the book provides a deep understanding on the different forms of representation particularly the relationship between descriptive women's representation (numbers) and substantive women's representation (impact). This will enable readers to understand the relevance of these forms of representation for protecting women's interests in Africa. Most books on women's representation in politics focus on increasing women's numeric participation, or factors that inhibit their participation, the uniqueness of this book lies in its investigation of women's representation as a holistic phenomenon that encompasses both their numeric representation in political institutions and substantive representation manifesting in how their interests are represented.

REFERENCES

Childs, S., and M.L. Krook. 2009. Analysing women's substantive representation: From critical mass to critical actors. *Government and Opposition* 44 (2): 125–145.

Clayton, A., and P. Zetterberg. 2018. Quota shocks: The budgetary implications of electoral gender quotas worldwide. *Journal of Politics* 80 (3): 916–932.

Dahlerup, D. 2006. *Women, quotas and politics*. London: Routledge.

Dahlerup, D., and L. Freidenvall. 2005. Quotas as a 'fast track' to equal political representation for women: Why Scandinavia is no longer the model. *International Feminist Journal of Politics* 7 (1): 26–48.

Gray, D. 2014. *Doing research in the real world*. Sage Publications.

International Institute for Democracy & Electoral Assistance. 2021. *Global database of quotas for women*. Stockholm University and the Inter-Parliamentary Union. https://www.idea.int/data-tools/data/gender-quotas.

Jones, M.P. 2009. Gender quotas, electoral laws, and the election of women evidence from the Latin American vanguard. *Comparative Political Studies* 42 (1): 56–81.

Krook, M.L. 2006. Reforming representation: The diffusion of candidate gender quotas worldwide. *Politics & Gender* 2: 303–327.

———. 2009. *Quotas for women in politics: Gender and candidate selection reform worldwide*. New York: Oxford University Press.

Mansbridge, J. 2005. Quota problems: Combating the dangers of essentialism. *Politics & Gender* 4: 622–638.

Nugent, M.K., and M.L. Krook. 2016. All-women shortlists: Myths and realities. *Parliamentary Affairs* 69 (1): 115–135.

O'Brien, D., and J. Rickne. 2016. Gender quotas and women's political leadership. *American Political Science Review* 110 (1): 112–116.

Paxton, P., M. Hughes, and A. Painter. 2010. Growth in women's political representation: A longitudinal exploration of democracy, electoral system and gender quotas. *European Journal of Political Research* 49 (1): 25–52.

Ritchie, J., and J. Lewis, eds. 2003. *Qualitative research practice: A guide for social science students and researchers*. London: Sage Publications.

Salkind, N.J. 2012. *Exploring research*. Pearson: Pearson Education.

Schwindt-Bayer, L.A. 2007. Review of women, quotas and politics. *Politics & Gender* 3 (2): 289–291.

———. 2009. Making quotas work: The effect of gender quota laws on the election of women. *Legislative Studies Quarterly* 34 (1): 5–28.

Umebinyuo, J. 2016. *Questions for Ada*. California: CreateSpace Independent Publishing Platform (CPSIA).

Yin, R. 2015. *Qualitative research from start to finish*. New York: Guilford Publications.

Zetterberg, P. 2009. Do gender quotas foster women's political engagement? Lessons from Latin America. *Political Research Quarterly* 62 (4): 715–730.

CHAPTER 2

Women's Political Representation and Its Different Forms

There's really no such thing as the 'voiceless'. There are only the deliberately silenced or the preferably unheard.

–Arundhati Roy (2004)

INTRODUCTION

Paxton and Kunovich (2003) assert that women's representation in the political system politics has not improved much, despite advancement made by the feminist movement on education, suffrage, etc. Olaitan (2024a) expands that the representation of women in politics is still low considering that BPfA called for increased women's participation in politics in 1995. Paxton (1997) asserts that a persisting problem with gender stratification is the underrepresentation of women in political institutions worldwide. Scholars highlight three justifications often given for the slow progress in women's political representation; they are social-structural, political and ideological (Kenworthy and Malami 1999; Reynolds 1999). Political explanations emphasise how accessible the political system is to women, while social-structural explanations concentrate on the pool of eligible women, and ideological explanations emphasise the public perceptions of women in politics and their viability as candidates and leaders. Randall (1987) and Norris (1997) affirm the social cultural explanation for low representation of women in political institutions; they argue that the underrepresentation of women in politics is believed to be caused by

© The Editor(s) (if applicable) and The Author(s), under exclusive license to Springer Nature Switzerland AG 2024
Z. M. Olaitan, *Women's Representation in African Politics*,
African Histories and Modernities,
https://doi.org/10.1007/978-3-031-76051-8_2

two factors: the supply of female candidates and the demand for female candidates. Paxton and Kunovich (2003) argue that structural factors dictate supply, given that political elites are disproportionately drawn from highly educated classes and specific professions. Consequently, if women lack access to educational and professional opportunities, they will lack the financial and human resources necessary to run for public office. This explanation posits that women's educational and professional level affect their representation or underrepresentation in politics.

The low representation of women in political institutions across different countries spurred women's organisations to consolidate their advocacy for the mainstreaming of women in politics. Paxton et al. (2006) report that while different institutions were used to advance the cause for increasing women's political representation, given the primacy of the United Nations as the apex intergovernmental organisation, women's organisations targeted it as a place to advocate for gender equality in the political system. According to Paxton et al. (2006), the UN was under pressure from the global women's movement to address issues pertaining to women, including their involvement in politics. Over time, as the UN and other global cultural institutions grew, so did the international women's movement. Increased pressure and influence were exerted on states by international actors to improve women's political representation. Towns (2004) notes that to achieve their aim, international actors and women's movement framed women's political representation as synonymous to modernity, which entails expectations of financial rewards in addition to enhanced global standing. Due to this framing and the emergence of a transnational actors and network of international organisations, states have come under increasing pressure to include women in politics throughout time (Meyer et al. 1997; Ramirez et al. 1997). This pressure focused on increasing the number of women in political institutions as a means to improve women's political representation.

The attention to women's representation in politics nonetheless does not acknowledge the different forms that representation takes, mostly because advocacy for women's inclusion in politics focused on increasing their numbers rather than ensuring holistic representation (Olaitan 2023). The need for holistic representation requires the understanding of representation as a concept and its different manifestations. Phillips (1995) asserts that representation has different dimensions; however, most feminist work focus largely on descriptive representation and the ways in which it can foster substantive representation. This dichotomy between descriptive and substantive representation embodies several themes on the link between the numbers and impact, the role that representatives perform and the extent to which they can represent or speak for the represented. Saward (2006) advocates for the shift from one aspect of representation to a rounded understanding in terms of representative claims, the impact of representatives, and the symbolism of their representation. Furthermore, feminists have utilised differing insights in their conceptualisation of women's political representation; these insights address the legislative behaviour of women, emphasising the connections between women's policy outcomes and their numerical participation (Celis et al. 2008). Without delving deeply into the factual or theoretical plausibility of this link, studies on women's representation prefer to focus on the surface, without discussing the possibility of women politicians acting for, speaking for and representing women.

The understanding of women's political representation and its different forms in this book is predicated on: (1) the need to establish the current context around women's underrepresentation in politics as a background to argue for increased participation of women in the political system and (2) examining the concept of representation and the different forms of political representation. The basis of research around how women can be represented in the political system stems from the acknowledgement that women are largely excluded from the system. Following this acknowledgement, democratic theorists and feminist theorists have delved into the discourse of representation and the different forms individuals or groups can be represented in within the system. Hence, this chapter starts by establishing the current context on women's underrepresentation in politics. It proceeds to examining the concept of representation and the different forms of representation to capture the means through which women's underrepresentation in politics can be addressed. Importantly, it delves into the debate on trustee-delegate, examining if representatives are mere delegates or trustees, i.e., do representatives just mirror the interests of their constituents or can they make decisions on behalf of their constituents? This debate is important to the book as it establishes the mandate of political representatives and the extent to which they can exercise that mandate.

Underrepresentation of Women in Politics

Women's underrepresentation in politics is still an important phenomenon as the average representation of women in parliaments globally is not up to 50%, signifying that they are still underrepresented in leadership positions. Pande and Ford (2011: 2) explain that although there have been notable achievements with regards to women's inclusion in politics, such as that of Angela Merkel of Germany, Ellen Johnson Sirleaf of Liberia, Dilma Rousseff of Brazil, women are still largely underrepresented in political spaces. Female heads of state or government are still a minority, although the number has increased from 12 to 21 over the past 20 years (European Parliament 2019). The electoral system, gender stereotypes, political culture, and preference for a gladiatorial style of politics may all be examples of elements that contribute to the discrimination against women in politics. Considering the additional difficulties of cross-sex mentoring and the need for social trust, frequently based on similarity, in such interactions, it may also entail a mentor shortage. These factors continue to perpetuate discrimination against women, which impedes their participation in their political system. When women are excluded from politics, it raises questions about discrimination and may even delegitimise decisions since the preferences and circumstances of those left out are not taken into account (UN 1995). The argument that is often advanced to advocate for increased representation is that women should make up half of all decision-making structures because they make up half of the population, echoing the logical principle of justice and equality. Like many equal opportunity arguments, it simply presupposes that talent is not confined to one gender and that discrimination, whether direct or indirect, is the cause of the underrepresentation of women in political positions. The basic argument for women's equal participation in public decision-making is that it is one of their rights that is recognised by international agreements. This argument does not rely on women making a difference to public life but on their natural rights to participate. This motivated women's international organisations to strengthen their advocacy to facilitate increasing number of women in legislatures.

Notably, as far back as the 1990s there was a surge in the interest in women to be included in political decision-making. This was due to the sudden drop in parliamentary participation of women globally following the overthrow of communism in the defunct Soviet Union and Eastern Europe (Sawer 2000: 23). This interest manifested in international organisations taking up the issue, which led to swift policy diffusion world-wide and mutual reinforcement of national and international agendas, such as Convention on the Elimination of All Forms of Discrimination Against Women (CEDAW) and Beijing Platform for Action (BPfA). Both instruments deal with women's equal rights in politics and public life. As of March 2000, 165 countries had ratified CEDAW, and as a result, they were required to report on how its provisions, particularly Article 7 that speaks to equal rights in political and public life, were being put into practice. The 1995 BPfA identified the implementation of measures to ensure the inclusion of women in political positions and equitable access to power structures as one of its strategic goals. Specifically, the BPfA advocated for the adoption of practical measures like quotas to push for increased women's participation in the political system. The BPfA stated that it is necessary to "ensure equal representation of women at all decision-making levels in national and international institutions" (UN 1995: 1). Pande and Ford (2011: 8) note that this provided opportunity for the adoption of gender quotas as a necessary and effective policy to enhance women's descriptive representation. The Millennium Development Goals (MDGs) adopted in 2000 also prioritised the increased proportion of seats held by women in national parliaments as one of the three targets of Goal 3, which is to promote gender equality and empower women. When the MDGs were replaced in 2015 by the Sustainable Development Goals, Goal 5 of the Sustainable Development Goals continued this emphasis "to ensure women's full and effective participation and equal opportunities for leadership at all levels of decision-making in political, economic, and public life" (UN Women 2021). Sawer (2000: 24) notes that "Article 25 of the International Covenant on Civil and Political Rights recognises the rights of both men and women to participate equally in public life". International organisations for women are yet another source of assistance for campaigns to increase the number of women in legislatures.

These various international instruments for women's political representation had an increasing impact on the global agenda for gender equality and women's empowerment. The rationale for enhancing women's participation in politics is built around the need to increase their numbers in political positions to ensure their interests are represented within these bodies. Sawer (2000: 23) argues that the underrepresentation of women "derives its force from the numerous layers of significance that are entwined in it, including the representation of interests, the representativeness of the legislative, and the equal right to act as a representative". In addition to seeking greater representation for women in parliaments, there is a need to improve the responsiveness of those bodies to the needs of women in the community. The advocacy for greater representation of women in political positions rests on understanding the importance of representation of marginalised groups within the political system.

UNDERSTANDING REPRESENTATION

Understanding the concept of representation is crucial to this book as it establishes what it means to represent or be represented. The concept of representation "is a rich brocade whose complex weave is not always appreciated" (Schwindt-Bayer and Mishler 2005: 407). Pitkin (1967) provides a succinct conceptualisation of what representation is by defining it as "to simply represent" which is to "make present again". Dovi (2018: 1) further expands this definition by asserting that "political representation is the activity of making citizens' voices, opinions, and perspectives present in public policy-making processes. It occurs when political actors speak, advocate, symbolise, and act on the behalf of others in the political arena. In short, political representation is a sort of political assistance". Pitkin (1967) references Hobbes's understanding of the concept of representation, and she posits that for Hobbes "representation is so intimately connected with action and governing an assembly in which each member has a veto power". Brennan and Hamlin (1999) attest that the establishment of a mediating assembly between the people and political decision-making is a crucial feature of political representation because it entails indirect decision-making or agency.

Representation has several components that are "some party that is representing (the representatives), something that is being represented (the interests), a setting within which the activity of representation is taking place (political context) and something that is being excluded (interests not voiced)" (Dovi 2018: 2). Democratic theorists of political representation often limit these components to only signify formal representation, such as representatives who hold elected offices. Rehfeld (2006) provided a general theory of representation and identifies representation based on reference to a relevant audience accepting a person as its representative. However, Dovi (2018: 3) argues that a consequence of Rehfeld's reference is that "it allows for undemocratic cases of representation as it does not specify what representatives do or should do to be recognised as representatives". In exemplifying what representatives do, Burke (1790:

115) states that "the parliament is not a congress of ambassadors from different and hostile interests, which interests each must maintain, as an agent and advocate, against other agents and advocates; but the parliament is a deliberative assembly of one nation, with one interest that of the whole". This can be used to argue that representatives in the parliament have common interests, which is to serve the country, but it does not recognise the diversity that exists within the population and its implication on interests.

The divide between whether representatives should serve as delegates or trustees is an important contribution to the concept of representation because it establishes the extent of responsibility. Madison et al. (1787) see representative government as the delegation of the government to a small number of citizens elected by the rest. This view of representatives as delegates considers that the people elected them for a purpose, but Burke's argument of the composition of the parliament signifies that representatives are trustees who follow their own understanding of the best action to pursue in representing the interest of their constituency. The difference in views concerning the responsibility of the representative places competing demands on the behaviour of representatives. Seeing representatives as delegates creates a platform for them to follow the interests of their constituencies but seeing them as trustees allows the representatives to prioritise their own judgement on what the interests of their constituency are.

The crux of this dilemma lies in the question of whether representatives are a mere reflection of the people's interests or are a determinant of the people's interests. Russo and Cotta (2020: 3) contribute to the debate by providing a historical perspective on representation. They narrate that Roman legal tradition offered significant insights into practices of representation and note that there was often the need for people (delegates) to stand for cities or estates in different political contexts (councils, parliaments). Particular importance was given to the ability of the ambassadors to consent to decisions taken in the council or parliament to ensure that the decisions are "binding on the communities they represented" (Russo and Cotta 2020: 3). They state that these ambassadors often received '*instructiones*' from the communities they represented, allowing them to contribute to the discussions that happen in the parliament. The significance of this to the trustee versus delegate debate is that Roman legal tradition or middle age Europe regarded representatives as both trustees and delegates of the people who represent the interests of their constituents but are able to make decision that are binding for their communities.

Pitkin (1967) weighs in that it does not matter greatly who represents as long as the ideas and preferences are represented. According to her, representation is not about the representative, for example, being a woman but rather about the representative capturing relatively accurately whatever ideas and preferences the women constituent has that relate to policies. However, Mansbridge (1999) posits that it is desirable for the representative to resemble the represented population in relevant characteristics. In Pitkin's (1967) discussion of representation as acting for, she highlights ideas on what the activity of a representative should be and what they should be doing. One important element is that representatives' opinions and actions should to some extent reflect the wishes, needs, or interests of the people they represent. To confirm this, Dahl (1989) asserts that representatives should be responsive to what the people want. However, Mansbridge (1999) contends that disadvantaged groups may want to be represented by individuals that share certain similarities or shared experience with them as they reflect some of the more typical group experiences and behaviours. The discourse on representation reveals that the responsibilities of representatives is divided between being a trustee that can use their initiative to act for their constituents or a delegate that aptly represents what the people want while sharing certain similarities with them. The implication of this is the context in which we view representatives or politicians, and this book notes that we see them as both trustees that can make decisions on behalf of their constituency and as delegates who represent the interests and opinions of the people.

In contributing to the delegate-trustee debate, Hamilton identified three modes of representation which are principal-agent, trusteeship and identification. The principal–agent relation is a situation where the group has an agency and a standard set of rules to act as a principal; they therefore appoint an agent to act in their stead to perform some prescribed tasks and functions. Consensus is important to this form of group representation, because the set of rules that shape the judgements and decisions of the groups is borne out of it. The flaw in this mode of representation is the assumption that groups are always organised, have the capacity to act prior to the action of the representatives. Trusteeship from 'trust' rooted in common law is an arrangement whereby money or property is managed by a person, sets of persons, or an organisation (the trustee) for the benefit of another person or organisation (the beneficiary). There is creation of a legal fiction, by which the representatives act in the group's name and on its behalf. In this mode, a beneficiary is involved and the trustee has independence of interpretation compared to the principal–agent where it is based on delegation. There is independence of the group interest and no supervision by the group. It does not require the group to always make decisions for themselves or be organised. Identification mode is one where an individual or a group of individuals bring forth a claim to represent a group, or a group makes someone/groups of individuals their representatives based on identifying with the shared interests or identities. Under this mode, the representatives do not necessarily share the same characteristics with the members of the group; also, the representative does not need to be a member of the group.

Forms of Representation

Pitkin (1967) provides the most widely used categorisation of representation that has been adopted by other scholars writing on political representation. She identifies four distinct but interconnected forms of representation. Dovi (2018) points out that while Pitkin did not provide an explanation of how these different representations relate with each other, she affirms that they are unified. The four types of representation identified by Pitkin (1967) are descriptive representation, formalistic representation, substantive representation, and symbolic representation. These forms provide different approaches for examining representation and allow for different standards when evaluating representatives. Russo and Cotta (2020) argue that disagreement concerning the responsibility of representatives happens because people adopt the wrong notion of the kind of representation these representatives engage in, and, hence, clarity on the typology of representation helps resolve this confusion.

Pitkin (1967: 38) refers to formalistic representation as the 'authorisation view' because the "representative is someone who has been authorized to act or represent others". In explaining this, Schwindt-Bayer and Mishler (2005: 407) note that formalistic representation "refers to the institutional rules and procedures through which representatives are chosen". This type of representation focuses on the institutional aspect of representation and on authorisation and accountability between the representative and represented without reference to the activities that the former is expected to carry out (Russo and Cotta 2020: 7). Descriptive representation "refers to the compositional similarity between representatives and the represented" (Schwindt-Bayer and Mishler 2005: 407). Schwindt-Bayer and Mishler (2005: 407) note that this type of representation focuses "on the extent to which a representative resembles those being represented". Substantive representation "refers to the compatibility between representatives' actions and interests of the represented. This relates to the activity of representatives, the actions taken on behalf of and in the interests of the represented" (Dovi 2018: 4). Schwindt-Bayer and Mishler (2005: 408) note that symbolic representation "refers to the represented's feelings of being fairly and effectively represented. The way that a representative stands for the represented, that is, the symbolic significance that a representative has for the represented". There are important differences among the four typologies, but Pitkin (1967) argues that they should be thought of as essential components of a coherent whole and further asserts that there are direct causal relationships among the forms of representation. Powell (2000) and Schumpeter (1943) note that the fact that proponents of formal representation stress the significance of credibility in elections is not only because it is important for democracy but also because they make descriptive representation possible, promote responsive policy making, and ensure legitimacy for the representatives. This is similar to the perceived link between descriptive representation and policy responsiveness as the former is deemed crucial for the latter, and symbolic representation is thought to be largely influenced by policy responsiveness (Mishler and Rose 1997).

The four types of representation have been identified, but there is the tendency among democratic theorists to focus on formalistic representation, translating to more attention being paid to the workings of representative democracy (Barber 2001; Guinier 1994). The implication of this is that discussions on political representation are substituted to mean elections and democracy. This is because political representation is seen as a way to establish legitimacy for democratic institutions and create institutional incentives for governments to be responsive to citizens. In response to this, Plotke (1997) suggests that it is necessary to broaden the scope of what is meant by political representation to include interest representation to capture the debate on what the proper activity of representatives should be. Mansbridge (2003) argues that understandings of representation are not keeping up with recent empirical research on democratic practices. She identifies new forms of representation, namely promissory, anticipatory, gyroscopic, and surrogacy representation. Mansbridge (2003: 515) defines gyroscopic representation as when representatives use their lived experience to understand the interests of their constituency. Surrogate representation is when legislators represent constituencies beyond their immediate districts even though they share similar interests. Anticipatory representation refers to instances where legislators prioritise what they believe their constituents would support in the next election rather than what they campaigned on promising to do. By identifying new forms of representation in modern democracy, Mansbridge (2003) attests to the fact that democratic representation should not be conceived as a monolith as there are multiple forms of representation. This traditional view often limits discourse on representation to the relationship between the representatives and the represented. From the different forms of representation presented above, the two that relate to the scope of this book are descriptive representation and substantive representation.

Descriptive Representation

Schwindt-Bayer and Mishler (2005: 408) explain that "descriptive representation, or representativeness, refers to the extent to which representatives resembles the represented". This means that the composition of the representatives should reflect the characteristics of those they are representing. Descriptive representation is the form in which a person or thing stands for others by being sufficiently like them. In this type of representation, representatives are in some ways a microcosm of the greater class of people they are meant to represent. Few scholars note that the term 'descriptive representation' can refer to shared experiences as well as observable qualities like colour and gender (see Mansbridge 2005; Schwindt-Bayer and Mishler 2005; Phillips 1995). As a result, a representative from a similar background is in some ways a 'descriptive representative' to their constituency (Dovi 2018). Schwindt-Bayer and Mishler (2005: 408) assert that "descriptive representation is arguably the most studied of Pitkin's (1967) four typology partly because the composition of the legislature is highly visible and easily measured". Russo and Cotta (2020: 8) argue that "Pitkin's account of descriptive representation is often misleadingly reduced to the idea of social representativeness".

Substantive Representation

Pitkin (1967: 209) defines substantive representation as "acting in the interests of the represented in a manner responsive to them". Most studies on substantive representative interpret it to mean 'policy responsiveness' or the extent to which legislators can make policies that address the interests of their constituency. Pitkin advocates that substantive representation is the most crucial form and the core of the integrated model of representation, though others disagree with this view.

Is There a Relationship Between Descriptive Representation and Substantive Representation?

Schwindt-Bayer and Mishler (2005: 410) assert that "one of the most widely studied hypotheses regarding representation holds that variations in descriptive representation have substantial effects on policy responsiveness". John Stuart Mill (1967: 22) argues that "in the absence of its natural defenders, the interest of the omitted is always in danger of being overlooked; and when looked at, is seen with very different eyes from those of the persons whom it directly concerns". Pitkin (1967: 63) makes a similar argument, claiming that it is only rational "to expect the composition of a legislature to determine the activities". She highlights that strong causal connection exists between these two forms representation. Literature on women's political representation confirms the importance of descriptive representation for policy responsiveness.

Descriptive Women's Representation: Increasing Their Numbers

Descriptive representation with regards to women's political participation focuses on increasing the number of women in political offices. The first step towards ensuring holistic women's representation is to increase the number of women participating in politics. Kanter (1977: 238) cites three predictions that arise when there is an increase in women's participation in any system. Firstly, increased participation allows women to form alliances and influence the group; secondly, they can start to differentiate themselves because of their collective strength; and finally, women who identify as feminist or are gender conscious can form supportive alliances and influence the group's culture. These predictions form the basis of the critical mass movement that presupposes that an increase in the number of women participating in politics will likely yield positive impact for women's representation. Based on Kanter's tipping point prediction, in addition with

Dahlerup's (1988) suggestion, 30% is often the stated critical mass for women's political representation. However, more recently, the need for a critical mass of women has been replaced by a more ambitious demand for gender balance or gender parity, which is 50/50 or 40% women and 60% men in political assemblies. The critical mass argument is still used in countries with low women's representation, and the clamour for gender parity occurs primarily in countries that already have a strong representation of women. Most studies identify additional aspects of the political context, such as hostile environments or unrecognised interests as factors that make descriptive representation more important to ensure substantive women's representation (Dovi 2002; Mansbridge 1999).

Substantive Women's Representation: Protecting Their Interests

According to Childs and Krook (2009), substantive representation transcends numbers and entails the quality of women's actual participation in politics by focusing on the outcomes of their participation and on the factors that impact their performance rather than on descriptive aspects of women's representation. This form of representation goes beyond debuting women in the political space to ensure numerical parity; it entails the qualitative representation of women on issues that affect their quality of life, such as financial inclusion, reproductive health, and freedom from GBVF. The distinction between descriptive and substantive women's representation is why attempts at ensuring representation of women should ensure that not only are women represented numerically but their interests are also protected. Unfortunately, the significant increase in the number of women taking up political positions is often assumed to mean equal or greater representation of women issues (Celis 2008). Studies examining legislators' behaviour often predict that women's increased presence in the parliament means that the interests of women will be addressed because they are motivated to advance the common interests women have (Celis et al. 2008: 105).

A major conceptual limitation of this form of representation is the contestation of what exactly constitutes women's interests. This contestation revolves around concepts like women's issues, feminist issues, gendered issues and women-friendly policies (Beckwith and Cowell-Meyers 2003); accountability to women, gender-sensitive policies, women's political effectiveness (Goetz 2003); strategic gender interests (Molyneux 2001); and feminising politics (Lovenduski 2005). Other ambiguous words, such as women-friendly legislation (Hernes 1987), the promotion of women's interests accountable to women, gender-sensitive politics, women's political efficacy (Goetz 2003), and strategic gender interests, are used in public discourse and even research (Waylen 1997). These different concepts reveal the need for an agreed definition on substantive representation, or rather, on what constitutes women's interests. Beckwith and Cowell-Meyers (2003: 3) assert that some scholars attempt to resolve this confusion by examining "the relationship that exists between the proportion of women in politics and making a difference". Tremblay (2006: 506) argues that the idea of making a difference, also known as the "difference fallacy, proposes underestimating the obvious possibility that women in politics, perhaps even more so when there are many of them, will be able to influence their male colleagues and change either the overall political agenda or the agenda of their individual parties (or both), with the result that there are relatively few gender differences in attitudes and behaviours". Some researchers support this claim with studies that reveal different policy preferences among male and female legislators (see Williams 1996). However, most empirical research highlight disparities among women, including those caused by ethnicity, class, age, and party affiliation, which hinder the development of a common legislative agenda. They contend that categories like women "are inherently exclusive and serve to reify one difference while erasing and obfuscating others" (Childs and Krook 2009: 131). They contend that gender is a partially manufactured and reproduced identity within the context of specific legislatures rather than a pre-political and fixed identity that women and men carry with them when they enter politics. Some scholars argue that women only have an impact when they behave differently from men. While "others reject a focus on difference on the grounds that it identifies women as the gender with 'special' interests and experiences" (Beckwith and Cowell-Meyers 2007: 555).

Olaitan (2024b) notes that the contestation on defining women's interests led feminist political theorists to advocate for a shared perspective among women as a group to consolidate calls for increased women's participation in politics. Going back to Saward's (2006) argument that representation is at least in part a performance of 'claim making' provides a way to break out of the deadlock on defining women's interests. These discourses are essential to understand what constitutes substantive women's representation because acting on behalf of women entails claiming to speak for them and framing issues in terms of how important they are to them. Irrespective of these discussions, a substantive representation of women can be seen as the act of articulating women's interests leading to the formulation of a wide range of viewpoints and interests, however those interests and perspectives may be described. As a result, it can have a variety of objectives and driving forces, such as enhancing the lives of women, pursuing gender equality, or emphasising difference and complementarity. Therefore, substantive representation of women can focus solely on women, on gender, or examine men and women's positionality in society. Squires (2008) describes this dynamic as the "constitutive representation of gender". It is crucial to stress that feminist issues are just one potential aspect of substantive representation of women; it can also consider 'practical interests' that result from the actual circumstances of women's lives (Celis 2008; Molyneux 1985). Weldon (2002) argues that collaborative procedures of interest articulation, rather than just the perspective of one legislator, are the best ways to define 'women's interests'. Wangnerud (2009: 53) suggests that "one way to handle such controversies is to let politically active women themselves define women's interests or what they perceive as gender equality; this strand of research relies on what are labelled subjectively defined interests". Other studies developed theoretically grounded classifications that take into account the diversity of women but also highlight some areas of agreement (see Lovenduski and Norris 2003; Wangnerud 2000). Olaitan (2024b) suggests that it is important that whatever the agreement on what substantive women's representation is should consider the nuance of women as a homogenous group and a group with intersectional interests that cut across other aspects of society.

RELATIONSHIP BETWEEN DESCRIPTIVE AND SUBSTANTIVE WOMEN'S REPRESENTATION

Reingold (2000: 2) asks the following fundamental question: "Does the election of more and more women mean that women will be better represented?" This question is the basis upon which much research has been done to understand the relationship between the number of women in politics and the representation of women's interests. Additionally, most feminist research on political representation focuses on descriptive and substantive representation as well as potential connections between the two types of representation (Carroll 2001; Young 2000). Research focuses on the question of whether adding more female representatives (descriptive representation) will result in greater attention being paid to women's policy issues (substantive representation) (Childs and Krook 2006; Dahlerup 2006; Grey 2006). The core assumption is that "numbers matter, an increase in descriptive representation of women in parliaments will generally even automatically translate into an increase in substantive representation of women" (Celis et al. 2008: 105). Beckwith (2007: 1) indicates "that the relationship between women's descriptive and substantive representation has attracted attention to the sheer quantity of women and number-based theories of women's representation". Mansbridge (2005: 622) asserts that "descriptive representation of women enhances substantive representation for women", noting that numbers have frequently been claimed to drive impact. By conveying to the represented that the political arena supports and represents them, descriptive representation activates substantive representation. According to Williams (1996: 106), a representative must have some understanding of how the privilege of masculinity affects the lives of women in her constituency to effectively represent their interests. The best way to understand this impact is to draw from her own experiences of gender inequality and the stereotypes attached to her gender. This demonstrates that descriptive representation of women is a necessity for adequate representation of women because representatives can better understand the needs of women. Studies have been carried out to demonstrate that female politicians feel that they are expected to represent women issues and influence the legislative agenda in favour of women. One such study is the Inter-Parliamentary Union [IPU] study on 200 female legislators from different countries, which found that 89% of them felt that they have an obligation to act for women and represent them (IPU 2000: 133–41). Lovenduski (2005: 5) rightly points out "that more women in descriptive roles may result in the inclusion of women's concerns. Increased participation of women in politics is the main mechanism of the many available ways to improve the substantive representation of women". The increased number of women entering politics leads to change in political agenda and the priorities of both male and female politicians and these agendas now include issues like public childcare, pay inequality, and violence against women in their policies and programmes. To better understand how numbers can translate to this, a structural explanation might be that more than 30% of women in politics can challenge stereotypes against them within positions of power, which leads to the development of a new parity-democracy norm. While an actor-oriented explanation might be that as there are more women in politics, they have more opportunities to hold positions of power within political parties and are more likely to recruit other women, either out of a sense of obligation to their own gender or as a temporary measure to counteract male dominance in politics.

Arguments about the need for increased women's participation in the parliament often turn into discussions about making a difference and for raising the parliamentary behaviour standards. This is because "gender is seen as relevant to the way representatives' roles are likely to be performed and it is expected that the presence of more women will reduce the level of aggression found in male-dominated parliaments. It is not only the people that expect women to make a difference, but the women MPs also themselves have this expectation" (Sawer 2000: 26). Sawer (2000) further notes that a study of some female MPs from Western Australia found that almost all of them thought that having more women would increase the focus on consensus politics. Women's interests are anticipated to be represented differently as a result of their presence. It is important to recognise that the participation of women in the political system is based on the need to ensure equality as well as to ensure that their interests are protected within decision-making structures (UN 1995: 181). Williams (2000) finds that women in the Australian Senate are five times more likely than their male counterparts to bring up concerns like domestic violence and paid parental/maternal leave.

Some scholars argue that there is no direct link between the number of women in politics and the representation of women's interests due to the lack of agreement of what women's interests are and the inability of female politicians to speak for women (Childs and Krook 2006; Dahlerup 2006). Childs and Krook (2006) point out that it is easier to question men's ability to speak for women and to wonder whether those who are given the role of women in society can ever truly be represented by those who have not had these experiences than it is to argue that women will be better able to represent women's interests. They further contend that even if women's interests or perspectives could be agreed upon, a more representative legislature does not guarantee that their interests will be more effectively represented because acting for is different from standing up for something (see Pitkin 1967). The other contention is that women are not a homogenous group, which affects the idea that women share common or specific experiences that can be protected by female politicians. As a result, some argue that female legislators pose a better possibility for addressing certain issues that affect women even though this contention exists (Phillips 1995: 53).

In contrast to this argument, some scholars note that women in the parliament see themselves as representatives of women who should act for the collective group; this is an acknowledgement that women have specific interests that bind them together (Carroll 2001; Reingold 2000; Skjeie 1991). Mateo-Diaz (2005) adds that female politicians often share the same policy opinions with women's organisations and their constituency due to their shared experience. This gave impetus to the notion that men and women have different interests, which feeds into the kind of policy goals they advocate (Lovenduski 1997; Swers 1998; Thomas and Welch 1991). Researchers discovered that women tend to behave differently than men most of the time, especially when defining the legislative agenda and introducing new measures that deal with issues that are important to women (Bratton and Ray 2002; Childs 2004). Additionally, their presence results in transformation of the legislative agenda (Grey 2002), as well as changes to parliamentary procedures and work schedules (Skjeie 1991). Mansbridge (2005: 625) explains that "in the cases of gender and race, legislators who themselves are members of a group respond to issues affecting that group with greater concern than do non-members". She notes further that issues like education and women's rights, which normally affect female constituents more than male constituents, "are given more attention by female legislators than by male legislators in practically every measured representative body, from the U.S. House of Representatives to the Indian panchayats". Descriptive representatives from groups who are most affected by certain issues tend to be more invested in those causes, devote more time to them, and work harder to bring them to the attention of legislators. Mansbridge (2005: 626) contends that "descriptive representatives have, moreover, several advantages in communicating with other legislators. They can react quickly and flexibly in response to what they hear from their constituents while also drawing on their own personal experience". When speaking, they can use examples from their own experiences to illustrate how a piece of legislation might affect their group. They have the ability to express information and emotion vividly through their speaking. They have the ability to speak and might be trusted. They can also rely on the bonds they have made with other legislators to provide them with the understanding of the descriptive representative's stance that they may require. Even when the descriptive legislator is passive, the other legislators are made aware of the opinions and priorities of the group that the descriptive member belongs to by virtue of the descriptive legislator's very physical presence.

While discussions are ongoing regarding the relationship between numbers and representation of women's interests, the popular notion is that increased number of women in politics provides grounds for women's interests to be better represented. Women politicians understand the needs and lived experiences of women, which makes it suitable for them to advocate for these issues in positions of power. While contestations continue regarding definition of women's interests, there are certain issues that generally affect women as a group, one of which is gender-based violence and femicide. The intersectionality that exists among women as a group does not shield them from being victims of violence; hence, there are numerous convergences that can be arrived at on what constitutes women's interests or substantive representation of women. Dahlerup (2006: 18) confirms that there are "five categories of observations about the relationships between descriptive and substantive representation which are: (1) expected effects of higher proportions of women; (2) enabling and constraining legislative contexts; (3) legislators' identities and interests; (4) definitions of women's issues; and (5) policy-making processes".

Conclusion

The resulting effect of increased women's representation in politics is the need to expand the scope of what representation means beyond numbers to ensure holistic and substantive representation of women. This chapter engages the discourse on women's underrepresentation in politics to provide context on the need for increased representation of women in politics. It embarked on a review of existing literature on women's political representation, the concept of representation and its forms with particular focus on descriptive and substantive representation. It provided a discussion on what representation is and the lens through which we can evaluate the role of representatives by delving into the trustee/delegate dichotomy. This chapter looked at the different types of representation and how they are different yet interconnected, and it focused on the relevant forms that relate to the book, which are descriptive and substantive representation. By reflecting on the underrepresentation of women in politics, this chapter established grounds to motivate for their increased participation in politics and the protection of their interests. It noted that when women are underrepresented in politics, their interests are often not attended to, further creating a link between women's political participation and the representation of women's issues. The relationship between descriptive women's representation and substantive representation was examined to understand whether the increase in the number of women participating in politics translates into the representation of women issues. This covered the contestation concerning the definition of women's interest considering the nuance that exists among women.

REFERENCES

Barber, K. 2001. *A right to representation: Proportional election systems for the 21st century*. Columbia: Ohio University Press.

Beckwith, K. 2007. Numbers and newness: The descriptive and substantive representation of women. *Canadian Journal of Political Science* 40 (1): 27–49.

Beckwith, K., and K. Cowell-Meyers. 2003. *Sheer numbers*. Paper prepared for the Annual Meeting of the American Political Science Association, Philadelphia, August 28–31.

Bratton, K., and L. Ray. 2002. Descriptive representation, policy outcomes, and municipal day-care coverage in Norway. *American Journal of Political Science* 46 (2): 428–437.

Brennan, G., and A. Hamlin. 1999. On political representation. *British Journal of Political Science* 29 (1): 109–127.

Burke, Edmund. 1790 [1968]. *Reflections on the revolution in France*. London: Penguin Books.

Carroll, S.J. 2001. *The impact of women in public office*. Bloomington: Indiana University Press.

Celis, K. 2008. Studying women's substantive representation in legislatures: When representative acts, contexts and women's interests become important. *Journal of Representative Democracy* 44 (2): 111–124.

Celis, K., S. Childs, J. Kantola, and M.L. Krook. 2008. Rethinking women's substantive representation. *Representation* 44 (2): 99–110.

Childs, S. 2004. *New labour women MPs: Women representing women*. London: Routledge.

Childs, S., and M.L. Krook. 2006. Should feminists give up on critical mass? A contingent 'yes'. *Politics and Gender* 2 (4): 522–530.

———. 2009. Analysing women's substantive representation: From critical mass to critical actors. *Government and Opposition* 44 (2): 125–145.

Dahl, R. 1989. *Democracy and its critics*. New Haven: Yale University.

Dahlerup, D. 1988. From a small to a large minority: Women in Scandinavian politics. *Scandinavian Political Studies* 11 (4): 275–298.

———. 2006. The story of the theory of critical mass. *Politics and Gender* 2 (4): 511–521.

Dovi, S. 2002. Preferable descriptive representatives: Or will just any woman, Black, or Latino do? *American Political Science Review* 96: 745–754.

———. 2018. Political representation. *In Stanford encyclopaedia of philosophy.* Stanford, CA: Stanford University Press.

European Parliament. 2019. Women in politics: A global perspective. https://www.europarl.europa.eu/RegData/etudes/BRIE/2019/635543/EPRS_BRI (2019)635543_EN.pdf

Goetz, A.M. 2003. Women's political effectiveness: A conceptual framework. In *No shortcuts to power: African women in politics and policy making,* ed. A.M. Goetz and S. Hassim, 29–80. London: Zed Books.

Grey, S. 2002. Does size matter? Critical mass and New Zealand's women MPs. *Parliamentary Affairs* 55 (1): 19–29.

———. 2006. Numbers and beyond: The relevance of critical mass in gender research. *Politics & Gender* 2 (4): 492–502.

Guinier, L. 1994. *The tyranny of the majority: Fundamental fairness in representative democracy.* New York: Free Press.

Hernes, H. 1987. *Welfare state and women power; Essays in state feminism.* Vojens: Norwegian University Press.

Inter-Parliamentary Union. 2000. *Politics: Women's insight.* Geneva: Inter Parliamentary Union. http://archive.ipu.org/pdf/publications/womeninsight_en.pdf.

Kanter, R.M. 1977. *Men and women of the corporation.* New York: Basic Books.

Kenworthy, L., and M. Malami. 1999. Gender inequality in political representation: A worldwide comparative analysis. *Social Forces* 78: 235–268.

Lovenduski, J. 1997. Gender politics: A breakthrough for women. *Parliamentary Affairs* 50 (4): 708–719.

———. 2005. *Feminizing politics.* Cambridge: Cambridge University Press.

Lovenduski, J., and P. Norris. 2003. Westminster women: The politics of presence. *Political Studies* 51 (1): 84–102.

Madison, J., H. Alexander, and J. John. 1787 [1987]. *The federalist papers.* Edited by Isaac Kramnick. Harmondsworth: Penguin.

Mansbridge, J. 1999. Should Blacks represent Blacks and women represent women? A contingent 'Yes'. *The Journal of Politics* 61 (3): 628–657.

———. 2003. Rethinking representation. *The American Political Science Review* 97 (4): 515–528.

———. 2005. Quota problems: Combating the dangers of essentialism. *Politics and Gender* 4: 622–638.

Mateo-Diaz, M.M. 2005. *Representing women? Female legislators in West European parliaments.* Essex: ECPR Monographs.

Meyer, J., J. Boli, G. Thomas, and F. Ramirez. 1997. World society and the nation state. *The American Journal of Sociology* 103 (1): 144–181.

Mill, J.S. 1861 (1967). *Considerations on representative ©Government.* London: Parker, Son, and Bourn Publishers.

Mishler, W., and R. Rose. 1997. Trust, distrust and skepticism: Popular evaluations of civil and political institutions in post-communist societies. *Journal of Politics* 59: 418–451.

Molyneux, M. 1985. Mobilization without emancipation? Women's interests, the state, and revolution in Nicaragua. *Feminist Studies* 11 (2): 227–258.

———. 2001. *Women's movements in international perspective: Latin America and beyond.* London: Palgrave.

Norris, P. 1997. *Passages to power: Legislative recruitment in advanced democracies.* Cambridge University Press.

Olaitan, Z.M. (2023). *Gender quotas and the substantive representation of women in African politics: Case studies of Botswana and South Africa.* Doctoral Thesis, University of Pretoria.

———. 2024a. Women of EndSars: Understanding women's participation in protests in Nigeria. *The International Journal of Law and Politics* 2: 25–49.

———. 2024b. *Engaging the concept of women's interests: What does it mean and who gets to define it.* Liberation Alliance Africa, 9 May. https://liberation-allianceafrica.com/engaging-the-concept-of-womens-interests-what-does-it-mean-and-who-defines-it/

Pande, R., and D. Ford. 2011. *Gender quotas and female leadership.* World Bank Development Report Background Paper on Gender Equality and Development.

Paxton, P. 1997. Women in national legislatures: A cross-national analysis. *Social Science Research* 26: 442–464.

Paxton, P., and S. Kunovich. 2003. Women's political representation: The importance of ideology. *Social Forces* 82 (1): 87–113.

Paxton, P., M. Hughes, and J. Green. 2006. The international women's movement and women's political representation, 1893–2003. *American Sociological Review* 71 (6): 898–920.

Phillips, A. 1995. *The politics of presence.* Oxford: Oxford University Press.

Pitkin, H.F. 1967. *The concept of representation.* Berkeley, CA: University of California Press.

Plotke, D. 1997. Representation is democracy. *Constellations* 4 (1): 19–34.

Powell, B. 2000. *Elections as instruments of democracy: Majoritarian and proportional visions.* Yale: Yale University Press.

Ramirez, F.O., Y. Soysal, and S. Shanahan. 1997. The changing logic of political citizenship: Cross-national acquisition of women's suffrage rights, 1890 to 1990. *American Sociological Review* 62 (5): 735–745.

Randall, V. 1987. *Women and politics: An international perspective.* Macmillan Education.

Rehfeld, A. 2006. Towards a general theory of political representation. *The Journal of Politics* 68 (1): 1–21.

Reingold, B. 2000. *Representing women: Sex, gender and legislative behaviour in Arizona and California*. Chapel Hill: University of North Carolina Press.

Reynolds, A. 1999. Women in the legislatures and executives of the world knocking at the highest glass ceiling. *World Politics* 51 (July): 547–572.

Roy, A. 2004. Peace & The New Corporate Liberation Theology. Lecture delivered at 2004 City of Sydney Peace Prize Lecture CPACS Occasional Paper No. 04/2.

Russo, F., and M. Cotta. 2020. Political representation: Concepts theories and practices in historical perspective. In *Research handbook on political representation*, ed. M. Cotta and F. Russo. Cheltenham: Edward Elgar Publishing.

Saward, M. 2006. The representative claim. *Contemporary Political Theory* 5 (3): 297–318.

Sawer, M. 2000. Parliamentary representation of women: From discourses of justice to strategies of accountability. *International Political Science Review* 21 (4): 361–380.

Schumpeter, J.A. 1943. *Capitalism, socialism and democracy*. London: Allen and Unwin.

Schwindt-Bayer, L.A., and W. Mishler. 2005. An integrated model of women's representation. *Journal of Politics* 67 (2): 407–428.

Skjeie, H. 1991. The rhetoric of difference: On women's inclusion into political elites. *Politics and Society* 19 (2): 233–263.

Squires, J. 2008. The constitutive representation of gender: Extra-parliamentary representations of gender relations. *Representation* 44 (2): 183–199.

Swers, M. 1998. Are women more likely to vote for women's issue bills than their male colleagues? *Legislative Studies Quarterly* 23 (3): 435–448.

Thomas, S., and S. Welch. 1991. The impact of gender on activities and priorities of state legislators. *The Western Political Quarterly* 44 (2): 445–456.

Towns, A. 2004. *Norms and inequality in international society: Global politics of women and the state*. PhD Dissertation, University of Minnesota.

Tremblay, M. 2006. The substantive representation of women and PR. *Politics and Gender* 2 (4): 502–511.

United Nations. (1995). *Beijing declaration and platform for action*. https://www.un.org/womenwatch/daw/beijing/platform/

United Nations (UN) Women. 2021. *SDG 5: Achieve gender equality and empower all women and girls*. https://www.unwomen.org/en/node/36060

Wangnerud, L. 2000. Representing women. In *Beyond Westminster and Congress: The Nordic experience*, ed. P. Esaiasson and K. Heidar, 132–154. Columbus: Ohio State University Press.

———. 2009. Women in parliaments: Descriptive and substantive representation. *Annual Review of Political Science* 12 (1): 51–69.

Waylen, G. 1997. Analysing women in the politics of the third world. *Review of Japanese Culture and Society* 9: 1–14.

Weldon, L.S. 2002. Beyond bodies: Institutional sources of representation for women in democratic policymaking. *Journal of Politics* 64 (4): 1153–1174.

Williams, M.S. 1996. Memory, history and membership: The moral claims of marginalized groups in political representation. In *Do we need minority rights?* ed. J. Raikka, 85–119. Netherlands: Kluwer Law International.

Williams, M. 2000. The uneasy alliance of group representation and deliberative democracy. In *Citizenship in diverse societies*, ed. W. Kymlicka and W. Norman, 124–153. Oxford: Oxford University Press.

Young, I.M. 2000. *Inclusion and democracy*. Oxford: Oxford University Press.

CHAPTER 3

Gender Quotas and Descriptive Women's Representation: Global and Continental Context

States Parties shall take specific positive action to promote participative governance and the equal participation of women in the political life of their countries through affirmative action, enabling national legislation and other measures.

—Article 9, Protocol on the Rights of Women in Africa (2003).

Introduction

Krook (2006) confirms that gender quotas have gained popularity in response to women's underrepresentation in politics. This is the result of increased advocacy by international women's movements, feminist organisations that pushed for the global adoption of gender quotas as a tool to increase women's political representation. The adoption of quotas while welcomed by most has also created discussions around their usefulness and implementation. Debates about gender quotas have surfaced in national politics across the globe (Baldez 2006). As of 2024, more than 100 countries have changed their constitutions or enacted new electoral laws mandating that women make up specific percentages of candidates, aspirants, or legislative seats, while political parties have imposed quotas on their own in many other countries (IIDEA 2024). The global adoption of quotas presents a number of normative and empirical issues, such as the appropriateness of gender quotas and the reasons for their adoption and

Z. M. Olaitan, *Women's Representation in African Politics*, African Histories and Modernities, https://doi.org/10.1007/978-3-031-76051-8_3

effectiveness (Schwindt-Bayer 2007). Increasing bodies of literature on quotas have sought to explain the mechanisms and motivations behind the adoption of quotas as well as, more recently, the reasons why some quota regimes are more successful than others at granting women access to political office.

Krook (2006) explains that the discourse on gender quotas are essentially normative, centred on divergent interpretations of gender, equality, and representation. Supporters of quotas typically argue that they benefit women as a group, advance equality of results, and establish gender as a category of political representation. While opponents of quotas contend that they prioritise certain groups over others, erode equality of opportunities, and overlook other more pressing social divisions. Two normative concerns are stated by both proponents and opponents of quota reform and permeate practically all quota campaigns, even though different normative settings offer different opportunities and restrictions for quota adoption and implementation (Krook 2006). The first and most evident criticism is that women elected under quotas might not want to amend laws in a way that benefits women. This is true, but it ignores the fact that these policies are gender quotas, or more accurately, sex quotas that aim only to increase the number of women in political decision-making, independent of any obligations to change policy outcomes (Krook 2006). This point highlights a great deal of research on the relationship between the descriptive and substantive representation of women. The second major criticism is that gender quotas could undermine the legitimacy of female politicians as active participants in politics, including those who were elected into office without affirmative action such as through more conventional methods of candidate selection (Mansbridge 2005).

While current conversations on the adoption of gender quotas are still focused on 'inclusion', women's organisations have started emphasising the need for a 'critical mass' and 'gender parity' which are increasingly being included in global discourse on women's political representation (Olaitan and Isike 2024; Olaitan 2023). It is argued that for women in the parliament to attain some level of power that enables them to influence policies or substantively represent women, a critical mass of 30% must be achieved (Dahlerup 2006a). As a result, the critical mass threshold is often used by the UN Commission on the Status of Women to assess member state progress towards women's political representation. Although, conversations on gender parity (50%) are increasingly dislodging the 30% threshold, with countries like Senegal passing a gender parity law to push for increased women's representation in politics (Toraasen 2017).

Baldez (2006) assert that the implementation of gender quotas could inadvertently lead to political transformation. Zetterberg (2013) argues that due to their transformational nature, quotas are not only impacted by the institutional context in which they are established but they also have the potential to help change political institutions. The dynamic relationship has implications for the examination of important representative democratic institutions: In certain instances, electoral quotas can put established analytical frameworks and methods of examining political life in jeopardy. Baldez (2006) opines that gender quotas have the potential to avert men's domination in political institution and their exclusive control over political power, at the same time, they may also serve to maintain the current quo which might not often be beneficial to women's representation.

The assumption that the implementation of gender quotas will facilitate the increased participation of women in politics has been peddled as a means to accelerate the adoption of quotas. This assumption provides ground for this chapter to delve into the discourse on gender quotas at a global and continental level to examine the validity of this claim. This chapter delves into the history and conceptualisation of gender quotas as a precursor to discuss its effect on descriptive women's representation. It provides a continental context to the discourse by explaining the history and adoption of gender quotas in Africa. This chapter highlights the intricate issues that enhance or affect the impact of gender quotas, such as electoral system. The historical overview of the implementation of quotas on the continent was engaged by zooming in on notable countries in the different sub-regions. It examines the different kinds of quotas adopted on the continent and provides country examples to illustrate it. It goes on to discuss how quotas have contributed to the significant increase in women's political participation in Africa. This discussion is relevant as it acknowledges the effect gender quotas has to ensure the increased number of women in African politics as a precursor for engaging the book's central questions. Drivers that facilitate the success of gender quotas are discussed to highlight that quotas are not a one-size-fits-all mechanism because certain factors determine its impact. It also identifies certain challenges based on country examples that impede the effectiveness of quotas. The discussion engaged in this chapter relates to the nexus between gender quotas and increasing women's participation in politics (descriptive women's representation) globally and in African politics.

GLOBAL CONTEXT ON GENDER QUOTAS

Gender quotas, often known as electoral gender quotas or quotas, are institutional forms of affirmative action aimed at resolving structural imbalances that limit the political representation of women (Krook 2004). Dahlerup (2006a: 6) states that they are 'fast-track' models meant to enable political representation that emanate from growing impatience on the slow pace of change in women's political power.

Quotas were initially implemented in Nordic countries when the Socialist Left Party of Norway set a 40% minimum goal for gender representation on electoral lists in 1975, other parties in Norway, as well as those in Denmark and Sweden, quickly followed (Pande and Ford 2011: 8). Ten countries implemented gender quotas between 1930 and 1980, and 12 other countries did the same in the 1980s. However, quotas were implemented in more than 50 countries in the 1990s, and since 2000, approximately 40 more countries have joined them (Krook 2006: 312–313). These waves directly interact with variations in the prevalence and timing of various quota measures. The first quota type designed to ensure women's representation were reserved seats, which became the primary quota type used between 1930 and 1970. However, since 2000, they have increased in popularity. Madsen (2019) notes that voluntary party quotas first appeared in the early 1970s but that they spread more widely in the 1980s and 1990s; legislative quotas emerged in the 1990s and gained popularity during the 2000s. Along with these time variations, the kinds of quotas implemented follow specific regional patterns and have comparable rules throughout the locations where they are present. Gender quotas are now widely used, and as of 2008, more than 100 countries had implemented them in one form or the other (IIDEA 2007). More recent statistics shows that 135 countries have implemented a form of quota system (IIDEA 2024). These patterns imply that quotas are not just a global phenomenon but are also related to other quota campaigns around the world or that they have significant things in common with them. Zetterberg (2009: 715) notes that "gender quotas have arguably been the most drastic and highly contentious reform in the field of gender equality in the last 50 to 60 years". By mandating that women represent a specific percentage of political candidates or officials, they impact the gender compositions of those who hold political office (Hughes 2011). Despite being different in many other aspects, most quota adoption cases have one thing in common: They frequently occur during times of change or crisis. Baines and

Rubio-Marin (2005) assert that in cases of constitutional reforms, quotas are often approved by national legislatures.

Quotas found expression when the "United Nations ECOSOC endorsed a target of 30% women in decision-making positions in the world by 1995 as well as several international declarations from the 1990s calling for a target or quota of 30%" (Pande and Ford 2011: 10). Dahlerup (2006a: 14) argues that "this target was far from met, since in 1995 only 10% of the world's parliamentarians were women, in 2005, only 16% which was still far from one-third, as a result, many countries adopted fast-track procedures like quotas". The UN BPfA and CEDAW are cited by proponents of gender quotas in politics to support their argument for quotas. The Platform for Action is described as advocating for gender quotas in politics, even though it does not use the contentious word 'quota', because it urges "special targets and implementing measures, if necessary, through positive action" (UN 1995: Art. 190a). Similarly, the 1979 CEDAW convention refers to 'special measures'. The percentages or figures used in electoral gender quotas vary widely, ranging from 5% in Nepal to 50% in Sweden and France. However, 30% is the most common proportion chosen for candidate quotas for both legal and voluntary party quotas (Dahlerup 2006b). There is a transition emerging from calls for minority participation of 30% to a more radical call for gender parity in politics of 50%. But while, for example, the Platform for Action represents this new line in its demand for equal representation, it nevertheless continues to argue for securing a critical mass of women in parliaments (UN 1995: Art. 181–95). The recent trend of enacting gender quotas in post-conflict states is frequently based on arguments that women must be included if democracy is to advance (Dahlerup 2006a).

TYPES OF GENDER QUOTAS

There are three main types of electoral gender quotas, namely legislated or constitutional, voluntary, or party quotas, and reserved seats quota. Krook et al. (2008: 3) notes that most of the research on gender quotas identifies the following three main categories of quota measures: Reserved seats, which designate seats in political assemblies for women and that men are not permitted to run for; party quotas, which involve party pledges to nominate a certain percentage of women; and legislated quotas, which call for a certain percentage of women to be nominated by all parties as mandated by law.

Legislated Quotas

Legislated or constitutional quotas, also known as legal quotas, are mandated by national legislations, and embedded in the constitution to specify that a certain percentage of candidate seats must be held by women (International IDEA 2024). They often set limits on where women can appear on the electoral list, such as mandating that every second person on the list must be a woman. Legal quotas, which control political representation of one or more groups using the power of the constitution, are the most used form of quotas, and more than 100 countries have implemented them. National gender quotas impact all political parties in a system, even those that frequently represent minority groups. These policies may increase minority women's representation more successfully than gender quotas that political parties freely adopt. An electoral gender quota legislation might, for instance, mandate that at least 40% of the candidates on the electoral lists be women. Since women are the underrepresented group in political institutions, most legislation strive to ensure that women have a minimum number of seats. This implies that there is a maximum set for the representation of men. Legal gender quotas are required either by the electoral law, as in several countries in Latin America, as well as Rwanda, Angola, Belgium, Bosnia-Herzegovina, Slovenia, and France, or by the constitution, as in Nepal and the Philippines. Krook (2004) notes that legislated quotas are typically prevalent in post-conflict societies, predominantly in Africa, the Middle East, and south-eastern Europe, and in developing countries, particularly Latin America. They are the most recent form of quotas and first appeared in the 1990s when the underrepresentation of women attracted attention on a global scale and made it onto the agenda of international organisations and transnational non-governmental organisations. Legislated quotas are similar to party quotas in that they address party selection processes, but they differ in that they are passed by national parliaments to require that all parties nominate a specific percentage of female candidates. They are frequently implemented through changes to electoral laws and occasionally constitutions. As a result, their provisions apply to all political parties and not only to those that opt to implement quotas. Legislative quotas, like party quotas, require women to make up a specific proportion of all candidates. However, they entail broader reform procedures that are more concerned with changing the language in constitutions and electoral laws than the specifics of party statutes, and therefore, some partisan support is necessary for their ratification. Depending on the electoral system, legislative quotas can be enforced in a way that affects party lists (Meier 2004). Legislative quotas are unique as they typically include penalties for violation and are subject to some level of external scrutiny given their legal standing (Baldez 2004; Jones 1998). For legislated quotas, distinction is made between quotas implemented through changes to the electoral legislation and those implemented through constitutional revisions because of certain inherent differences in the legislative process (Dahlerup 2006a).

Voluntary Quotas

Voluntary or party quotas are often set by political parties, allowing them to nominate a specified number of female candidates for their electoral lists. The most prevalent kind of gender quotas are party quotas (Childs and Krook 2012). A small number of socialist and social democratic parties in Western Europe originally adopted them in the early 1970s. However, during the 1980s and 1990s, they arose in a wide range of political parties around the world, including green parties, social democratic parties, and even certain conservative parties. For voluntary quotas, political parties have the authority to decide the modalities that surround the quota, and often the adoption of quota by one party creates a diffusion wherein other parties adopt them too. Party quotas, at their core, are voluntary policies set by certain parties that bind the party to strive for a specific percentage of female candidates for elected office. They change party procedures in this regard by establishing new criteria for candidate selection that oblige elites to acknowledge pre-existing prejudices and take into account other domains of political recruitment (Krook 2005; Lovenduski and Norris 1993). The prerogative of how many women to be included in the party list is left to the whims of the party and depends on how dedicated they are to increasing women's participation. A number of political parties have implemented quotas for their own lists in several countries, including Germany, Norway, Sweden, and South Africa. It is interesting to note that only one or two parties often choose to use quotas in many other cases. Nonetheless, the overall rate of female representation may be significantly impacted if the country's dominant party employs a quota, such as the African National Congress (ANC) in South Africa (Dahlerup 2004). Sometimes, party quotas are adopted in conjunction with other quota systems in various countries to advance women's representation. Aspirants' quotas, which limit the number of women who can be considered for nomination in the pre-selection process, and candidate quotas, which mandate that parties include a certain percentage of women in their final lists of candidates, are categories that fall under party quotas (Matland 2006).

Reserved Seats System

Reserved seats are positions that are solely open to female candidates. These seats are used as a more direct means of controlling the proportion of women in elected posts and are backed by law (Pande and Ford 2011:8). Countries that use the reserve seats system fill seats in parliaments through special election lists, distinct party lists, or unique direct appointment procedures (Htun 2004). Reserved seats are mostly used in the Middle East, Asia, and Africa (Krook 2004). In countries like Jordan, Uganda, and Rwanda, gender quotas are increasingly being implemented using reserved seat systems, and the women elected under these systems are elected rather than appointed. There are no reserved seats in Western Europe, North America, Australia, or New Zealand. The majority of scholars contend that reserved seats should be considered a type of quota because their regulations give clear guarantees as to who may enter political life rather than influencing candidate nomination processes (Dahlerup 2006a). Related to reserved seats system is the idea of 'double quota', which is used to characterise quota systems that not only call for a particular proportion of female candidates to be included on the electoral list but also work to keep them from being relegated to the bottom of the list with little prospect of winning. Examples of countries that have constitutional requirements for double quotas are Belgium and Argentina. Unlike legislated or party quotas that do not guarantee that women will be elected to political positions, reserved seats ensure that women occupy a certain percentage of political positions.

Discussions on the forms of quotas address the following two questions: Who mandated the system, and at what stage? It also indicates that the degree to which quotas are regulated varies: Some are controlled by constitutional provisions or electoral laws, and others are controlled by party regulations. By changing the fundamental definitions of equality and representation that guide the candidate selection process, quota policies make significant strides toward legitimising positive actions and recognising gender as a political identity.

Effectiveness of Gender Quotas for Descriptive Women's Representation

Despite significant efforts to promote women's political engagement, women, minorities, and minority women continue to be notably under-represented in high-level political roles globally (Paxton and Hughes 2007). As a result, there was an increased need to explicitly encourage women to participate in decision-making using practical instruments. Hence, most countries implemented quota laws and policies requiring women to be included on candidate lists or in representative bodies to address ongoing disparities (Dahlerup 2006a). The main goal of quotas is to increase the number of women in political positions, which is descriptive women's representation. Quotas help to ensure numerical similarity between political bodies and the people they represent in terms of characteristics such as gender. As more and more countries adopt quotas as corrective instruments to address the underrepresentation of women in politics, the call for descriptive representation of women gained momentum (Squires 1996). Political quotas vary greatly across the globe because of their influence to ensure the political representation of former excluded social groups. Krook and O'Brien (2010) assert that quotas promote representation by gender, colour, ethnicity, etc. Quotas seek to ensure that women make up a sizeable minority of 20%, 30%, or 40% or ensure a 50/50 split in political positions, notable of which is in the parliament. Schwindt-Bayer (2009) confirms that the descriptive representation of women is significantly improved via quotas.

Some countries use quotas as a temporary measure until the obstacles hindering women's political participation are resolved, but most quota-using countries have not resolved these obstacles over time, thereby prolonging their use (Tripp 2004). Since the underrepresentation of women is typically a problem that needs to be addressed, most quotas attempt to increase the representation of women, which is especially relevant given that women typically make up 50% of the population. Pande and Ford (2011: 11) argue that quotas are designed to improve the proportion of women in positions of leadership. By formally requiring that certain roles be reserved for women, prejudice is avoided. They explain that quotas enable fair representation of women in leadership roles when the political system's structure hinders women's political advancement. Quotas are implemented in countries where women make up a small minority in the parliament to ensure an increase in their numbers. Dahlerup and

Freidenvall (2005: 27) assert that "we are currently witnessing historically significant increases in women's representation, such as the rise of Costa Rica's female representation in the parliament from 19 to 35% in just one election, or South Africa's 30% female electorate in the country's first democratic parliamentary election". The effectiveness of quotas motivated scholars to claim that due the prevalent adoption of quotas, new paths for equal political participation for women are now viable, in contrast to earlier experiences.

Women's organisations typically mobilise in favour of quotas when they learn that they are effective at promoting an increase in women's political representation. These women may be represented by women's groups inside political parties, women's movements within civil society, women's organisations abroad, or even just one or two powerful women (Bruhn 2003). Krook and O'Brien (2010) highlight that implementing quotas that demand a certain amount of representation for women, racial and ethnic minorities, or other underrepresented groups on the ballot or in the decision-making body is one way to increase the descriptive diversity of political bodies. According to O'Brien and Rickne (2016), quotas ensure that specific number of seats in the parliament be set aside for women while also encouraging political parties to delimit some constituencies for female candidates. This led to declaration that the overall objective of quotas to raise the proportion of women in office has been achieved.

Women's empowerment has been aided by the adoption of certain political measures such as quotas to guarantee a better gender balance. Out of 279 posts globally, there were 55 women in charge of national parliament chambers in 2018 (IPU 2008). In countries with special measures like quotas, the representation of women in parliaments has dramatically increased. For instance, France, which is in the EU, has had the highest increase in the proportion of women in the parliament by passing legislation that promote gender parity in elected positions. At the end of 2008, there were 24.1% more women serving in the parliament than there were 20 years prior, a rise of 13% (IPU 2008). Quotas have also been used to enhance women's involvement in political leadership in Africa. For instance, studies of both Tanzania (Yoon 2011) and Rwanda (Burnet 2011) suggest that quotas have transformed negative cultural and social beliefs about women's participation in politics and granted women access to leadership positions from which they had traditionally been excluded. In Niger, the quota law increased the number of women in elected office from 1.2% in 1999 to 12.4% in 2004, and there are more females in executive cabinet and other government positions (Kang 2013).

Quotas have been useful in facilitating the achievement of a 'critical mass', which is considered to be established with roughly 30% representation, which is beneficial for improving overall mobilisation along gender lines (Peschard 2003: 26). Whether it be a candidate list, legislative assembly, committee, or government, quotas for women must make up a specific number or percentage of the membership. The system's main goal is to elevate women into political leadership roles and make sure that they are more than just a bystander to politics. Critical mass suggests "that women should make up 30% of all political bodies which according to international organisations, transnational networks, party politicians, women's activists, and even regular citizens, is the magic number where female legislators are supposedly able to make a difference" (Dahlerup 1988: 280). It assumes that as their numbers rise, women will be able to work together more effectively, and in some cases, women do seem to make a difference, sometimes even more so when they represent a small minority of legislators, either because their numbers increase, and male legislators retaliate or because their numbers rise and allow individual women to pursue other policy goals. Improved representation of women's policy interests can be achieved by increasing the proportion of female leaders through quotas (Pande and Ford 2011: 11). The relevance is that quotas help increase the number of women in the parliament, which enables the critical mass needed to represent women issues.

ROLE OF THE ELECTORAL SYSTEM IN THE SUCCESS OF GENDER QUOTAS

When discussing the effectiveness of quotas in facilitating women's descriptive representation, it is important to include the impact the electoral system has on such effectiveness. The type of electoral system in place affects the success of the quota system adopted. A proportional representation (PR) system is most compatible with a quota system as it enables the inclusion of women in party lists, which would be difficult to achieve in a first-past-the-post (FPTP) simple majority system. Dahlerup and Friedenvall (2005: 36) attest that "even though quota provisions are being tested in majority systems like the UK, France, India, Bangladesh, and Nepal, quota provisions are unquestionably more compatible with PR electoral systems than with majority systems". PR is the electoral system where quotas are most easily implemented; for instance, 67 out of the 135 countries with quota systems have a PR electoral system, and the other 68 are divided among other electoral systems such as FPTP, Parallel, MMP, etc. (International IDEA 2024) (Fig. 3.1).

This is not to say that quotas are impossible with majority systems, but the operationality does not lead to significant increases in women's representation. Taking into account only the 89 countries that Freedom House (2006) rates as free, parliaments established under simple majority had an average female membership of 10.8% in October 2005, mixed system assemblies had a rate of 17.7%, and PR-based parliaments had a rate of 21.1%. In other words, parliaments created by PR have two times as many women in them as legislative assemblies created through majority systems (particularly with party lists). This data supports several research findings that PR has a better ability to feminise parliaments than majority systems (Matland 1998; Norris 2004: 179; Rule 1994). Therefore, PR appears to be better suited than majority systems to facilitate the formation of a critical mass of female MPs. While electoral systems, descriptive representation, and critical mass do have substantial correlations, the same cannot be said for the substantive representation of women. Ideally, PR appears to provide a more favourable environment for the substantive representation

Quotas & Electoral systems

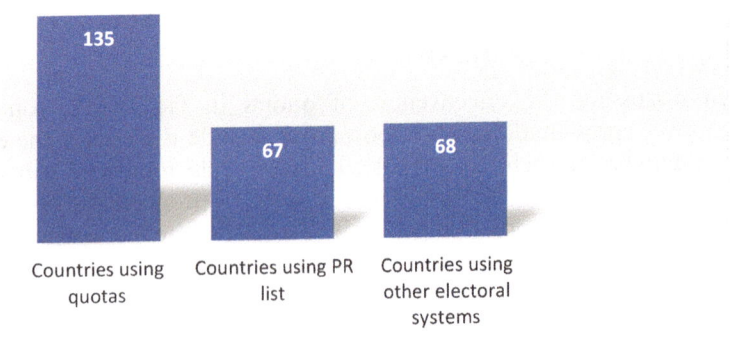

Fig. 3.1 Overview of countries using quotas and electoral system. (Source: International IDEA 2024)

of women. However, studies of female politicians who were elected using a variety of electoral systems and who made up wildly varying percentages in their national parliaments (13% in France compared to 50% in Wales) point to the common conclusion that they understood their obligation to represent women. A critical mass of women appears to be a condition that enables substantive women's representation because PR often produces higher proportions of female parliamentarians than majority systems, and thus, the former has greater potential to improve substantive representation of women than majority systems. The compatibility of PR system with quotas is not absolute because depending on the kind of quotas adopted in the PR systems, some political parties may find it difficult to implement quotas since they may be perceived as interfering with party politics. For instance, if a legislated quota is provided for without consolidating it with party quotas, those parties may argue that the law is interfering with the composition of their party list.

LIMITATIONS OF QUOTAS

There is frequently disagreement among women as a group over the merits of gender quotas. Feminists, both inside and outside political parties, have been some of the sharpest opponents, arguing that quotas do not further the cause of women empowerment or are not based on merit and competence (Amar 1999; Huang 2002; Kishwar 1998). Murray (2014) responds to concerns about quotas not based on merit, she argues that this furthers the notion that men are expected to be in politics without having to prove themselves which gives them an unfair advantage. She notes that competence or merit is not asked from men when conversations on gender quotas are raised.

Contestation regarding the use of gender quotas touches on theoretical discussion of "women as a group and highlight the issue of whether it is ethically appropriate to continue referring to one specific group of women as we. One may argue that women as a group are both the Achilles' heel of the feminist movement and its raison d'e^tre (Dahlerup and Freidenvall 2005: 31). Because quotas only address one aspect of inequality at a time, they may reinforce intra-group disparities. In addition, "because women and minorities are disproportionately underrepresented in politics, a measure to increase their participation may increase the likelihood that a more diverse group of women or minorities will be elected" (Mansbridge 1999: 636). Quotas have drawbacks because while certain quotas are linked to improved minority women's parliamentary representation, other quota systems disadvantage minority women. The specific groups targeted and the level (national, party, or both) at which quotas are regulated, may help to clarify how quotas affect the descriptive representation of minority women. Mansbridge (2005: 631) argues that while "quotas can disprove some essentialist theories by, for instance, allowing enough women of various types to participate in politics such that both men and women can see them as capable leaders". They can also strengthen essentialist attitudes by claiming that "only women can represent women for essentialist reasons and therefore that women cannot represent men". The most apparent manner that quotas might rigidify group lines is by requiring members of one group to vote exclusively for members of that group and not for members of other groups. On the other spectrum of re-enforcing disparities, critics of quotas in countries where they are seen as a way to advance equality and equitable access have contended that they are unconstitutional or illegal because they discriminate against men (Guadagnini 2005).

Institutional factors often hinder the effectiveness of quotas, which is why Dahlerup and Freidenvall (2005: 37) note that while some countries have seen significant gains in the number of women parliamentarians since the implementation of gender quotas, others have seen more modest improvements or even declines. This is because decision-makers often give the implementation procedure intended to make quotas effective little thought. If the execution of quota restrictions is not regulated and there are no penalties for non-compliance, passing them can only be a symbolic gesture. Women's movements must play a significant part not just in the passage of the quota regulations but also in their implementation. When gender quotas were first implemented, they frequently resulted in the appointment of women who were predominantly from powerful political families, and some quotas were openly considered a technique for raising submissive women (Carrió 2003). Carrió (2003) further argues that in these situations, women elected under quotas speak up on women's interests less frequently than women elected in open elections against men. If quota policies advance female lawmakers who are seen as submissive or redundant by their voters and colleagues, women elected through this process may avoid pursuing "legislative agendas that are counter-cultural, such as taking a firm stance on women's rights" (Carrió 2003: 170). Researchers identify instances where quota-elected women show excessive loyalty to ruling elites, frequently in authoritarian or semi-authoritarian contexts that limit their liberty to speak out on issues beyond the party chapter dominated by men (Bauer 2008; Walsh 2012). Another problem is that women may be reluctant to speak up about issues that disproportionately affect women for fear that doing so may hinder their ability to grow in their careers. Clayton (2015: 340) argues that "under these circumstances, negative quota effects which highlight difference between women who enter into legislative office with and without quotas, damper the potential for quotas to be used to increase women's descriptive representation". The degree to which a certain culture at a specific point in history may recognise quotas as legitimate also affects how effective they are (Mansbridge 2005: 629); for instance, "in the United States, the name quota itself suggests that merit, individual worth, and fair competition are not important, besides the fact that the state should not interfere with people's freedoms".

Continental Context on Gender Quotas and Descriptive Women's Representation

Historical Overview of Adoption of Gender Quotas in Africa

Tripp (2004: 70) notes that "the introduction of quotas in Africa largely began in 1996, with most countries implementing them from 2000". This adoption is attributed to regional parliamentary conventions and the 1995 BPfA, which aimed for 30% female representation by 2005. By recognising the exclusion that African women face in politics while acknowledging the many barriers preventing them from entering politics, we can begin to understand that quotas are not discriminatory toward men, but rather a restitution for all the challenges that women face (Ballington 2004). It is maintained that quotas are necessary until all these barriers are addressed, and therefore, they are a temporary measure to ensure women's political participation. However, removing all social, cultural, and political obstacles to equitable female representation might take decades because the obstacles that limit women's political participation in Africa are deeply entrenched in cultural and religious norms, making them difficult to totally eradicate. Hence, quotas provide face value solution to this problem. Moreso, because the issue to be addressed is the underrepresentation of women in African politics, quotas strive to increase their representation. Given that women typically make up 50% or even more of the population on the continent, this measure is very important (Dahlerup 2004: 19). Ballington (2004) notes that most African countries that have adopted gender quotas did so after 1995. This coincided with the UN conference for women and the insertion of Article 7 in the CEDAW. These two monumental instruments that established principles for enhancing the political representation of women were widely mentioned by the countries and parties that enacted quotas. They provided unequivocal evidence of the influence of the global movement for women on the implementation of quotas in Africa. Prior to 1995, just three African countries had quotas, with notable mention of Uganda. This does not include the Convention People's Party's endorsement of a quota of 10 women in Ghana in 1960 or the implementation of 8% quotas in Egypt from 1979 to 1986. African regional organisations were pressured by female activists to urge their member states to increase female representation. Equal gender representation was demanded under the 2003 African Union Protocol on the Rights of Women in Africa, the 1997 Southern African Development Community (SADC) Declaration on Gender and Development, and the 2001 Economic Community of West African States (ECOWAS) Protocol on Democracy and Good Governance. Additionally, there have been initiatives to increase the proportion of women in these regional bodies to one-third. Furthermore, the Female Parliamentary Association in the ECOWAS region advocated for more women in national legislatures, and the East African Legislative Assembly demanded one-third female representation (Ballington 2004).

A quota system generally signifies a departure from the common gradual equality efforts to a more fast-track model (Dahlerup 2006a). This is based on the backdrop of recommendations from international organisations and changes in various national contexts, which have increasing impact on the choice of whether or not to implement a quota. In terms of examining the triumphs and failures connected to quota implementation, Africa is an interesting region. Women's organisations at local and regional levels actively advocated for quotas in a number of the countries where discussions regarding the implementation of quotas are now taking place. Governments in Africa, for their part, have frequently sought quotas for two reasons: Firstly, mostly for symbolic reasons in an effort to win over female voters and convey a concern for women's rights and voices; and secondly, in reaction to shifting worldwide standards for female representation. The former relates to government officials trying to establish new channels of patronage by appointing women who will remain loyal to them, such as in Uganda (Tamale 2004). Irrespective of the initial intent for the adoption of quotas, it is crucial that they are implemented in a way that prioritises the needs of women and that the conditions are acceptable to them (Tripp 2004). Dahlerup (2004: 17) highlights that the continental adoption of quota systems signals a change in strategy from 'equal opportunity' to 'equality of results'. She notes further that it is preferable to consider electoral gender quotas as an example of 'equal opportunity' since most quota systems only stipulate the amount of women and men to be presented to voters on electoral lists and not the gender distribution after the election. Both men and women have an equal opportunity to introduce themselves to voters, and in majority and open list PR systems, voters may choose to support a female or male candidate. In a closed list system, quotas really determine which candidates will be chosen, but the electorate still decides how many seats should be given to each party. But for equality of results, quotas ensure that women are represented in political offices after the elections.

Adoption of Quotas in Africa

Important examples of quotas that exist in institutions other than national legislatures include the SADC Policy Forum and the African Union (AU). Although it may be too soon to discuss a continent-wide tradition of quota implementation, there are several instances where quotas have helped ensure women have access to decision-making structures.

For the AU, Maboreke (2002 cited in Ballington 2004) emphasises that during the Inaugural Session of the Heads of State and Government in 2002, the AU paved the way for gender parity quotas by adopting a 50% gender equality quota. This 50% gender quota for women was to be applied to all major decision-making levels, from commissions to senior appointments. She explains that the 1990s-adopted African and Global Platforms for Action provided impetus for the AU to adopt a quota system and that the recommendation of 30% women in decision-making structures was increased to 50%. She states that "instead of resulting from the organised lobbying efforts of women, it was dialogue with civil society, teamwork, and the political will of the leadership that were the factors responsible for the equality rule entering into force" (Maboreke 2002 cited in Ballington 2004: 29).

Southern Africa

The SADC region serves as an important example for the adoption of gender quotas to facilitate women's political participation in Africa. The region's Declaration on Gender (SADC 1997) provides an essential element for the advancement of women's political participation in the region, which was drawn from the BPfA. The declaration enjoined SADC member states to meet a target of 30% of women in decision-making bodies by 2005. To ensure the goal is reached, a number of action programmes were created, of which gender quotas were an important part. This declaration came about in the wake of women's constant mobilisation for practical instruments to ensure increased political participation of women. The SADC heads of state and governments committed to using "all techniques available to raise the participation of women at all levels of decision-making to 30% by 2005" when they signed the Declaration on Gender and Development in 1997 (Kethusegile-Juru 2004: 20). The heads of state and government pledged in Article 8 that they and their respective countries would, among other things, "ensure the equal representation of women and men in the decision-making of member states and SADC structures at all levels and the achievement of at least 30% women's representation by the year 2005" (SADC 1997: Art. 8).

Kethusegile-Juru (2004: 21) highlights that the declaration was a response to the call to action by the BPfA, which aimed to ensure 30% women's participation in decision-making structures and also addressed the growing inequalities between men and women. After the SADC Declaration on Gender and Development was signed, there were more calls for particular steps to be taken to help fulfil this pledge of which gender quotas were suggested as a viable option for women (Kethusegile-Juru 2004). As a result of the adoption of quotas, the minimum target of 30% female representation in the parliament in SADC was achieved. The regional mobilisation of women in support of the 30% aim outlined in the SADC Declaration on Gender aided the achievement of 30% women's political participation (Gender Links 2005). SADC countries that passed quotas into law or implemented constitutional amendments to include women at the party or national level have seen considerable increase in the number of women in the parliament. For instance, SWAPO in Namibia, ANC in South Africa, and the Zimbabwe African National Union-Patriotic Front (ZANU-PF) made it a requirement that women hold 30% of all positions with decision-making structures. The opposition parties in

Botswana, such as the Botswana National Front (BNF) and the Botswana Congress Party (BCP), also implemented minimum quotas of 30% of women inside their party structures in Botswana. However, compared to their counterparts, neither party in Botswana established any measures to guarantee that these clauses are effectively carried out (Ntseane and Sentsho 2005).

It is interesting to note that most African countries' adoption of quota systems has been directly correlated with women's movements, and most documented instances of the efforts of women's groups come from Southern Africa. The ANC Women's League in South Africa led the effort to raise the proportion of women in the parliament and achieved a quota of 30% (Hendricks 2004). Prior to the 1999 Namibian elections, the Namibian Women's Manifesto Network, a group of women's movements and other NGOs, lobbied several parties to adopt resolutions requiring party lists with 50% female candidates, which increased female representation in the parliament from 12.5% in 1994 to 26.4% in 1999 (Electoral Institute for Sustainable Democracy in Africa 2009). However, parties in Namibia did not adhere to the resolutions, which affected the number of women that were elected. For example, only 20 of the ruling party's 72 candidates were women. Following this, the Namibian Women's Manifesto Network launched the 50/50 campaign to fight for 50% female representation in the legislature in 2000. The BCP Women's Congress discussed several implementation tactics and recommended reserved seats as the best method for making the quota easier to execute, but the party leadership rejected this. There is a general tendency in Southern Africa to use quotas or other proactive measures that were mostly advocated for by women's movements across the region. These efforts have yielded a positive result for the region, and most of the SADC members states increased women's political participation, except for Botswana, which has the lowest (Kethusegile-Juru 2004).

West Africa

Ballington (2004: 54) argues that Senegal is performing relatively better than many of its West African neighbours. As of 2024, the country boasts 46.06% female MPs in its national parliament because of its adoption of a legislated candidate quota with a parity law that was adopted in 2010 (IPU 2024). Toraasen (2017) writes that the parity law mandated political parties to include women and men in an alternating format on their lists aiming towards 50:50. This achievement is lauded to be due to the strong women's movement in Senegal known as Conseil Senegalais des Femmes founded in 1994. Prior to this, Kassé (2004) examined the slow improvement in women's access to the legislature as well as Senegal's limited attempt at political party quotas. For instance, in 2003, women represented 19% of MPs, which was up from a 12% participation in 1993. To address this, some parties decided to enact female candidate quotas, ranging from 25% to 40%, in advance of the 1998 elections. However, this quota was only applicable to the PR portion of the poll due to Senegal's mixed electoral system that combines PR lists with constituency elections (Kassé 2004). As with any PR system, the selection panel and members of the party's decision-making bodies plays a key role in determining the quantity and placement of women on lists. Furthermore, even if the national party leadership may in theory support quotas, their execution is frequently opposed by the party's local structures or grassroots as well as by women who view quotas as discriminatory. Similar to Southern Africa, women's movements advocated for political parties to include women in their party lists, banking on the support of the international and regional community (Diop 2001). Kassé (2004) notes that the Senegalese Council for Women devised ways to cooperate with diverse political players with the capacity to expand women's representation because there were no legislative provisions to ensure the promotion of women to elected office. These included the media, civil society in general, women's groups, political parties, and women's political movements. A coalition of women's organisations launched a citizen campaign during the Senegalese parliamentary elections in 2001 to draw attention to the underrepresentation of women in the legislature. They aimed to change the situation when only 19 of 140 legislators (13.5%) were women. During the run-up to the 2001 legislative elections, the majority of Senegal's 25 political parties fielded over 20% female candidates on national lists, and the Parti Démocratique Sénégalais list reached over 33%. This was an unprecedented development. As a result of this effort taken by women, Senegal was able to increase women's presence in the parliament to 19.2% of the seats, an increase of nearly 6%. (Kassé 2004: 67). The case of Senegal lends credence to the diffusion factor discussed in the literature review wherein parties are likely to adopt quotas when one party implements quotas. In African countries, it is particularly clear that if one party implements quotas, other parties can feel pressured to follow suit in order to retain the support of women voters. Senegal also serves as an example of the importance of political will towards increasing women's representation, the government showed its commitment by passing the law on parity which aided the increased representation of women in politics.

East Africa

Tamale (2004) explains that electoral quotas in Uganda are strongly backed by the law. Article 32(1) of the Ugandan Constitution explicitly provides for the implementation of affirmative action; it states that "the State shall take affirmative action in favour of groups that are disadvantaged on the basis of gender, age, disability, or any other basis resulting from history, tradition, or custom, with a view to redressing imbalances that are in their favour" (cited in Tamale 2004: 38). By allowing for a certain number of reserved seats in the national parliament equal to the number of districts in the country, the 1995 constitution codified the quota system. It ensured women would hold one-third of the seats in municipal councils. In addition, women benefit from the restricted number of quota seats set up for workers, youth, and people with disabilities. Reserved seats for women were introduced in 1986 in Uganda as a pioneering step to increase women's presence. These combined efforts put women's representation in Uganda in the top 12 countries in Africa at 33.9% (IPU 2024). Rwanda is another notable East African example of the adoption of gender quotas. In 2003, Rwanda amended its constitution to include the provision of quotas by pledging to increase women's participation in decision-making structures. This constitutional provision mandated that women make up at least 30% of all political positions at different levels of governance. It ensured that a certain number of seats were reserved for women without any competition to those seats as in the case of Uganda (Powley 2008). To this end, Rwanda combined the power of the constitution and a reservation system to increase women's participation. This feat yielded the desired result when in 2003 it successfully surpassed the Nordic countries in women's political representation. Women's participation in political positions in Rwanda is currently at 61%, which is the highest in the world (IPU 2022)

North Africa

Abou-Zeid (2004) asserts that Egypt was one of the first countries in Africa and one of the first Arab countries to implement reservations for women; although they are no longer in effect. In 1979, there was a presidential decree that reserved 30 of the 360 seats in the parliament for women. This was against the backdrop of the momentum generated by the first World Conference on Women held in Mexico in 1975 and the CEDAW of 1977. She notes that the law on reserves for women was repealed in 1986 but that it was still in effect when the electoral system was examined in the 1980s. Due to the reserves getting repealed, the percentage of women in the parliament decreased from 10% to 2.2%, and locally similar losses were noted. Akin to Uganda, the idea behind the adoption of reserves was to give women descriptive representation in addition to the seats that had previously been set aside for workers and farmers (Abou-Zeid 2004: 46).

Types of Quotas Adopted in Africa

Several types of quota systems have been adopted in Africa, ranging from legislated, voluntary to reserve seats system. All these systems aim to increase women's political participation.

Legislative Quotas

Out of the 45 countries in Africa that have adopted quotas, more than 30 use legislated quotas to ensure the inclusion of women in national parliaments. These countries include Algeria, Djibouti, Kenya, Senegal, Uganda, and Rwanda (International IDEA 2024). Legislative quotas were implemented in Africa for a variety of reasons by different actors. They are a result of shifting international standards for female representation, which are reflected in numerous conventions and resolutions as well as in the legislative goals set by regional organisations like the AU, the SADC, and the Economic Community of West African States. Legislated quotas were used to pave new ways for female voters as well as to develop new grounds for patronage networks due to the emergence of multi-partyism and the loss of large-scale women's organisations linked to a single party (Tripp 2004: 72). This type of quota is embedded in the constitution, and enjoys the legitimacy of the constitution, they cannot be overridden by any statute and are required and enforceable across all parties and the current administration. Looking at the proliferation of legislated quotas on the continent, it can be argued that African countries understand that legitimising the use of quotas via the constitution ensures better result for women's representation than leaving it to the mercy of political parties. Tanzania serves as an illustration of this: Its constitution requires that 33% of local representatives and 20% of MPs are female (Meena 2004). Another feature of the adoption of this form of quota is that they are often combined with other kinds of quota; for instance, Rwanda and Uganda adopted both legislated and reserved seats quotas, and Angola, Benin Republic, and Zimbabwe adopted voluntary quotas in addition to legislated quotas (International IDEA 2024).

Voluntary Quotas

Sixteen African countries have voluntary party quotas, e.g., South Africa, Namibia, Malawi, and Botswana (International IDEA 2024). The benefit of a voluntary party quota is that it significantly increases the possibility of women's entry and participation in the parliament, especially when implemented by the ruling party, such as in the case of the ANC in South Africa (Dahlerup 2006a; Hendricks 2004). Political parties typically implement voluntary quotas on their own either as a result of provisions in the party's policy documents and practices or as a result of the 'goodwill' of the party leadership. The party is not required to carry out the provision by any law, as in the case of BCP and BNF in Botswana. These two parties included a provision for 30% quota without putting in place practical mechanisms to actualise it (Ntseane and Sentsho 2005). Party quotas are often included in party constitutions or election mandates. The ANC in South Africa and the Front for the Liberation of Mozambique in Mozambique are two successful examples from the SADC region. Kethusegile-Juru (2004) argues that the drawback of party quotas is that it depends on the party maintaining its commitment to upholding it and winning a majority of seats in upcoming elections. Sometimes parties only enact quotas because of pressure from rival parties to remain competitive.

Reserved Quotas

This is a form of legislated quotas as it provides that women occupy a specified number of seats in the parliament. Uganda and Rwanda are notable examples of countries using reserved seats. The intrinsic uniqueness of this type of system is that it can be used by both democratic and undemocratic or semi-democratic governments to foster women's political participation. Tamale (2004: 39) explains that the National Resistance Movement

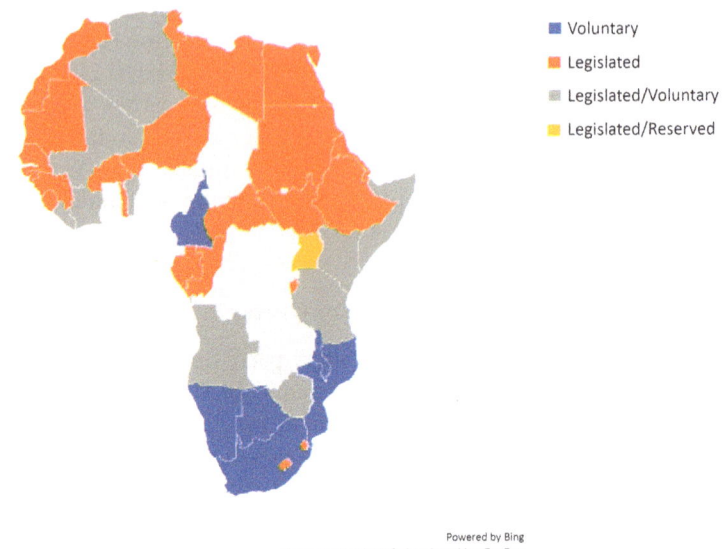

Voluntary
Legislated
Legislated/Voluntary
Legislated/Reserved

Powered by Bing
© GeoNames, Microsoft, OpenStreetMap, TomTom

Fig. 3.2 Overview of quota types used in Arica. (Source: International IDEA 2024)

in Uganda introduced affirmative action for women in 1986 but launched the reserved seat system in 1989. The system provides that "each district is required to elect a female parliamentary representative as well as permit women to run against men in open seats as a result of the government's affirmative action policy". This system guarantees that women hold 27% of the seats in the parliament. In addition to the reserved seats for women, they are allowed to contest in the open election that is available for everyone. The percentage of women in Uganda's parliament has increased to 33.9% as a result of these allocations (IPU 2024). Apart from women, reserved seats are allocated to other groups such as farmers, trade unions, and women's organisations. Voters may or may not have a choice between candidates who belong to a particular group when there are reserved seat quotas (Fig. 3.2).

Quotas and Increased Women's Political Participation in Africa

Tripp and Kang (2008) argue that to enable women's greater access to parliaments, some form of electoral gender quota has been adopted in most African countries. Over the past 40 years, Africa has experienced the highest growth in women's representation in national legislatures. Women made up 1% of African lawmakers in 1960, by 2003, this proportion had increased to 14.3% and as of 2024, the continental average is 26% (Africa Barometer 2024). In terms of the percentage of women in the parliament, four of the top 15 countries in the world are in Africa, with Rwanda leading the pack with 61.3% (Table 3.1).

This achievement can be credited to the increased adoption of quotas, which is partly a result of the influence of the global women's movement. The establishment of international norms on the necessity of including women in politics, which have found expression in conventions and resolutions on a worldwide scale, has considerably aided lobbying efforts. Also, the rise in multiparty elections has increased pressure on political parties to attract women voters and appeal to a wider base. The impacts of

Table 3.1 Top 15 countries for women's representation in the parliament

Country	Quota type	% of women in the parliament
Rwanda	Legislated Reserved	61.3%
Cuba	–	55.74%
Nicaragua	Legislated	53.85%
Mexico	Legislated	50%
Namibia	Voluntary	50%
UAE	None	50%
Costa Rica	Legislated Voluntary	49.12%
Grenada	–	47%
Sweden	Voluntary	46.70%
Bolivia	Legislated	46.16%
Senegal	Legislated	46.06%
Finland	None	46%
New Zealand	Voluntary	45.53%
South Africa	Voluntary	45.04%
Norway	Voluntary	44.38%

Source: IPU (2024); International IDEA (2024)

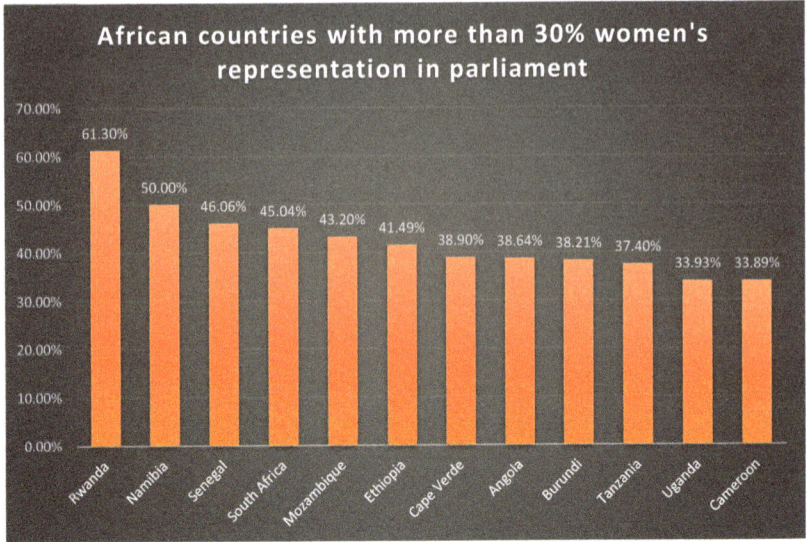

Fig. 3.3 Top African countries for women's representation in the parliament. (Source: IPU 2024)

quotas are evident: The average rate of female representation in quota-enforced countries is over 20%, compared to 10% in countries without quotas (IPU 2024). The average increases to 30% when only countries with quotas of over 20% are included. The percentage of women in the parliament has increased significantly in countries with 30% reserved seats and over 30% quotas for the ruling party or top two parties. This affirms that quotas have been instrumental in increasing women's political participation in most African countries (Fig. 3.3).

Tripp (2004) traces the impact of gender quotas on the descriptive representation of women in Africa. From 1% in 1960 to 14.3% in 2003, there were 10 times more women legislators than there were in 1960. The biggest growth occurred between 1990 and 2003 when the proportion of female seats increased from 8% to 14.3%. In 2003, Rwanda overtook the Nordic countries to become the country with the highest percentage of female legislators when women held 48.8% of parliamentary seats. The growing use of various quotas is one of the key elements responsible for this increase. These quotas are partly the consequence of pressure from both domestic and international women's movements, particularly in

African countries. An excellent example of reaching over the established quota is Rwanda, where Article 9 of the Constitution commits the government of Rwanda to set aside 30% of posts in decision-making bodies to women candidates and Article 82 reserves 30% of seats to women in the Senate (IIDEA 2009). After the 2003 elections, women made up 48.8% of the Lower House and 30% of the Senate, and after the 2008 election, women made up 56.3% of the Lower House and 34.6% of the Senate, making Rwanda the country with the highest percentage of women parliamentarians in the world (IPU 2008). Burnet (2011: 318) asserts that due to its commitment to the established gender quotas, Rwanda was able to equalise gender representation in political positions.

QUOTAS IN AFRICA: DRIVERS

Post-conflict Transition

Several countries in Africa with quotas had just come out of civil conflicts, such as Eritrea, Mozambique, Rwanda, Somalia, and Uganda, or wars of liberation, such as Namibia and South Africa, and as a result, they had to rewrite their constitutions and start new legislatures, which made it easy to include quota provisions for women (Tripp 2004: 70). Tripp (2004: 71) argues that "in Africa, the end of major turmoil and conflict meant that there was greater openness in relation to creating new rules that included female leadership. The drawing up of new constitutions and the redrafting of legislation have created important opportunities for women", and this opportunity allowed women to demand better measures to ensure the increase in women's political representation. More so, the introduction of quotas in this context allows women to run for open and uncontested seats in the case of reserved seats rather than directly challenging a male incumbent. It has historically been challenging to implement female quotas in places where a high percentage of incumbents are male and need to be re-elected. As a result, constitutions adopted during post-conflict transition makes it easier for gender quotas to be implemented to allow for the inclusion of women in legislative bodies. The role of an active women's movement is also important in weaponising the transitory process for gender quotas.

Pressure from Women's Movements

Another factor that often aids the success of gender quotas is the extent to which women's movement push for it. Some scholars argue that women's increased access to political offices is a result of their increased influence in political parties (Morna et al. 2009; Tripp 2004). They note that women's movements have been closely associated with the adoption of gender quotas in most African countries (Tripp 2004: 75). Women want to exercise a well-earned right not because they feel they are due something in return, which is why they strive for leadership and influential positions inside political parties. The reason women, especially in Southern Africa, argue they want to transcend beyond the hospitality right is that they are the ones who support and form the foundation of political parties. An interesting observation is that most countries with gender quotas have very active women's movements because they are able to lobby and push for measures to increase women's representation; examples are South Africa, Senegal, and Namibia.

Electoral System

The electoral system is said to influence women's ability to gain legislative representation, thereby identifying it as an important variable for the success of quotas. A little over 33% of African countries use PR, compared to 31% who use FPTP plurality systems, 18% who use two-round majority voting, and 10% who use FPTP semi-proportional voting (International IDEA 2024). Notable African countries like Liberia, Ghana, Nigeria, Kenya, Botswana, Uganda, and Ethiopia use FPTP voting systems. Ghana and Nigeria have been struggling to adopt any form of quotas that will ensure increased women's participation (Madsen 2019). Apart from Ethiopia (41.3%) and Uganda (33.9%), countries with the FPTP system and without quotas all have below 20% women's political representation. The ones with quotas have relatively low representation compared to countries using the PR system. In general, countries with PR systems have had the most success with quotas, provided that the party leadership exhibits the required political will. Impressive outcomes have come from the voluntary quotas accepted by the ANC in South Africa and the Front for the Liberation of Mozambique in Mozambique. Party quotas in

Table 3.2 Top 12 African countries with quota type, electoral system, and % of women's representation

Country	Quota type	Electoral system	% of women in the parliament
Rwanda	Legislated Reserved	PR	61.3%
Namibia	Voluntary	PR	50%
Senegal	Legislated	Parallel	46.06%
South Africa	Voluntary	PR	45.04%
Mozambique	Voluntary	PR	43.20%
Ethiopia	Legislated	FPTP	41.31%
Cape Verde	Legislated	PR	38.9%
Angola	Legislated Voluntary	PR	38.64%
Burundi	Legislated	PR	38.21%
Tanzania	Legislated Voluntary	FPTP PR	37.40%
Uganda	Legislated Reserved	FPTP	33.93%
Cameroon	Voluntary	FPTP	33.89%

Source: IPU (2024), International IDEA (2024)

constituency electoral systems, on the other hand, have had less success; in Botswana and Zimbabwe, women face off against men in the districts. Another way that women have entered the parliament is through the presidential appointment system, which is used in Zimbabwe, Botswana, and Swaziland. Two countries that have paired a voluntary party quota with a PR electoral system are Mozambique and South Africa. Because of the combination of a PR and a list system, every third person on their respective list is a woman (Kethusegile-Juru 2004). This combined strategy of PR system with voluntary quotas has ensured increased levels of female representation with South Africa at 45.04% and Mozambique at 43.2%, the two highest in the region (International IDEA 2024). Most countries with more than 30% women's political representation use a PR system, notable of which are Rwanda, Mozambique, South Africa, and Namibia (Table 3.2 and Fig. 3.4).

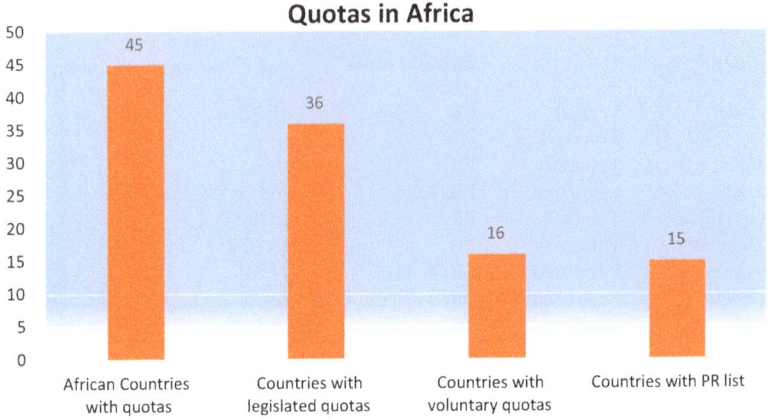

Fig. 3.4 Overview of quota types and electoral systems in Africa. (Source: International IDEA 2024)

Quotas in Africa: Challenges

Kethusegile-Juru (2004) notes that while voluntary quotas by the ruling party is important for increased women's representation, it is not absolute because often the high percentage seen at the national level are not reflected at local levels. For instance, in Mozambique, success at the legislative level has not been mirrored at other levels because even in a PR electoral system, a voluntary quota's success depends on the 'goodwill' of the leadership, the makeup of the party, and the political environment at the time. Kethusegile-Juru (2004: 23) notes that "Zimbabwe, like the ANC in South Africa and Liberation of Mozambique in Mozambique, has a voluntary quota for women and youth. However, because of the constituency-based electoral system, the 'zebra stripe' system for the selection of candidates" (alternating male and female candidates) has not translated into increased women's participation due to lack of proper implementation. As a result, despite the fact that ZANU-PF is the majority party, women have not been as well represented. Similar to this, the two opposition parties (the BCP and the BNF) in Botswana both set a target of 30% women in political positions (Bauer 2011). However, they did not aggressively ensure that the quota was fulfilled by examining their practices to improve access for women, actively seeking out women candidates, encouraging them to run, and creating a supportive environment for them in the primary elections. These parties continue to nominate very few women candidates in the national elections. On the other hand, the Botswana Democratic Party (BDP), which is the governing party, does not have a quota system for women; however, it bowed to pressure from female party members and women's organisations to field more female candidates in the 1999 elections. Many of these candidates were elected and are currently serving in the cabinet and parliament (Kethusegile-Juru 2004: 24). The BDP's success depends entirely on the leadership's 'mercy', party whims, and sensitivities. It may also depend on the regional quota pledge in the SADC Declaration on Gender and Development, which the government of Botswana had ratified. This demonstrates that, while quotas are useful, political parties must also take action, either voluntarily or in response to outside pressure, to ensure their cultures and organisational structures support and encourage women to run for office. Due to the shortcomings of a voluntary quota, a legislated quota is preferable to a voluntary quota that is adopted by one or more parties in a PR system. This suggests that legislated quotas and a PR system are a better combination for achieving gender parity in politics, which is the ultimate objective (Kethusegile-Juru 2004: 24).

Conclusion

The chapter provided a global and continental context on the adoption and implementation of gender quotas. It established the relationship between the adoption of gender quotas and its effectiveness in ensuring descriptive women's representation at the global and continental level. The chapter confirmed that quotas have been useful in facilitating women's political participation, though certain factors, such as electoral system and the extent of implementation, can consolidate or impede its effectiveness. It noted that quotas enable the constituting of a critical mass of women needed to ensure substantive representation. A historical overview of the adoption of quotas in Africa showed that countries across the different sub-regions had adopted some form of quota system. Contextualising the discourse on gender quotas in Africa revealed that the adoption of quotas did not start with the 1995 Beijing Platform for Action as some countries on the continent already adopted some forms of quotas. Most of the literature argues that the adoption of quotas accelerated following the UN BPfA and the signing of CEDAW, due to the fact that both of these instruments advocated for women's increased political participation as a necessity for achieving gender equality. The chapter provided a continental discussion on the impact that gender quota has on increasing women's political participation in Africa. It noted that quotas allow for equality of opportunity as well as equality of results as the latter ensures that women are represented in political positions after election while the former does not. The chapter highlights that the SADC region has been the most successful with quota adoption as most of its member states have increased presence of women in their parliaments. The discussion identified different kinds of quotas adopted, varying from legislated quotas to voluntary party quotas and the reserved seats system, which is a variation of legislated quotas. It argued that proportional representation (PR) is the most suitable electoral system for the implementation of quotas because countries with the highest rate of women's political participation use it. It further noted that the combination of a PR system with a voluntary quota adopted by the governing party enables the significant participation of women in politics. However, this system is not without faults as the mechanism of the quota is left to the goodwill of the party, and therefore, it is necessary for such systems to include quota provisions in the constitution. Recognising that certain drivers were also responsible for the adoption of quotas in Africa, such as post-conflict transition, advocacy by women's movements, etc., helps to provide a holistic understanding to the continental discourse on quotas. While these drivers can ensure the adoption of quotas, the chapter acknowledges that there are challenges that can impede the effectiveness of gender quotas in Africa.

REFERENCES

Abou-Zeid, G. 2004. Introducing quotas in Africa: Discourses in Egypt. In *The implementation of quotas: African experiences*, ed. J. Ballington. Stockholm: International Institute for Democracy and Electoral Assistance.

Africa Barometer. 2024. *Women's political participation.* Second edition of report for the International Institute for Democracy and Electoral Assistance.

Amar, M. 1999. *Le Piege de la patriate: Arguments pour un debate.* Paris: Hachette Literatures.

Baines, B., and R. Rubio-Marin. 2005. Introduction: Toward a feminist constitutional agenda. In *The gender of constitutional jurisprudence*, ed. B. Baines and R. Rubio-Marin. Cambridge: Cambridge University Press.

Baldez, L. 2004. Elected bodies: The gender quota law for legislative candidates in Mexico. *Legislative Studies Quarterly* 24: 231–258.

———. 2006. The pros and cons of gender quota laws: What happens when you kick men out and let women in? *Politics and Gender* 2 (1): 102–109.

Ballington, J. 2004. *The implementation of quotas: African experiences.* Stockholm: International Institute for Democracy and Electoral Assistance.

Bauer, G. 2008. Uganda: Reserved seats for women MPs: Affirmative action for the National Women's Movement or the National Resistance Movement? In *Women and legislative representation: Electoral systems, political parties, and sex quotas, 27–39*, ed. M. Tremblay. New York: Palgrave Macmillan.

———. 2011. Update on the women's movement in Botswana: Have women stopped talking? *African Studies Review* 54 (2): 23–46.

Bruhn, K. 2003. Whores and lesbians: Political activism, party strategies, and gender quotas in Mexico. *Electoral Studies* 22: 101–119.

Burnet, J. 2011. Women have found respect: Gender quotas, symbolic representation, and female empowerment in Rwanda. *Politics & Gender* 7 (3): 303–334.

Carrió, E.M. 2003. *Argentina: A new look at the challenges of women's participation in the legislature.* Presented at the IDEA Workshop, Lima.

Childs, S., and M.L. Krook. 2012. Labels and mandates in the United Kingdom. In *The impact of gender quotas, 89–102*, ed. S. Franceschet, M.L. Krook, and J.M. Piscopo. New York: Oxford University Press.

Clayton, A. 2015. Women's political engagement under quota-mandated female representation: Evidence from a randomized policy experiment. *Comparative Political Studies* 48 (3): 333–369.

Dahlerup, D. 1988. From a small to a large minority: Women in Scandinavian politics. *Scandinavian Political Studies* 11 (4): 275–298.

———. 2004. Quotas are changing the history of women. In *The implementation of quotas: African experiences*, ed. J. Ballington. International Institute for Democracy and Electoral Assistance.

———. 2006a. *Women, quotas and politics.* London: Routledge.

———. 2006b. The story of the theory of critical mass. *Politics & Gender* 2 (4): 511–521.

Dahlerup, D., and L. Freidenvall. 2005. Quotas as a 'fast track' to equal political representation for women: Why Scandinavia is no longer the model. *International Feminist Journal of Politics* 7 (1): 26–48.

Diop, A.S. 2001. *Senegalese women want to be elected not electors.* Pan-African News Agency (PANA).

Electoral Institute for Sustainable Democracy in Africa. 2009. South Africa: Women's representation quotas. https://www.eisa.org/wep/souquotas.htm

Freedom House. 2006. www.freedomhouse.org

Gender Links. 2005. *Fact sheet on governance.* Available at: https://genderlinks.org.za/wpcontent/uploads/imported/articles/attachments/09275_fs2005-2governance.pdf

Guadagnini, M. 2005. Gendering the debate on political representation in Italy: A difficult challenge. In *State feminism and political representation*, ed. J. Lovenduski, 130–152. Cambridge: Cambridge University Press.

Hendricks, C. 2005. Women and party representation. In *South Africa's 2004 election: The quest for democratic consolidation*, ed. L. Piper. EISA Research Report 12.

Htun, M. 2004. Is gender like ethnicity? The political representation of identity groups. *Perspectives on Politics* 2: 439–458.

Huang, C. 2002. *Democracy and the politics of difference: Gender quota in Taiwan.* Paper presented at the Annual Meeting of the American Political Science Association, Boston, MA, August 29–September 1.

Hughes, M.M. 2011. Intersectionality, quotas, and minority women's political representation worldwide. *American Political Science Review* 105 (3): 604–620.

International Institute for Democracy & Electoral Assistance (IIDEA). 2007. Global database of quotas for women. http://www.quotaproject.org.

———. 2009. Global database of quotas for women. www.quotaproject.org

———. 2024. *Global database of quotas for women.* Stockholm University and the Inter-Parliamentary Union. https://www.idea.int/data-tools/data/gender-quotas.

Inter-Parliamentary Union (IPU). 2008. Women in Parliament. www.ipu.org

———. 2024. New Parline, open data platform. https://data.ipu.org/

Kang, A. 2013. The effect of gender quota laws on the election of women: Lessons from Niger. *Women's Studies International Forum* 41 (2): 94–102.

Kassé, A.F. 2004. Women in politics in Senegal. In *The implementation of quotas: African experiences*, ed. J. Ballington. Stockholm: International Institute for Democracy and Electoral Assistance.

Kethusegile-Juru, M. 2004. Quota systems in Africa: An overview. In *The implementation of quotas: African experiences*, ed. J. Ballington. Stockholm: International Institute for Democracy and Electoral Assistance.

Kishwar, M. 1998. Women's Reservation Bill is a setback to feminist. *India Abroad*, July 31.

Krook, M.L. 2004. Gender quotas as a global phenomenon: Actors and strategies in quota adoption. *European Political Science* 3 (3): 59–65.

Krook, M. 2005. *Politicizing representation: Campaigns for candidate gender quotas worldwide.* PhD dissertation,. Columbia University.

Krook, M.L. 2006. Reforming representation: The diffusion of candidate gender quotas worldwide. *Politics & Gender* 2: 303–327.

Krook, M.L., and D. O'Brien. 2010. The politics of group representation: Quotas for women and minorities worldwide. *Comparative Politics* 42 (3): 253–272.

Krook, M.L., J. Lovenduski, and J. Squires. 2008. *Gender quotas and models of political citizenship.* Paper presented at the Midwest Political Science Association National Conference, Chicago, IL April 3–6. http://mlkrook.org/pdf/KLS_MPSA_2008.pdf

Lovenduski, J., and P. Norris, eds. 1993. *Gender, and party politics.* Thousand Oaks: Sage.

Madsen, D. 2019. *Women's political representation and affirmative action in Ghana.* Nordic Africa Institute Policy Note no. 1.

Mansbridge, J. 1999. Should Blacks represent Blacks and women represent women? A contingent 'Yes'. *The Journal of Politics* 61 (3): 628–657.

———. 2005. Quota problems: Combating the dangers of essentialism. *Politics & Gender* 4: 622–638.

Matland, R. 1998. Enhancing women's political participation: Legislative recruitment and electoral systems. In *Women in parliament: Beyond numbers,* ed. A. Karam, 65–88. Stockholm: International IDEA.

———. 2006. Electoral quotas: Frequency and effectiveness. In *Women, quotas and politics,* ed. D. Dahlerup. New York: Routledge.

Meena, R. 2004. The politics of quotas in Tanzania. In *The implementation of quotas: African experiences,* ed. J. Ballington, 82–86. Stockholm: International Institute for Democracy and Electoral Assistance.

Meier, P. 2004. The mutual contagion effect of legal and party quotas: A Belgian perspective. *Party Politics* 10: 583–600.

Morna, C.L., K. Rama, and L. Mtonga. 2009. Gender in the 2009 South African elections. Gender Links, 11 May. http://www.genderlinks.org.za/attachment_view.php?pa_id=1056

Murray, R. 2014. Quotas for men: Reframing gender quotas as a means for improving representation for all. *The American Political Science Review* 108 (3): 520–532.

Norris, P. 2004. *Electoral engineering: Voting rules and political behavior.* Cambridge: Cambridge University Press.

Ntseane, D., and J. Sentsho. 2005. Women's representation in parliament and council: A comparative analysis. In *40 years of democracy in Botswana,* ed. Z. Maundeni. Gaborone: Mmegi Publishing House.

O'Brien, D., and J. Rickne. 2016. Gender quotas and women's political leadership. *American Political Science Review* 110 (1): 112–116.

Olaitan, Z.M. 2023. *Gender quotas and the substantive representation of women in African politics: Case studies of Botswana and South Africa.* Doctoral Thesis, University of Pretoria.

Olaitan, Z.M., and C.A. Isike. 2024. Gender quotas as a mechanism for engendering political transformation in Africa. *The African Review* 1: 1–21.

Pande, R., and D. Ford. 2011. *Gender quotas and female leadership.* World Bank Development Report Background Paper on Gender Equality and Development.

Paxton, P., and M. Hughes. 2007. *Women, politics and power: A global perspective.* Sage Publications.

Peschard, J. 2003. An overview of the quota systems in Latin America. In *The implementation of quotas: Latin American experiences,* 20–30. Quota Workshop Report Series no. 2. Stockholm: International IDEA.

Powley, E. 2008. *Demonstrating legislative leadership: The introduction of Rwanda' gender- based violence bill.* The initiative for Inclusive Society. Available at: https://www.inclusivesecurity.org/publication/demonstrating-legislative-leadershiptheintroduction-of-rwandas-gender-based-violence-bill/.

Protocol to the African Charter on Human and Peoples' Rights on the Rights of Women in Africa 2003.

Rule, W. 1994. Parliaments of, by, and for the People: Except for women? In *Electoral systems in comparative perspective: Their impact on women and minorities*, ed. W. Rule and J.F. Zimmerman, 15–30. Westport, CT: Greenwood Press.

Schwindt-Bayer, L.A. 2007. Review of women, quotas and politics. *Politics & Gender* 3 (2): 289–291.

———. 2009. Making quotas work: The effect of gender quota laws on the election of women. *Legislative Studies Quarterly* 34 (1): 5–28.

Southern African Development Community (SADC). 1997. *Declaration on gender and development.* https://www.tralac.org/documents/resources/sadc/1263-sadc-declaration-on-gender-and-development-8-september-1997/file.html

Squires, J. 1996. Quotas for women: Fair representation? In *Women in politics*, ed. J. Lovenduski and P. Norris, 73–90. New York: Oxford University Press.

Tamale, S. 2004. Introducing quotas: Discourses and legal reform in Uganda. In *The implementation of quotas: African experiences*, ed. J. Ballington. Stockholm: International Institute for Democracy and Electoral Assistance.

Toraasen, M. 2017. *Gender parity in Senegal—A continuing struggle.* Chr. Michelsen Institute (Insights CMI no.2). https://www.cmi.no/publications/6230-gender-parity-in-senegal-a-continuing-struggle

Tripp, A.M. 2004. The changing face of Africa's legislatures: Women and quotas. In *The implementation of quotas: African experiences*, ed. J. Ballington. Stockholm: International Institute for Democracy and Electoral Assistance.

Tripp, A.M., and A. Kang. 2008. The global impact of quotas on the fast track to increased female legislative representation. *Comparative Political Studies* 41 (3): 338–361.

United Nations (UN). 1995. *Beijing declaration and platform for action.* https://www.un.org/womenwatch/daw/beijing/platform/

Walsh, D. 2012. Party centralization and debate conditions in South Africa. In *The impact of gender quotas*, ed. M.L. Krook, S. Franceschet, and J. Piscopo, 119–135. New York: Oxford University Press.

Yoon, M. 2011. More women in the Tanzanian legislature: Do numbers matter? *Journal of Contemporary African Studies* 29 (1): 83–98.

Zetterberg, P. 2009. Do gender quotas foster women's political engagement? Lessons from Latin America. *Political Research Quarterly* 62 (4): 715–730.

———. 2013. The dynamic relationship between gender quotas and political institution. *Politics & Gender* 9 (3): 316–321.

CHAPTER 4

Theorising the Impact of Women's Political Representation

Feminism is the radical notion that women are people.

–Marie Shear (1986)

INTRODUCTION

Literature on women's political representation focuses on the need to foster their increased participation and understanding how that participation benefits them. The theorising of the impact of women's political representation primarily looks at the different theoretical underpinnings on how to ensure the protection of women's interests. More specifically, it looks at whether the participation of women in politics is a necessity for substantive women's representation (protection of women's interests) and why it has to be female politicians that foster this protection within the broader political system. These questions have informed debates on the relationship between the participation of women and the substantive representation of women. To better organise the discourse on this subject, this chapter adopts two theories, namely the theory of the politics of presence and the relational feminist theory, to guide the theorising.

The theory of politics of presence and relational feminism explain the need for women's participation in the political system and the best way to foster the substantive representation of women. The theory of politics of presence is an important democratic lens through which to understand the symbolism of women representing women in democracy, and relational feminism justifies the notion that only women can adequately represent women. Using two distinct yet interrelated theories helps this book to argue how the descriptive representation of women can impact their substantive representation. Considering that the book aims to examine the relationship between gender quotas and the substantive representation of women in African politics, these theories provide the needed lens to engage in the analysis. The first section of the chapter discusses the theory of the politics of presence in the form of a review of Anne Phillips's (1995) book *The Politics of Presence*, the justification for the theory and why it is relevant to the subject of women's representation in politics. The second section discusses relational feminism, its central tenets, and justification for women's representation in politics. This section features a critique of the theory as relational feminism includes elements of homogenisation and essentialisation of women. Finally, this chapter explains why both theories are relevant to the book and how they can be applied analysing women's representation in politics.

THEORY OF THE POLITICS OF PRESENCE

The theory of politics of presence was introduced in the 1995 book titled *The Politics of Presence* by Anne Phillips, which focuses on democratic theory and women's political representation. Erzreel (2015) notes that Phillips's seminal work on the politics of presence still inspires many scholars of democratic theory, political representation, citizenship, and multiculturalism. She explains further that "its basic tenet that the politics of ideas is incapable of dealing with political exclusion challenged common assumptions that democracy functions well without the presence of historically disadvantaged groups in elected assemblies" (Erzreel 2015: 1). Nonetheless, it should not be expected that the presence of more women in politics will translate to sudden change. The theory suggests that the presence of women in politics is important as it legitimises democracy and enables it to function well. Wangnerud (2009: 52) states that the theory establishes that "female politicians are best equipped to represent the interests of women thereby predicting a link between descriptive and substantive representation". Lovenduski (1997) highlights that the presence of women in the legislatures offers possibilities that women are not just 'standing as' women but also 'acting for' women as a group. Wangnerud (2009: 52) further notes the following:

Phillips's argument is built upon differences between women and men in their everyday lives, such as differences relating to childcare, education and occupations, divisions of paid and unpaid labour, exposure to violence and sexual harassment, and the fact that female politicians, at least to some extent, share the experiences of other women.

This argument is frequently made when it is assumed that women politicians prioritise and express different types of values, attitudes, and policy priorities because of their unique lived experiences in the home, workplace, and public sphere, such as a greater concern for childcare, health, or education, or a less combative and more collaborative political style. Lovenduski and Norris (2003: 87) highlight that "the understanding that women as a group are far from being homogeneous and that men and women have complicated sets of interests that both coincide and diverge, spurred Phillips to argue that the variety of women's interests does not disprove the idea that gender influences interests". Phillips (1995: 68) asserts that the argument from interest hinges on proving there is a difference between the interests of men and women rather than proving that all women have a single, undivided interest. However, if women are split along major cross-cutting cleavages like those of socio-economic class, region, ethnicity, or religion, as well as along ideological lines between the left and right, these variables may take precedence over any shared or common interests related to gender.

JUSTIFICATION FOR POLITICS OF PRESENCE THESIS

Phillips (1995: 1) starts by explaining how traditional views of liberal democracy see a problem with representation in terms of how well voters' beliefs and preferences are reflected and see differences among groups as a matter of ideas. Phillips criticised how the politics of ideas views difference in democracy. She notes that based on traditional interpretations of liberal democracy, difference has been seen in terms of ideas that was more or less sufficient, depending on how well it captures the opinions, preferences, or beliefs of voters. However, this has been questioned by an alternate view of political representation that prioritises proportionate representation based on characteristics such as gender or ethnicity. Held (1997: 530) expands that for politics of ideas it does not matter who the representatives of the constituents are as long as they are able to represent them appropriately. Phillips (1995: 6) notes that when considered in isolation from presence, politics of ideas fails to fully address the experiences of certain groups that have been marginalised and feel excluded from the democratic process due to their race, ethnicity, or gender. She argues that while politics of ideas is insufficient to address political exclusion, it should not be outrightly rejected for political presence. She states that "the biggest mistake is to set up ideas as the opposite of political presence: to treat ideas as totally separate from the people who carry them; or worry exclusively about the people without giving a thought to their policies and ideas" (Phillips 1995: 25). Phillips points out that the discussion has long moved beyond an either/or axis, thereby suggesting complementarity between ideas and presence. She states that "it is in the relationship between ideas and presence that we can best hope for a fairer system of representation" (Phillips 1995: 25). This means that while we can acknowledge the inadequacy of politics of ideas to solve the political marginalisation of certain groups, it should not be abandoned in its entirety because the presence of marginalised groups and the competing ideas of how they can be represented are what will ensure adequate representation of their interests.

Having critiqued the inadequacy of ideas, Phillips (1995) establishes the importance of presence for solving political exclusion. She states that due to the need for a more nuanced understanding of the relationship between ideas and experience, political exclusion becomes a problem that can only be addressed by political presence. The notion that people's interests and opinions are generally unproblematic underlies the division between who (subject) and what (object of representation) is to be represented and the subordination of one to the other. She explains that most modern theorists avoid the significance of "an essential female subject or black subject that can be represented by any one of their own" when confronted, for instance, with the 1789 assertion claim "that between the representatives and the represented, there must be an absolute identity of interests" (Phillips 1995: 53). This means that politics of ideas has given way to politics of presence in which members of the politically excluded and marginalised demand that they not only be the object of representation but also that the people who represent them be from their social group. For instance, it means that women want more of their kind in legislative bodies as it is not acceptable that they are excluded from positions of power.

This premise on presence provides background for the theory of politics of presence. Phillips (1995) notes that presence can be fostered by ensuring an increased number of women and other members of underrepresented groups in political structures because their descriptive representation, the extent to which representatives can be relied on in political negotiations concerning their interests, the necessity for better advocacy of the interests of minority groups, and the potential for changing political agendas are what consolidate the politics of presence. Although Phillips (1995: 63) expresses doubts for justifying presence solely based on the need for role models, she considers the arguments for symbolic representation to be particularly persuasive for politics of presence. Guinier (1994) makes the strongest argument for politics of presence by stating that "Blacks cannot enjoy equal dignity and political status until black representatives join the council of government". Phillips attests that notions such as dignity and equality should be used to undo the marginalisation and enable increased recognition for all even if their increased participation in politics "has no discernible consequences for the politics adopted". Furthermore, she notes that it is important to understand that the effects of having more women in politics are not automatic but that they can exist and manifest in specific situations.

Phillips (1995) uses Kanter's (1977) study on gender relations within industrial corporations to illustrate how presence can lead to transformation. She draws from the group categorisation done by Kanter concerning skewed and tilted groups to exemplify how the increased number of a minority group can begin to influence institutional culture. According to Kanter, skewed groups have a significant gender imbalance between men and women, with women often making up to 15% of the group, in the tilted group the numbers are between 15% and 40%, and finally, balanced groups include 40% to 50% of each gender. Kanter further recommends that when a group reaches a particular size, for instance in a tilted group, the minority begins to assert itself, and as a result, the institutional culture gradually changes. Kanter's submission means that instead of a gradual transformation, "there is a critical tipping point that depends on numbers. This is because when a group constitutes a tiny minority within a larger society, its members are tokens who will try to fit in by abiding by the established rules of the game". They will not take any action to increase the size of their group. The quantity of tokens will likely be maintained by their several potential techniques in what is termed 'the queen bee or assimilation'. However, once the group reaches a particular size, the minority begins to express itself and changes the institutional culture, norms and values, resulting in changes in available options and thereby causing a qualitative shift in the nature of group interactions. Phillips points out that Kanter falls short in articulating why a shift in the proportion of men to women will result in institutional, societal, and policy change. Phillips (1995) explains that rather than exclusively attributing this shift to their rising numbers, it is better to acknowledge that it was made possible by processes of mobilisation arising from the presence of women in a traditionally male institution. Based on feminist studies, it is often referred to as the effect of gender, which is seen as the distinctly assigned social traits between men and women.

POLITICAL CONTROL AND POLITICAL EQUALITY AS FOUNDATIONS FOR POLITICS OF PRESENCE

Phillips (1995) argues that the ideas of political equality and political control offer a solid foundational basis for the politics of presence because without the presence of people, control is impossible to achieve, and equality is hard to attain when some groups are excluded or when certain groups have much more power than others. It is important to point out that inability of control without people and lack of equality without balance is constrained by two significant initial issues. The first has to do with representative democracy's current state and how that has altered the parameters for popular control. Phillips (1995: 30) notes that "control, within the context of direct democracy is a function of presence since the ability to affect political decisions is purely dependent on attendance at the appropriate meetings, and those who are not there forfeit their chance to exercise control". However, in order to deal with the larger citizenry of the modern state, the emergence of representative institutions radically altered this equation and changes it rather deliberately. The question then becomes: does the emergence of representative democracy wherein presence is not a prerequisite for control undermine the significance of political presence. The idea that "everyone should count for one and none more than the other is a notable trait of political equality, rather than some people counting more than others. As always, count for one sounds like a largely procedural principle to be attained by making sure that each person has the same voting right as the next person" (Phillips 1995: 30). In contrast to this, Phillips (1995: 30) raises the following fundamental questions:

> What of those individuals who form a permanent minority, whether in their constituency or in the society as a whole? What if their preferences are always discounted because they happen to vote in the wrong place? Does counting

equally refer only to our starting positions, or does it extend to our influence on outcomes? Does the emphasis on individual equalities also extend to equalities between social groups?

This means that while political equality prides itself on everyone having the same voting right, this right does not extend beyond the vote as there is an inequality of outcomes. This is because the lack of equality among groups affects the extent to which interests of the marginalised can be reflected in decision-making.

Political equality can be interpreted in a variety of ways, and some emphasise balancing the size of various voting constituencies, while others emphasise balancing the likelihood that each voter will cast the deciding vote, and still others emphasise giving each voter an equal say in the makeup of the government that is elected. Phillips (1995: 31) highlights that because political equality is not well-defined, it is difficult for it to serve as the foundation for politics of presence. However, she agrees that principles of control and equality undoubtedly serve as the foundation for any politics of presence, but the crux of the contention is found in a more in-depth examination of historical exclusionary institutions and representational arrangements.

DISTINCTION BETWEEN PARTICIPATION AND REPRESENTATION

A further justification for presence is that the absence of certain groups poses challenges for the operation of democracy. Phillips (1995: 31) notes that studies on democracy and participation often begin with the premise that equality in participation is needed to ensure some degree of political equality because the systematic exclusion of some social groups is regarded as an obvious flaw of democracy. The definition of social group is unclear; however, feminists have taken advantage of this to mean the low participation of women. The discussion on equality of participation leads Phillips to engage in the difference between participation and representation. Phillips explains that the idea of participation already carries an implicit description of how groups in society can engage with the system, such as voting, signing petitions, joining political parties. On the other hand, it is difficult to judge representation based on these same criteria because a social group can be engaging with the system, but their voices are not represented. Phillips attests that the two are connected, and in a society where everyone had actual access to joining political parties, pressure groups, and meetings, there would very likely be an equitable distribution of power among those who are elected. However, in theory, they are different "since representative democracy has removed itself from physical presence as the standard of political equality in favour of participatory democracy" (Phillips 1995: 34).

She adds that the politics of presence may well appear as an odd repetition of the discussion on participation and representation given the following difference between direct and representative democracy: All citizens are given the same value, and therefore, the equal right to participate is a logical extension of that value. Therefore, any departure from the general proportionality seems to be grounds for legitimate worry (Phillips 1995: 35). However, representation has fundamentally changed the political landscape, and a proportionality that would have seemed fairly suitable in earlier situations does not seem to be a key concern anymore. Pitkin (1967) makes a convincing case for the correlation between fair representation and proportionate representation, but this is just one interpretation of what representation entails. Additionally, even while that particular interpretation may be entirely legitimate, it cannot be said that it inherently results from the equal right to engage in politics (Phillips 1995: 35). Phillips (1995: 36) notes that "an equal right to participate in politics as well as an equal right to be politically present accompanies political equality. To translate this into an equal right to represent is to assume what has not yet been shown". In a certain sense, the underrepresentation of certain groups of individuals is just a matter of empirical fact: They do not make up elected assemblies in the same numbers as they do in the voters (Phillips 1995: 39). She argues that the changing patterns of representation make it imperative for marginalised groups to have advocates who understand their needs and come from within their group. She adds that it is not that members of other groups cannot act for the marginalised groups but in cases where adequate representation is sought, it is beneficial for members belonging to the affected group to represent their needs. Expanding on if members of other groups can represent marginalised groups, she notes that parties have clear commitments on how they will address minority exclusion and gender or racial inequality, which forms the basis upon which politicians are elected. The question is whether it matters who the politicians are if there are clear party mandates for such policies. This question is likely to argue that efforts should be directed at accomplishing such mandates rather than worrying about who they are, or if they look like the people they are representing. However, Phillips (1995: 43) responds that the first answer lies in the significance of symbolic representation because it is very unusual for a democracy to claim responsibility towards addressing political exclusion and disadvantage but never considers the affected group as the best candidates to do it. The second part of the answer speaks to a founded scepticism about the limitations of party commitments and mandates. She argues that there are constantly new concerns and problems along with unforeseen limitations, and it might be quite important who the representatives are in the subsequent balancing of interpretations and priorities (Phillips 1995: 44). It is important to note that when disadvantaged groups are disproportionately underrepresented at the point of decision-making, this can and often does have negative effects. This is closely related to the need for a more equitable distribution of representative roles. Any politics of presence must be based on these ideas. She explains that:

> The first part relates to the symbolic significance of who is present, and the independent importance that has to be attached to including groups that have been previously denied or suppressed. The second and third refer more directly to the policy consequences we can anticipate from changing the composition of elected assemblies. Political preferences do not fit neatly into the categories of party politics, so it is essential to achieve that additional element of representation that results from the presence of previously excluded groups in order to achieve more adequate and fair representation of those interests that were previously excluded or not explicitly discussed during election campaigns as well better advocacy when decisions are being made. (Phillips 1995: 45)

To better illustrate her argument, she states that "consider the following very stark assertion, which was the basis on which a group of Frenchwomen laid claim to a place in the Estates General in 1789: Just as a nobleman cannot represent a plebeian and the latter cannot represent a nobleman, so a man, no matter how honest he may be, cannot represent a woman" (Phillips 1995: 52). This means that there must be complete interest identity between the representatives and the represented. The importance of shared experience over shared ideas is evident in this situation and no amount of consideration or empathy, no matter how cautious or sincere, could overcome the effects of prior experience. Conversely, it appears that experience was sufficient as a guarantee: The degree to which that experience was shared determined the sufficiency of the representation (Phillips 1995: 52). It goes without saying that those who currently monopolise positions of power cannot stand in for those they have excluded. Additionally, even if the challenges are structural, such as the distinct roles that men and women play in the sexual division of labour, it still seems improper to rely solely on one group to fill in for the other. Goodin (2004: 465) argues that "these locations will generate significantly different experiences, and, unless the range is reflected in the decision-making assemblies, decisions will express the preoccupations of those already there". Even with the greatest of intentions, people struggle to put themselves in another person's shoes (and all too frequently, we cannot rely on this). When our preconceptions are more strongly exposed, we may get better at such acts of mental transcendence, but this only occurs when the other is adequately represented.

A POLITICS OF PRESENCE THESIS FOR ANALYSING SUBSTANTIVE WOMEN'S REPRESENTATION

The thesis of politics of presence embodies the aim of this book, which is to understand the significance of the participation of women in the parliament on legislative and policy outcomes or the protection of women's interests (SRW). The acknowledgement of the historical underrepresentation of women in politics sheds lights on their marginalisation as a group. This exclusion from the political system is a function of the gender stereotypes that restricts the inclusion of women in the political system. A consequence of their exclusion is the domination of politics by men who mostly occupy political positions as representatives of the whole people. As argued by Phillips (1995), such a system shows signs of a failing democracy because no matter how honest at governance they are, male politicians cannot represent women issues the way female politicians would. This is due to the difference that exists between both genders and the positionality of lived experiences that influence the approach to policy making. Therefore, to ensure political equality in the system, it is necessary for women as a group to be represented in politics for two reasons. Firstly, their participation enables symbolic representation of women in the system, which, as confirmed by Pitkin (1967), is an important typology of representation. Secondly, by virtue of being included in the system, their presence in considerable number allows them to strongly advocate for their interests. The push for symbolic representation is premised on the importance of women as a group enjoying equality and dignity as contributing members of the society. Furthermore, their inclusion in the polity helps undo years of exclusion and underrepresentation in the system.

The importance of this theory to the book lies in its premise of presence for substantive representation of women. It argues that the participation of women in politics produces 'presence', which offers the opportunity for these representatives to act for women. It argues that their presence will lead to action on behalf of women due to their experiences as women. The prioritisation of women issues stemming from their lived experiences when they get into positions of power is a notable justification for the presence of women. Women in Africa have historically been excluded from public decision-making because of gender stereotypes stemming from post-colonial African patriarchies. Which is why different corrective instruments were adopted, notable of which is gender quotas to ensure there are increasing numbers of women participating in politics. This is in recognition that women are equal members of society who should also be involved in determining issues that affect them. This theory thereby provides an epistemic foundation on which to argue that the presence of women is important for protecting women's interests because their participation produces a sort of symbolic representation for women as a group and that they are mirrored in the political system. Furthermore, it argues that the presence of women is significant for women's issues as the representatives are likely to act in the interest of their group. This is consolidated by the need for critical mass of women to advocate strongly for women in the system. It is safe to assume that female MPs in the selected case studies because of their lived experiences as women offer opportunity for the protection of women's interests. The politics of difference, which is predicated on the difference between how women perceive GBVF and how men perceive it, creates this possibility. Secondly, the fact that the unique difference between men and women creates space for women representatives to act for women as men are incapable of understanding such. By using gender quotas to ensure equitable gender distribution in national parliaments, there are policy consequences that will be derived from this distribution that is likely to benefit women. The policies produced from this redistribution allow for the enabling of the substantive representation of women. We can argue on the context specificities that might arise from this but applying the politics of presence to the book provided reasonable ground that women are more likely to act as representative of other women when they are elected to positions of power.

RELATIONAL FEMINISM

Relational feminism, also known as 'maternal feminism', is a term that is frequently used to refer to the prevailing ideas of the old women's movement in Europe before World War II and the emergence of the new women's movement with its individual feminism since the 1960s (Trott 2019: 1). Having studied the Eurocentric history of feminism, Offen (1988: 135) highlights that this variant of feminism appears to have been the main school of thought in the West prior to the twentieth century as it dominated the middle- and upper-class women's movement in Europe until the 1950s. Relational feminism was a component of the first wave of feminism, which saw women call for political engagement (Offen 1999). It placed strong emphasis on the rights of women based on their status as mothers and their natural propensity to care for others compared to men. It also emphasised the unique contributions made by women in these roles to society as a whole and made claims of the commonwealth based on these accomplishments (Trott 2019). Mary Wollstonecraft, a British author on women's rights who lived in the late eighteenth century, and Elizabeth Cady Stanton, an American suffragist who lived in the nineteenth century, were two prominent proponents of relational feminism. In her 1792 book *Vindication of the Rights of Women*, Wollstonecraft consolidates her stance on the roles and responsibilities of women as mothers while in 1869 Stanton advocated for the inclusion of women in national affairs because men and women are the complement of one another, and women's contributions are needed to create a secure and reliable government (Offen 1988: 136).

The central tenet of the relational feminist theory has a direct link to politics of presence, which according to Offen (1988: 136), is the assumption that "while men and women are fundamentally different, the distinctive contribution that women make to society, specifically as women, entitle them to equal rights". Relational feminists such as Mary Wollstonecraft and Helene Lange believed that because of their 'maternal', 'nurturing', and 'gender character', which they had independent of real motherhood, women needed to have much more influence in the economy, society, culture, and politics, and are best suited to work in spheres like education, health, and welfare. Additionally, their concept of 'spiritual motherhood' allowed them to campaign for rights based on the 'natural' differences between women and men. They advocated for protective labour legislation, demanding a reduction of the working hours of mothers. They also advocated for state-sponsored childcare facilities for working mothers and family allowances for all mothers in need (Offen 1988). This same thesis is what some modern-day feminists such as Dahlerup (2006), Childs and Krook (2009), and Celis (2008) argue for when it comes to issues of representation. They advance the claim that women in government impact women's issues and that women are a homogenous group who need to be represented in discussions that result in policy making and implementation as their experiences are unique and different from men. However, this notion homogenises women without considering the inherent diversity that exists amongst them. Women have other intersecting social identities such as race, class, sexuality which leads to diversity and complexity of their experiences. Hence, it is problematic to ignore these intersecting identities for the sake of homogenising women. Celis et al. (2008) explain that in conceptualising their research on the political representation of women, scholars have delved into discussions surrounding the relationship between women's presence in politics and their ability to transform legislative agenda to favour women.

Offen (1988) asserts that the essential tenet of relational feminism is the notion that despite the fact that men and women are fundamentally different, they are entitled to equal rights because of the unique contribution that women make to society as women. Its central assumption is predicated on the difference that exists between men and women, and these difference started to be understood in terms of biology in the late eighteenth century. Natural scientists and philosophers alike argued that men and women had distinct but complementary character traits that in turn led to gender-specific roles in the 'separate spheres' of men and women in society and culture. These arguments were based on the discovered 'biological' differences between men and women. This manifested in the notion that men belonged in the public domains of commerce, trade and paid job, politics, and war, while women belonged in the private sector of the home and the family as mothers and caregivers (Trott 2019). The argument that women's voices needed to be represented in politics because only they could bring the maternal viewpoint and spirit that men lacked dates back to the middle of the nineteenth century in Europe, where women and women's groups also started making the case for political equality. For instance, Jeanne Schmahl and Helene Lange both believed that women's influence in national issues was necessary to create a safe and stable government. At the end of the nineteenth century, relational feminism-based moderate suffrage groups and their campaigns were founded throughout Europe (Trott 2019). The way that women viewed their relationships with their spouses was also impacted by relational feminism. Women claimed that their status as mothers and wives should be honoured, and they contested the idea that men were the masters of women and worked to promote the idea that men and women were equal partners in society, each in charge of a distinct area of influence. Due to the movement's broad appeal to both men and women, relational feminists in middle-class and upper-class women's movement were able to raise awareness of problems like domestic violence and abuse (Trott 2019). The early feminists established control and power inside the domestic realm using this gender order ideology.

JUSTIFICATION OF THE RELATIONAL FEMINIST THESIS

Relational feminism is built on the importance of relationships in people's lives and politics of difference. It argues for societal and legal involvement in relationships that are harmful to people as well as for the nurturing of relationships that are beneficial to people. However, insisting on one or the other frequently results in distinct views of relational feminism as it begins with a careful examination of human nature and the various ways that women and men experience personhood. The foundational claims of relational feminism reached its historical apex with the idea of 'equality in difference', or equity as opposed to equality, which at first glance appears to be incompatible (Offen 1988: 139). The fundamental tenets included the notion that there were both biological and cultural distinctions between the sexes, based on a concept of womanly or manly nature, of a sharply defined sexual division of labour, or roles, in the family and throughout society. Relational feminism included demands "for women's right to vote, to participate in all professions, and to work outside the home, as these concepts were developed in conjunction with the discourse surrounding the democratic and industrial revolutions of the last two centuries" (Trott 2019: 1). It also incorporated demands for equality in civil law pertaining to property and people. This was done in alignment with earlier calls for unrestricted moral and ethical development as well as equitable access to formal education. Offen (1988: 139) asserts that "relational feminism paired a case for moral equality of women and men with an explicit awareness of distinctions in women's and men's sexual functions in society or to borrow Catharine MacKinnon's excellent term, the difference that difference makes".

Offen (1988) argues that proponents of relational feminism possessed a feminist consciousness based on previous evidence. She believed that protest and political action could transform the collective condition of women in the culture, which they perceived as unfair and blamed on institutions of social and political power created by men. However, she insisted that women played a unique role that was separate from men (Offen 1988: 141). She adds that the tenet of the relational feminist theory is "rooted in sexual dimorphism and based on a vision of specific, complementary responsibilities within an organised society that could even supersede claims for personal liberty that went beyond moral equivalence in European history, particularly in the nineteenth century" (Offen 1988: 141). These were not only embraced by progressive men and women in that culture, but also served as the basis for making the most expansive claims for women's empowerment and radical shifts in the power dynamics between men and women (Offen 1988: 141–142). It fosters the need to pay more attention to gender in order to comprehend politics and power. The ideas and actions of relational feminists to influence state-sponsored maternity benefits and government-enacted protective legislation for women workers must now be understood within this new history of politics and power. Offen (1988: 1) notes that efforts to recognise the impact of relational feminism must include the following:

"Their advocacy for equal pay for equal work, demands for compensation for housework, formation of housewives' union, must recognise all political efforts to expand the welfare state to better serve women's needs as wives and mothers (e.g., payment of family allowances to mothers, establishment of childcare facilities, movements for improved housing, and the like); as well as efforts to end state control of women's bodies e.g., contesting anti-abortion laws and regulated prostitution."

CRITICISM OF RELATIONAL FEMINISM

Judges (1995: 1330) states that "relational feminism is sometimes premised on the view of female identity, based on Carol Gilligan's work" that women frequently perceive themselves as connected to, and even accountable for, many other people. Their moral thinking therefore refers to an ethics of care. Because of this, it has been criticised by feminist writers who are concerned that its support of traditionally feminine traits will hinder women's progress toward equality and limit their ability to assert their sexual reproductive rights. This is because of its appraisal of a uniquely feminine approach to advocating for the inclusion of women in politics, which embodies an ethics of care. More generally, Gilligan discovered that men typically associate morality "with a negative view of the rights of others to non-interference with life and self-fulfilment while women typically see it as characterised by a responsibility to recognise and provide the need for care" (Judges 1995: 1339). Arguments based on sexual difference, women's parenting responsibilities, nurturing thinking, and, particularly, the assumption that physiological or hormonal differences between the sexes or female sexuality itself have social ramifications are often condemned by contemporary feminist research. Ultimately, relational feminist arguments have been a problem for late-twentieth-century feminist theorists because they seem to cut both ways: Even though they support a case for women's uniqueness and complementarity of the sexes, they can be used by political opponents to support male privilege. In the past, those opposed to women's emancipation have appropriated certain aspects of arguments based on "women's special nature, physiological and psychological distinctiveness, the importance of motherhood, and a clear sexual division of labour within the family and society" to support arguments for their continued subordination (Offen 1988: 154).

Another fundamental flaw with the relational feminist theory is the justification of representation of women based on maternal instincts and biological difference. Its premise on maternal instincts excludes women who are not mothers, further entrenching the marginalisation of certain groups from the political system. The maternal and biological premise has been rejected by modern liberal feminists who argue for women's representation based on equality and justice rather than difference. Trott (2019: 1) submits that irrespective of its flaws "relational feminism should not be regarded as a philosophy confined to the eighteenth and nineteenth century because women today often still advocate for rights and legislation based on their role as mothers". Maternity leave, for example, rests on the understanding that women need time off to care for their new-born children.

In the face of the criticisms raised, it is important to note that the complexity and variety of women's experiences cannot be adequately addressed by a single definition or philosophy due to their intersecting identities based on class, race, sexuality, etc. Considering that feminist discourses on intersectionality has to do with how different systems of oppression intersect to construct multiple identities and social locations amongst women. All attempts at understanding feminism must consider this intersectionality and strive to eliminate all types of oppression that women face. As a result, we must be critical of these philosophies while taking the historical setting into consideration when looking at the history of feminism. Irrespective of its fundamental flaws, relational feminism is incredibly useful for understanding the historical struggles of women. To better understand the status of women now, we need to be aware of the hardships women have encountered throughout history (Trott 2019). In any given society, feminism advocates for rebalancing the social, economic, and political power between men and women in favour of both sexes, not just for their similarities but also for their differences. The difficulty is basically a humanistic one that raises questions about personal freedom and accountability, a person's collective accountability to others in society, and interpersonal communication styles (Offen 1988: 151–152). By respecting women's own interpretations of 'different' in all of its multifaceted complexity, the relational way of approaching women's emancipation may offer some answer to overcoming current feminism resistance (Offen 1988: 153).

A Relational Feminist Thesis for Analysing Substantive Women's Representation

Similar to the thesis of politics of presence, relational feminism rides on the difference in lived experience inherent between men and women to advocate for the inclusion of women in the political process. It uses the exclusivity of women's lived experience as a justification to argue that women are likely to act for women. Also, it employs the ethics of care narrative that women are likely to represent women issues, which enables them to advocate for better policies on childcare, sexual and reproductive rights, and so forth. As a result, they should be included in the political system to enable the development of gender-sensitive laws and policies. What can be drawn from this for the book is that female politicians, because of their lived experience as women understand the problems that bedevil women, which allows them to cater for issues that affect women as a group. Their participation in the system fosters great attention that can translate to policies to address women issues, as they are likely to advocate for rights and legislations based on their role as women. While this should not be used to further the inequality that exists between men and women, it allows for new approach to ensuring substantive representation of women. The assumption that women are better at handling women issues because of the commonality of their lived experience particularly in relation to gendered violence creates possibility for this book. GBVF was selected as the index to measure substantive representation because it affects all women irrespective of the identity they embody. Women's experience of violence allows them to better advocate for more legislations and policies that address this prevailing menace. To ensure the substantive representation of women, women need to be included in the political process because they bring with them a different approach to dealing with issues that uniquely affect women as a group. This confirms the politics of presence thesis, which is that the inclusion of women as a group leads to policy consequences in the interest of women because women can apply their lived experience as women to the policy process. This also establishes women as critical actors that can advance women's interest in the system based on existing gender differences. It contends the possibility of men acting for women as they are unlikely to relate to the struggles women go through. The argument that only women can represent women finds expression within the relational feminist theory as a precursor to argue for the participation of women in politics. While the debate on critical mass and critical acts continue on how best to ensure substantive representation of women, relational feminism tilts towards combining the debate, claiming that there is a need to push for the inclusion of women in politics because it is only then that gender-sensitive legislations can happen. It does not agree with the assumption that men can act for women, which is a notion that can be drawn from the critical acts movement. It primarily places the responsibility of protecting women's interests on women as they understand their struggles better than anyone and can better represent themselves.

This theory also sets the ground for arguing that female MPs are in a good position to advocate for the protection of women's interests when looking at the problem of GBVF. It explains that their experience as women in relation to GBVF will push them to advocate for better legislations and policies to address the increasing rate of GBVF in Botswana and South Africa. It can be assumed that the constant push for harsher punishment for GBVF perpetrators in Africa often comes from women as they are the most affected. The endemic hegemonic masculinity that perpetuates violence against women affects female MPs too as their gender makes them susceptible to such. There have been reports from female politicians that they have been harassed and abused in Africa, testifying that GBVF is a problem to which they can relate. Based on the thesis set by relational feminism, it can be argued that female politicians will be predisposed to act for women in the parliament because they can relate to the scourge of GBVF that women go through, which may manifest in them pushing for better policies. This assumption creates a new lens for the discourse on how best to ensure substantive representation of women. While the theory of the politics of presence pushes for the presence of women to enable policy consequences for women, relational feminism argues that because of women's lived experience as women, they are in a better position to represent women issues. The area of convergence between politics of presence and relational feminism is in the appropriateness for women to represent women and that the quality of representation can only be assured if women participate in politics.

CONCLUSION

To enable a rich theoretical explanation for the book, two distinct yet interrelated theories were selected to understand the relationship between numbers and impact. The concept of representation forms a central conceptual frame for this book as it sought to understand how one type can lead to the other. It employed the theory of the politics of presence by Anne Phillips (1995) and the relational feminist theory to argue for enabling substantive representation of women. The theory of politics of presence is premised on the politics of difference that interests of groups within the political system are often different. This motivates the need for such groups to be equally present in the system. It situated its thesis within national legislatures to argue that women, as a previously marginalised group, must participate in the system because their presence provides both symbolic representation as well as substantive representation. The theory uses political equality and political control to argue that to ensure the legitimacy of any democracy, all groups within it must be equally represented in national council. The theory further asserts that the presence of women in politics not only creates a form of mirror representation where women can identify with the representatives but also that this presence allows the representatives to act for women, and not just to stand for them in terms of descriptive or symbolic representation but to advocate and act on behalf of women. This indicates that the mainstreaming of women into politics through gender quotas allows for the presence of women in politics which has further implications for their substantive representation.

The relational feminist theory was engaged to justify the assertion that only women can represent women. Relational feminism, which is premised on the difference in lived experience that exists between men and women, advocates for the participation of women in politics for them to influence legislations and policies that affect them. While the differences that exist between men and women are often used to perpetuate essentialist notions, which translate to gender inequality, the difference analogy makes it clear why it is necessary for women to represent women. It also helps clarify the critical acts debate to say that only women can act for women because of their lived experiences as women. So, any definition of critical actors in relation to women's substantive representation must recognise that only women can accurately represent women.

This chapter created a convergence between the two theories that there is need for women to participate to protect their interests, and because of the politics of difference, only women can represent women. It created grounds for addressing the book's research objectives concerning the relationship between numbers and impact and whether the participation of women fosters the protection of women's interest.

References

Celis, K. 2008. Studying women's substantive representation in legislatures: When representative acts, contexts and women's interests become important. *Journal of Representative Democracy* 44 (2): 111–124.

Celis, K., S. Childs, J. Kantola, and M.L. Krook. 2008. Rethinking women's substantive representation. *Representation* 44 (2): 99–110.

Childs, S., and M.L. Krook. 2009. Analysing women's substantive representation: From critical mass to critical actors. *Government and Opposition* 44 (2): 125–145.

Dahlerup, D. 2006. The story of the theory of critical mass. *Politics & Gender* 2 (4): 511–521.

Erzreel, S. 2015. *Intersectionality, citizenship and multiculturalism.* Panel discussion on Diversity, Intersectionality, and the Politics of Presence. https://ecpr.eu/Events/Event/PanelDetails/3814

Goodin, R.E. 2004. Representing diversity. *British Journal of Political Science* 34 (3): 453–468.

Guinier, L. 1994. *The tyranny of the majority: Fundamental fairness in representative democracy.* New York: Free Press.

Held, V. 1997. Book review: The politics of presence. *Ethics* 107 (3), 530–532.

Judges, D.P. 1995. Taking care seriously: Relational feminism, sexual difference, and abortion. *North Carolina Law Review* 73 (4): 1323–1480.

Kanter, R.M. 1977. *Men and women of the corporation.* New York: Basic Books.

Lovenduski, J. 1997. Gender politics: A breakthrough for women. *Parliamentary Affairs* 50 (4): 708–719.

Lovenduski, J., and P. Norris. 2003. Westminster women: The politics of presence. *Political Studies* 51 (1): 84–102.

Offen, K. 1988. Defining feminism: A comparative historical approach. *Signs* 14 (1): 119–157.

———. 1999. *European feminisms, 1700–1950: A political history.* California: Stanford University Press.

Phillips, A. 1995. *The politics of presence.* Oxford: Oxford University Press.

Pitkin, H.F. 1967. *The concept of representation.* Berkeley, CA: University of California Press.

Shear, M. 1986. Review of A Feminist Dictionary in New Directions for Women.

Trott, K. 2019. *Relational feminism. Towards emancipation: Women in modern European history.* A Digital Exhibition and Encyclopaedia. https://hist259.web.unc.edu/relational-feminism

Wangnerud, L. 2009. Women in parliaments: Descriptive and substantive representation. *Annual Review of Political Science* 12 (1): 51–69.

Substantive Representation of Women in African Politics: Issues and Debates

Ours must be
a politics of revolution
freedom can't exist
until the most disadvantaged are free.

–Rupi Kaur (2015)

INTRODUCTION

Shim (2022) notes that the percentage of women serving in political offices has long piqued the curiosity of political scientists who study gender relations. Despite making up slightly more than 50% of the global population, women hold less than 40% of elected political positions on average. As a result, there have been calls for action to raise the proportion of women in national parliaments based on the need for justice and the assertion that increasing women's numbers in political offices will significantly alter the procedures and results of decision-making. There has been contention on whether women in parliaments need to reach a 'critical mass' to effect meaningful change in the political system. This contention is based on the assumption that the presence of female politicians in parliaments will significantly impact political decision-making, i.e., what Phillips (1995) terms the 'politics of presence'. Women politicians are perceived as not only "standing as" women but also "acting for" women as a group once elected (Lovenduski and Norris 2003; Pitkin 1967). In these arguments, both the messenger and the message are valued (Catt 2003). The

Z. M. Olaitan, *Women's Representation in African Politics*, African Histories and Modernities, https://doi.org/10.1007/978-3-031-76051-8_5

assumption that the presence of women in politics can trigger political transformation is part of the discourse on fostering substantive women's representation (Olaitan and Isike 2024). Substantive representation of women is complicated by the awareness that women are by no means a homogenous group and each female lawmaker has varying cross-cutting identity traits that influence her worldview (Grey 2006). Regardless of this reservation, it is crucial to determine the extent to which a critical mass of women can trigger substantive representation and how well they can represent women, and what part numbers play in empowering politicians to speak for and on behalf of women.

Discussions on substantive representation must recognise the value that quotas have in ensuring the qualitative representation of women. According to Krook (2006), a closer look at gender quota laws around the globe shows that these laws frequently have a significant impact on increasing the number of women in political offices and how women are substantively represented in politics. For instance, quota systems that place a strong focus on numbers have changed the political agenda and the political engagement of female voters as well as the gender consciousness of female legislators in different countries. The political context must be taken into consideration when evaluating the effect of gender quotas as well as their effects on women and their interactions with the electoral system. In discussing the value of quotas, there is need to acknowledge countries that have adopted quotas to mainstream women in their political system. It is noteworthy that quotas helped Rwanda achieve gender parity in the legislature during a pivotal period in the country's history. While we can recognise the success of quotas in increasing women's representation in national parliaments, there is need to consider their value beyond numbers for substantive representation. Quotas change the dynamics that cause women to be viewed less favourably as candidates because they do not appear to be as similar to the majority of male elites as men are, rather than because they are comparatively rare in high-ranking positions. This made it previously unlikely that women would make significant progress towards representation as long as men constituted the majority of political elites (Baldez 2006).

Other issues around the concept of substantive representation of women focus on the contestation around women's interests. Although there is a consensus on the need for women politicians to speak for women, however, there is no agreed definition of what speaking for women means or women's interests. Additionally, the discourse on how best to ensure substantive women's representation often starts from assessing the qualitative impact of gender quotas. Studies on quotas focus majorly on the quantitative effect that it has, i.e., increasing descriptive women's representation without expanding the scope to how quotas can foster impact.

Therefore, this chapter interrogates the discourse on substantive women's representation and corresponding debate on the concept. It examines the extent to which quotas can enable impact beyond the number of women participating in the political system. This examination delves into the debate between critical mass and critical acts as they continue to dominate studies on qualitative women's representation. The critical mass thesis posits that to ensure the substantive representation of women, a critical mass of women is needed in the political system. The critical mass thesis focuses on the impact that quantity has for women and the power of numbers. On the other hand, the critical acts thesis posits that for there to be impact there is need for critical actors to champion issues/legislations that are of pertinent importance to women. The critical acts thesis focuses on the intentionality of acts carried out by individuals rather than the power of numbers. Within this frame, it is therefore important for this chapter to examine the ongoing discourse on substantive women's representation as well as the critical mass vs critical acts debate in a bid to assess the relevance of gender quotas beyond numbers. Specifically, it establishes ground for analysis of both the quantitative and qualitative impact that gender quotas have on substantive women's representation in African politics.

Beyond Numbers: The Value of Quotas for Impact

The deeper impact of quotas has been the subject of an ongoing debate, notably whether they alter how institutions function (Verge and Claveria 2016) or are only intended to ensure descriptive representation (Nugent and Krook 2016). In addition, studies on substantive women's representation often concentrate on the relationship between the proportion of women in elected office and the potential representative roles they may have. These studies are based on theoretical justifications that contend that as women come from a variety of experiences and backgrounds, they are better situated and more motivated to speak for all women (Mansbridge 1999; Phillips 1995; Pitkin 1967). These claims are supported by a substantial body of empirical research that reveals that female lawmakers, compared to their male colleagues, express a greater desire to represent the interests of women and initiate and sponsor legislations related to gender equality (Bratton and Ray 2002; Childs 2004; Thomas 1994). However, many of these studies stress that while numbers are necessary, they are an insufficient condition to ensure women's issues are given more consideration during the legislative process. The concept of a critical mass and the emphasis on female legislators as the only agents of change recently gave way to a greater emphasis on other elements that may affect how well women's interests are represented, such as "legislators' personal characteristics and party affiliation as well as broader institutional contexts" (Bratton 2005: 100; Celis et al. 2008: 115). This raises the following question: "Do quotas just enhance descriptive representation, or do they produce comprehensive changes in the characteristics of those who serve in political office?" (Barnes and Holman 2020: 1). Barnes and Holman (2020: 1) argue that quotas make considerable changes beyond ensuring descriptive representation because they "change how parties work, how networks operate and how individuals engage with politics through complementary mechanisms". Alexander (2012) argues that by reshaping the legislature descriptively, quotas help redefine perception of what an ideal candidate is in the eyes of political leaders and political parties. Particularly, as the proportion of women holding political offices rises, so does the awareness that a more diverse set of politicians with different backgrounds can lead. This creates a direct link between the increase in women's descriptive representation and the diversity of political leaders who hold legislative offices.

Hawkesworth (2003 cited in Barnes and Holman 2020: 2) attests that "quotas require parties to change their recruiting strategies and break gendered institutional patterns or the idea that institutions behave in ways that are constrained and restrictive of gender". The diversity of elected officials increases as long as a quota is in place that has further implications for diversity in policy. The role of parliamentary diversity in sparking change in policy cannot be overemphasised because the more representative and diverse a parliament becomes, the higher the likelihood that such diversity will reflect in policies. This argument is predicated on the idea that by increasing the representation of women, the diversity of individuals holding political power will also increase. Quotas are basically a strategy for boosting women's descriptive representation, which over time ensures political diversity. Advocates of gender quotas often refer to data showing that quota reforms the legislative landscape by normalising women's political participation, resulting in new political cultures, a broader political agenda, and more attention to women's issues among both women and men (Franceschet 2011; Mackay 2008). Quotas may influence the personal legislative agenda of specific female legislators, pushing them to focus on matters that directly affect women's welfare and to implement laws that take into account the political and economic preferences of female citizens (Childs and Krook 2012; Devlin and Elgie 2008). Other studies show how gendered power structures may actually be cemented or even be made worse by quota reforms. Beckwith (2007) notes that quota changes may provoke opposition from male lawmakers who, in response to quotas and the increased presence of women, attempt to maintain control by closing off places for substantive women's representation and marginalising female entrants. Male legislators may delegate women's issues to women in response to the unexpected influx of women, which would eventually result in less legislative focus on these matters. Furthermore, the stigma of needing a quota policy may delegitimise the women who benefit from it and limit their capacity to serve as legislators (Clayton 2015). There are several studies that document occasions where quota-elected MPs have been viewed as second-class or unnecessary lawmakers, making women's causes a less important or less significant legislative agenda (Childs and Krook 2012; Childs 2004).

Mackay (2008: 127) explains that the dependence on female legislators to advance change only "emphasises the link between women's descriptive and substantive representation". Tremblay (2006: 509) found that "although attention to women's interests may be descriptively marginal or led by only a small number of female MPs, female legislators are more likely than their male colleagues to bring up topics linked to gender equality in their legislative discourse". Based on data collected from Argentina, Piscopo (2011) found that discussions around sexual health changes in the National Congress of Argentina tend to view the interests of female constituents via various ideological lenses. While Phillips (1995) affirms that women advocate for quotas based on normative and practical grounds because they believe that more women in politics is necessary to advance justice, advance women's interests, and use women's resources for the benefit of society. Krook (2006) argues that given the lack of a natural trend toward change, it can only be accomplished by adopting carefully focused measures (quotas) to support female candidates. The introduction of gender quotas is seen by some scholars as being consistent with concepts around equality and fair access. Gender quotas are frequently compatible in a variety of ways with normative frameworks. Hassim (2002) notes that because policies like quotas align with the overarching objective of promoting social equality, left-wing parties are more receptive and open to them. During moments of democratic innovation, quotas frequently merge (Meier 2000), which makes them useful for establishing the legitimacy of new democratic institutions (Bauer and Britton 2006).

Evidence from numerous instances suggests that attempts to nominate more female candidates very seldom take place in the absence of gender quotas. This is why adoption of quotas is seen as part of development of current ideas relating to representation and equality. Others see gender quotas as part of a wider set of representational safeguards designed to acknowledge gender diversity and the necessity for PR (Inhetveen 2009; Meier 2000; Sgier 2003). Barnes and Holman (2020: 3) highlight that "by redefining candidate quality, the implementation of gender quotas may challenge these gendered practices of political recruitment. Expanding women's access to elected office may change how party leaders and prospective candidates assess who is viewed as an appropriate leader". This change in opinions about candidate quality can help break down gendered trends in candidate supply and demand. The implementation of quotas alone is probably insufficient to bring about a shift in the gender dynamic. However, if there is considerable turnover, quotas will impact the recruitment process because parties will eventually need to refill the supply of women on their lists. Therefore, quotas combined with a high rate of legislative turnover are likely to result in greater diversity over time, and "if it is true that quotas encourage changes in political recruitment patterns, it follows that the longer quotas are in place in political contexts with high turnover, the more parties will need to recruit women from a wider range of networks, and as a result, the more diversity observed among those in positions of power" (Barnes and Holman 2020: 4). Hawkesworth (2003) argues that an extensive body of research on gendered institutions contradicts the notion that merely ensuring descriptive representation of women without altering other institutional mechanisms will change the gendered nature of politics. This indicates that much more needs to be done beyond numbers to ensure substantive women's representation. Ndlovu and Mutale (2013: 75) argue in relation to the African context that "while quotas are important in addressing the exclusion of women from the public political sphere, women have not fully benefitted from the system in most African countries".

The central submission of this section is that the conversation on quotas must shift beyond descriptive representation to the use of quotas in engendering substantive women's representation. The representation of relevant groups in a political system via quotas can result in substantive representation whenever the speaking for, representing of the group's ideas, and acting on its behalf are done by people who understand what it means to be a part of this group. Quotas also help ensure diversity in composition of political bodies as well as expand recruitment standards for political parties. The consequential effect is that these contribute to the inclusiveness and responsiveness of policies developed. The myopic conception of the relevance of gender quotas does not bid well for the argument of how numbers create impact. If we begin to understand quotas within the broader objective of women's political representation rather than just participation, there will be progress in protecting women's interests. Summarily, the explicit inclusion of members of relevant groups in the political sphere using quotas is important for their substantive representation, and thus, it bids well to posit that gender quotas can help foster substantive representation.

CRITICAL MASS VERSUS CRITICAL ACTS

Part of the discussion about how best to ensure the substantive representation of women is the debate about critical mass versus critical acts. The former argues that a certain percentage of women is needed to make considerable change in the political system, and the latter posits that we should focus on certain acts that advance the interests of women. A brief overview of critical mass and critical acts or actors is provided in the following subsections to set the background for examining the debate.

Conceptualisation of Critical Mass

The concept of critical mass became popular in political science following Dahlerup's (1988) article *From a Small to a Large Minority: Women in Scandinavian Politics*. Dahlerup draws inspiration from Rosabeth Moss Kanter's 1977 study that looks at the inter-relationships within groups made up of people of various cultural categories or statuses to demonstrate how the composition of a legislative assembly influences its procedures and policies. Based on Kanter's research, there are two group types: The 'skewed group' in which the minority make up a maximum of 15% of the membership and are considered 'tokens', and 'the tilted group' in which the minority make up between 15% and 40% of the membership and is "becoming strong enough to begin to influence the group's culture" (Kanter 1977). The tilted group emerged as the most significant group interaction in critical mass debates. While Kanter's research is crucial and foundational to critical mass, her stated percentages seldom appear in critical mass studies. On the other hand, Dahlerup's 30% suggestion as the point for critical mass has gained momentum in both political science and the quota policies of many countries (Childs 2004; Grey 2002; Studlar and McAllister 2002; UN ECOSOC 2004). The critical mass argument was mostly used in the 1980s in cases where the percentage of women in parliaments or local councils was less than 30%. Dahlerup (2006: 515) makes the argument that "because a small number of women in politics tend to be tokens, it was impractical to foresee significant improvements until the percentage of women participating in politics had reached a critical mass". The discussion among feminist political scientists in the 1980s about using a critical mass theory to inform future studies of women in politics was inspired by Helen Mayer Hacker's (1951) article on women's minority position in society at large. Dahlerup (1988: 283) highlights that Hacker's article "offered six other aspects of potential changes that might result from changes in the relative number of women and men, widening the research topic in response to the current, very limited, discussion of why women do not make more of a difference in politics". The critical mass argument has undoubtedly had an impact as it has been and continues to be crucial for the global advocacy of raising women's representation since the 1980s. The concept of critical mass suggests that women need to make up a sizeable proportion in legislative bodies before they are able to influence policies that benefit women. It argues that a token of women is needed for women politicians to ensure substantive women's representation.

Conceptualisation of Critical Act(or)s

Childs and Krook (2006: 528) define "critical actors as those who initiate policy proposals on their own, even when women form a small minority, and embolden others to take steps to promote policies for women, regardless of the proportion of female representatives". They consolidate this definition by stating that they are "those who act individually or collectively to bring about women-friendly policy change" (Childs and Krook 2009: 127). In rare circumstances, they may not even be women, as specific men may play a significant role in furthering the policy needs of women (Tamerius 1995). Critical actors are far more driven than others to advocate for policy reforms on behalf of women, even though they hold attitudes similar to those of other representatives (Childs and Withey 2006). They further note that although they might work alone, they could also inspire others to take action, creating momentum for policy change, or they incite opposition to fundamental transformation. As a result, their shape and impact are relative. For example, smaller groups of women in the legislature may work together to successfully advance shared objectives, but bigger groups may increase the possibility of critical acts while also having the potential to undermine their outcomes. The recruitment of additional women, the implementation of female quotas, favourable gender policies, and the protection of women's interests are all critical acts often carried out by critical actors. Critical acts are dependent on "the willingness and capacity of the minority to mobilise the resources of the organisation or institution to improve the situation for themselves and the entire minority group" (Childs and Krook 2009: 129).

Debate on Critical Mass and Critical Acts

According to Kanter (1977), the size of a group affects the way people interact with one another. When a group is still a distinct minority within a larger society, its members will want to fit in by abiding by the majority social norms. Critical mass therefore suggests that when groups get larger and the minority begins to express itself, it creates considerable change in the character of group interactions as its numbers enable it to change institutional cultures, norms, and values. This is consistent with the idea that when the proportion of women elected to the parliament exceeds a certain threshold, the institutional culture and policy priorities will change (Lovenduski and Norris 2003: 2–3). Based on the central idea that when a threshold number is reached it will have a substantive effect on policy making, critical mass connects descriptive women's representation to policy change (Beckwith 2007). In a nutshell, the critical mass model proposes a connection between numbers and impact. Beckwith and Cowell-Meyers (2003: 3) argue that critical mass depends on the following factors:

> First, the number of elected women serves as the independent variable, operationalised by a measure of women's participation in national or state legislatures; second, the proportion of women in a legislature relative to its total size, or the percentage of women, generates a critical mass; third, most

scholars propose a critical mass that can be encompassed by a critical representation threshold, ranging between 15 and 30%.

The critical mass argument is strongly tied to the conviction that having more women in politics will have an impact since it is presumed that when there are enough women in politics, women will benefit. Even with the conceptual disagreement of what exactly it means for female politicians to make a difference, Sawer (2000) argues that women will always be expected to pull their critical mass into making a difference for the general women populace. The critical mass is often used to push the agenda that when women are numerically represented in politics, their numbers can be used for change. Dahlerup (2006: 514) assert that parties using gender quotas should ensure the nomination of significant numbers of women to reach a critical mass because the represented demand that their voices be proportionally represented.

Whether women in legislature need to attain a critical mass to affect change in the political sphere has been the centre of discussion in the debate concerning significant changes in political decision-making. According to Grey (2006), critical mass is only beneficial if we give up the notion that a certain percentage of women participating is the answer to all women's representation needs and if we give up the idea that numbers alone can significantly change policy processes and outcomes. The idea that women politicians will significantly influence political decision-making can be found in discussions concerning the "politics of presence" (Phillips 1995). The critical mass argument forms a significant part of the politics of presence. The idea that "both the messenger and the message are considered crucial" is a major part of discussions on critical mass (Catt 2003). Furthermore, once elected, female parliamentarians will be seen as not only 'standing as' but also as 'acting for' women as a group (Lovenduski and Norris 2003; Pitkin 1967). This notion is centred around how women experience the world and the way this influences how they would act if elected as political representatives and not on the idea that there is a necessary connection between sex and representation. In examining the role that the critical mass of women plays in influencing policy making, four factors stand out as being particularly crucial to look into: the position of the female politicians; their tenure in office; their personal beliefs and that of their party; and, finally, the responses of and to the female politicians. When the number of women in politics reaches a critical mass, Dahlerup

(1988: 283–287) argues that attitudes about them will change from both inside and outside legislatures.

Tremblay (2006: 502) points out that the "concept of critical mass has been subjected to abusive interpretations, becoming interchangeable with a causal relationship between presence and ideas (or between representation and responsiveness), leading one to believe in the existence of a sisterhood among female politicians and a discussion on their representational activities". The critical mass theory is one of the many manifestations of how the critical mass argument has been abused. Dahlerup (1988) agrees that there is a tipping point where women can begin to form alliances to influence the system, and theorists used this to develop a theory of critical mass. The problem with the theory is that it predicts that the increase in number of women will automatically transform legislative agenda for women. This creates a false assumption that to ensure substantive representation, all that needs to be done is to increase the number of women in positions of power, further legitimising instances where measures to protect the interests of women are collapsed into the single solution of increasing the number of women in politics. However, this misconception was corrected by Dahlerup (2006: 520) when she argues that while the number of women in politics is an important factor, it is not an absolute means to protect the interests of women.

Problem with Critical Mass Theory

The critical mass theory that assumes that increased percentage of women participation in politics will lead to better representation of women issues has been duly critiqued by scholars because of its shortcomings. Childs and Krook (2009: 126) state that the problem with the critical mass theory lies in "its assumption that there is a linear relationship between numbers and outcomes as well as a precise tipping point at which feminised change occurs". Dahlerup (1988: 279) argues that women politicians are confronted with two contrasting expectations because of this theory: they must demonstrate that, firstly, they are equal to male politicians, and secondly, that if elected, they will have an impact. Even without this dilemma, there will be devastating consequences if people believe that female politicians just stand up for women's interests or even feminist interests. It is important to note that women are by no means a cohesive group, and female politicians have cross-cutting identity features that affect their perspectives, making it more difficult to enable substantive representation based on critical mass. In an effort to improve the substantive representation of women, there has been too much focus on the percentage of women in national parliaments, and, as a result, the complexity of power relations in politics and how it affects female politicians' capacity to speak and act as and for women have been neglected. Even though numbers are vital for establishing any legislative majority, the proportion of women in parliaments is definitely not the most important aspect because numbers interact with other factors (Childs and Krook 2009; Dahlerup 2006). Mateo-Diaz (2005: 160) presents another justification for the convergence assumption and implicitly challenging the critical mass hypothesis by arguing that "as the proportion of women legislators rises, the likelihood of achieving greater socio-demographic and ideological diversity in the parliament rises as well". This diversity in ideology affects the understanding of what women's interests are among female legislators. Similar arguments have been made by others who claim that when the number of female politicians increases, the group may become more diverse, which might not produce a cohesive agenda on women's interests (Childs and Krook 2009: 129).

The critique of the critical mass theory does not suggest that increasing the number of women in politics is irrelevant in terms of concerns of representation, equality, and inclusion because women need to be represented in the political system for their interests to find expression in decision-making structures. Gender and Media (2006: 1) attests that "the mere representation of women in politics is not equivalent to gender transformation; however, there is a firm belief that transformation cannot begin to take place when over half the population is effectively excluded from decision-making". Therefore, the observation regarding critical mass is that while a certain proportion of women is needed to ensure representation of women within the political system, the assumption that this proportion will automatically lead to the substantive representation is subject to criticism as it poses a theory of critical mass for women's representation. Secondly, this observation feeds into the argument that researchers should consider both the limitations that exist as well as the beneficial effects that arise as the proportion of women in a legislature increases.

CRITICAL ACT(OR)S

Scholars such as Lovenduski (2001) and Childs and Krook (2006) contend that there is little evidence that a 30% critical mass is the absolute solution for ensuring the representation of women in national politics. However, others argue that critical acts are the most important element when fostering substantive representation of women (Childs and Krook 2009; Dahlerup 1988; Lovenduski 2001). Childs and Krook (2009) note that it might be possible for female politicians to influence the political agenda by winning 15% of the seats in a legislative body; however, they would need to constitute 40% of the legislature to introduce women-friendly policies. This is unlikely because there are few women in the most democratic legislatures. Additionally, this school of thought notes that it is difficult to fully investigate whether critical mass is required to secure the substantive representation of women, and, hence, it is safer to look towards critical acts.

Dahlerup (1988) tests the tipping point hypothesis using insights from Kanter in a bid to apply it to the field of women and politics but ultimately rejects the idea of critical mass in favour of critical acts on the grounds that increased percentage of women appear to be less significant than individual policy initiative in expressing women-friendly policy. In arguing for critical acts, Dahlerup (2006: 520) asserts that numbers and percentages are only of minor importance for policy outcomes. Under the correct circumstance, even a token of women in politics can have a significant impact, whereas a sizeable number of female lawmakers might not want to or be able to influence the political agenda in a particular political system at a particular time. Consequently, it is unlikely that having more women in parliaments is the most important factor. Childs and Krook (2009: 143) assert that the goal therefore should be "to move beyond an exclusive focus on the numbers of female legislators to identify the critical actors or critical acts espoused by individuals who may seek, successfully or unsuccessfully, to represent women substantively".

Studlar and McAllister (2002: 248) posit that "the substantive representation by female politicians requires an increase in feminist attitudes in the legislature not just a rise in the number of female politicians". This suggests that a critical mass of women in politics does not always translate to substantive representation for women because it depends on a number of factors such as gender identification, party allegiance, and the legislative positions held by women. Dahlerup (2006) collapsed Kanter's (1977) three hypotheses into one, believing that greater numbers will encourage women to form coalitions but does not argue that it will lead to policy responsiveness. While Dahlerup really makes an argument for focusing on critical acts, almost all critical mass theorists present her work as though she had produced a compelling case for critical mass. She argues that regardless of whether it is set at 25%, 30%, or 33%, it is time to discard the notion of a specific turning point. Lovenduski adds that political transformation involves acts and actors in general, demonstrating that there is no automatic effect arising from a particular proportion. Working with numbers and looking for effects before and after a specific numerical level or change in proportion of women's representation appear problematic. The involvement of more women in political assemblies as well as critical actors who execute critical acts are what should be focused on (Childs and Krook 2009; Dahlerup 2006). Pitkin's (1967) contribution on the typologies of representation lends credence to the critical acts argument, and she states that emphasis should be on what representatives do rather than on what they are.

To consolidate the debate on critical acts, some scholars are investigating Phillips's (1995) thesis that the gender of a representative influences their behaviour, even when it is not the only or most important factor. While most people concur that women are likely to be the key political players who advance women's substantive representation, this does not imply that they will or must be biologically female (Young 2000). Even though Dahlerup (2006) disagrees with the central thesis of the critical mass argument, she agrees with Kanter's (1977) submission that feminist women can act critically if they come together to act as one despite their small proportion. Therefore, to change the legislative agenda in favour of women, critical acts must be taken by these women, which stress actions rather than numbers (Dahlerup 2006). The body of research on critical acts also observe that "given various restrictions related to party affiliation, institutional norms, legislative inexperience, and the overall political environment, a simple increase in the number of women elected does not always translate into policy gains for women" (Beckwith and Cowell-Meyers 2007; Celis 2008; Childs 2004; Kathlene 1995). This means that the existence of critical actors is what is important for women's representation.

WHO CAN CONSTITUTE CRITICAL ACTORS?

Understanding who can be a critical actor requires paying careful attention to a broad spectrum of players, which includes male politicians, government officials, bureaucrats, and members of CSOs. Broadening the range of critical actors for the substantive representation of women also raises significant questions about the circumstances in which they could emerge and adequately represent women as a group. Beckwith (2002: 10) opines that "acting for women is not universally or eternally available to political actors, as many scholars have increasingly come to understand, nor is it exclusively reliant on political will". It is therefore worth considering what and who might constitute conditions that are more conducive to the substantive representation of women. One theory is that critical actors are more likely to bring about feminised change when they hold influential positions in politics, collaborate with players in other fields through various 'strategic alliances', and support policies that share the same ideologies as the governing party (Beckwith and Cowell-Meyers 2007). Recognising that men have political incentives to support gender-related policies that appeals to female voters in order to win over their female constituents and represent women is also vital. Furthermore, because of their majority numbers, men are frequently more active in policy discussions "that affect the well-being of their female constituents and hold influential legislative positions, making them potentially effective advocates for women's issues if they so choose" (Celis 2014: 160). Additionally, men are encouraged to actively participate in these policy discussions because women's issues occasionally or frequently have direct ramifications for them, such as inheritance rules.

Researchers in the gender and representation field frequently focus on either the conduct of women in government or the work of women's policy organisations as constitutive of critical actors. Weldon (2002: 1160) argues that "women's movement and government need to work together to achieve substantive representation, and that the former must not be congruent with the state in order to be able to criticise government policy, because women's policy agencies must have resources, authority, and a degree of independence". The interplay of these two agents can create critical acts that are effective in fostering women's substantive representation. The argument further notes that in the most effective cases of substantive representation of women "there is an independent women's movement that enhances the institutional capacity of government in addressing women's issues, as well as a strong women's policy agencies that provide extra resources to women's groups" (Weldon 2002: 1162).

The understanding of critical actors highlights the several potential domains of substantive representation that could be used to advance women's policy concerns. These sites could cooperate, compete, or even replace one another. They also open up new possibilities for examining a wider range of activities linked to the substantive representation of women as a group in terms of form, content, and place when combined with the idea of critical actors. Studies that sought to understand substantive women's representation often focus on the attitudes of female parliamentarians in national legislatures. While some men do, it is commonly known that not all female parliamentarians work to advance women's issues. The work of women's movements also indicates that non-parliamentary actors can work to advance women as a whole, at least as much as female politicians, if not more. Childs and Krook (2006) submit that it is better to look for critical actors who we describe as people or organisations that propose policy changes than relying on specific individuals. This reveals that critical actors may not necessarily be women in government as long as they get the job done. The context of substantive representation of women in question is also important because it gives actors a platform to act for or make representative claims on behalf of women as a whole.

ACHIEVING BALANCE BETWEEN CRITICAL MASS AND CRITICAL ACTS

In balancing both arguments, Childs and Krook (2009) acknowledge that the concept of critical mass may still have a place in studies of women's legislative behaviour despite their plea for better conceptual precision by changing the focus from critical mass to critical actors. This is because critical actors, as they describe them, are individuals who either initiate policy changes on their own or play a crucial role in inspiring others to support such policies. Additionally, as argued before, it is important to note that an increased percentage of women in politics should not be abandoned in the quest for critical actors as the transformation of the political system cannot happen without the debut of women in the sphere (Gender and Media 2006). Thus, a critical mass of women is still needed to effect change for the general populace of women, which establishes the necessity for quotas as a means to an end; alternatively, numbers are needed to make impact. The relationship between descriptive and substantive representation has drawn criticism from theorists, who contend that female lawmakers are not always better suited to represent the interests and policy preferences of women (Swain 1993; Young 1994). In light of this, discussions on how critical mass and critical acts can be combined to yield significant results for women's substantive representation need to start. The acknowledgement that a certain number of women are needed in legislatures to ensure gender-sensitive policies positions critical mass as an important component in protecting women's interests. While critical acts enable the actualisation of such interests by bringing up policy debates on women issues and introducing gender-related policies, the alignment of these two strategies will produce more results than the tendency to critique the ineffectiveness of one. Hence, the debate on critical mass and critical acts need to look beyond what is most suitable and move to how they can be combined to work together for the greater good.

EXAMINING QUALITATIVE IMPACT OF WOMEN'S POLITICAL REPRESENTATION IN AFRICA

Scholars have identified a number of substantive and symbolic representation consequences of more women in African parliaments. Bauer (2012) asserts that proponents of women's increasing representation in parliaments claim that they will represent women's interests and serve as significant role models. Bauer and Britton (2006: 20) argue that there are several instances where female MPs in Africa have advocated for gender issues and influenced legislative agendas. Devlin and Elgie (2008) attest that the increased number of women in parliaments allows for the political agenda to change in favour of issues that are applicable to women, such as ending GBVF, promoting sexual freedom, and reducing poverty. They argue that female MPs in Africa have effected changes in ways that have not been witnessed in circumstances in the West, and state that "in general, concerns such as land rights, eradicating poverty, HIV/AIDS, sexual freedom, and violence against women are different and more urgent for women in Africa than in the West" (Devlin and Elgie 2008: 240). Creevey (2006) notes that critics argue that because African national legislatures are weak, a greater representation of women may not mean much. Others argue that women's increased presence has often been cynically embraced by dominant parties in single-party-dominated regimes to boost their own popularity (Goetz and Hassim 2003) or has aided in executive control in many of those countries with more women in the parliament. Muriaas and Wang (2012) note that gender quotas provide women an opportunity to join the legislature; however, they do not remove gender discrimination and diminished legitimacy, which are two significant obstacles for women.

Longwe (2000: 27) discusses the different kinds of discrimination female politicians are exposed to by virtue of their participation in politics that impede the extent to which they can make an impact. He argues that gender prejudice still exist for even the smaller percentage of women who are elected to municipal or national office. It is likely to take the shape of verbal sexual harassment in many different forms, such as persistent innuendos about the morality of women in politics and assertions that the women have advanced through sexual relations with influential men in politics. Furthermore, Murray (2010) points out that because women begin their professions later and have considerably shorter careers in politics, they are seen as perennial outsiders in the political process. For instance, reduced perceptions of the legitimacy of female representatives are linked to reserved seat quotas, and because women exclusively compete with other women for seats under the reserved seat quota system, the system has less legitimacy. Clayton (2015) provides a corresponding argument for Lesotho where the government approved a law stipulating that 30% of all single-member districts be designated entirely for female councillors. She highlights that affirmative action policies that are seen as discriminatory undercut the authority of elected authorities and may have unforeseen negative effects. According to Matemba (2005), even though there are not many women in elected office in Botswana, the ones who do serve as role models, encourage other women to get more involved in politics and promote the potential of women in politics. This is evident, for instance, in the rise of female chiefs during the past 10 years in the country where historically women have never held the position of chief in their own right, except as regents. She notes that "the appointment of women as chiefs recently should be viewed within the wider framework of the remarkable and significant progress the country is making in boosting the status of women in social, economic, and political life". Interviews done across Botswana in 2009 and 2011 corroborated this, and Seboko, the country's first female paramount chief, states that when she was elected chief in the early 2000s, her people and other tribal leaders did not object because women were already serving as MPs and one of them was even the minister of local government, to whom chiefs answer (Bauer 2016).

Seboko further attests that female MPs and women ministers have paved the way for more women to enter politics. As in the case of former MP and Minister Gladys Kokorwe, who sponsored the Domestic Violence Bill in 2007, the only time in Botswana that a private member has sponsored a piece of legislation, demonstrating that women MPs have also been in charge of guiding particular pieces of legislation through the parliament.

Abou-Zeid (2004) argues that the presence of women in Egypt's reserved seats during the two legislative cycles was hardly noticeable and had no bearing on the position of women or on the councils in general. However, this has not dissuaded advocates of quotas from pushing for their implementation in Egypt because they understand the effect it has on women's political representation. Tamale (1999) argues that in Uganda, the National Resistance Movement's introduction of quotas for women in the National Assembly only aimed to produce "descriptive representatives who stood for" women. This was in order to maintain the uneven gender relations that existed in Uganda because the patriarchal state was not ready to have female MPs who politically 'acted for' women. This is evident from the restrained language of Article 78 of the Constitution, which identifies a woman representative for every district as a parliamentarian who represents women through affirmative action. By highlighting the descriptive nature of female representatives, the constitution creates 'status-quo' representatives rather than 'emancipationists'. The National Resistance Movement 'allows' women to take part in decision-making but forbids them from advocating on their behalf or taking on additional responsibilities.

Burnet (2011) notes that after the 2003 parliamentary elections in Rwanda, which saw considerable increase in the number of women in political leadership, women and girls have more access to school than they did before the introduction of gender quotas. Rwanda has gender parity at primary school level, and the gender gap is narrowing at secondary and higher levels (Burnet 2011: 318–19). Due to their increased political participation, "women in Rwanda discovered increased autonomy as economic subjects and enjoy greater involvement in decision-making over domestic resources" (Burnet 2011: 319). Burnet (2011: 320–1) further explains that "there has been a general change in the status of women in Rwandan society thanks to the increased representation of women in Rwanda. In short, women have found respect in their families and in their communities". In addition, Rwanda is said to promote quotas as a success symbol, which actively contributes to the dissemination effect of quotas.

However, apart from the symbolic effects, female MPs, whether they sat in reserved seats or not, were more obedient to the Rwandan Patriotic Front political party than to the people who elected them, and hence, they tended to follow legislative proposals coming from the government and stay away from sensitive topics (Burnet 2011: 330). Furthermore, the women who were elected as part of the party lists had no connection to rural Rwanda because they lived in cities and had interests different from rural women, particularly farmers in the countryside. For instance, in 2003 and 2004, a new land policy and law were being discussed, and the Forum of Rwandan Women Parliamentarians failed to recognise the substantial gender implications of the law. Despite the fact that most women in Rwanda are subsistence farmers whose traditional land rights were mediated by men, female parliamentarians saw land to be a problem "for all Rwandans" rather than a problem exclusive to women (Rwanda Initiative for Sustainable Development 2013). Many women outside the government were dissatisfied by their lack of support for women on a potentially divisive issue of critical importance to rural women, and this served as more evidence to rural women farmers that the parliament had little impact on their lives (Burnet 2011; Pottier 2006).

Meena (2004) argues that female MPs in Tanzania have been successful in pushing for laws that address women's issues in a number of areas, despite the low representation of women in the legislature. First, a bill on maternity leave for both married and unmarried mothers was introduced and supported by female MPs. They were also successful in changing a law that required high school graduates to stay at home for two years before enrolling in college. The decision had a significant impact on the enrolment of women at institutions of higher learning. This bill was amended by the parliament to let female candidates enrol in universities straight out of high school. Female MPs who had ties to women's non-governmental organisations pushed a sexual offence bill through the parliament that increased the harshness of sentences for sexual offenders. Similar to this, a provision in the land law reform ruled invalid gender-discriminatory customary practices.

To examine the usefulness of critical mass in converting women's political representation into effectiveness in the policy and reform arenas, particularly on those that directly affect women, Goetz and Hassim (2003) use the cases of South Africa (36%) and Uganda (30%) to make a comparative analysis. For instance, they contend that while the state and party structures   can   promote   women's   political   participation   and representation, the sustainability of progress obtained ultimately depends on how strongly society as a whole supports gender equality (Goetz and Hassim 2003). In a similar spirit, post-conflict societies like Rwanda and Mozambique, with 49% and 31% of their national parliaments made up of women, respectively, have been used as examples to highlight the short-comings in the critical mass argument (Powley 2005). For instance, Powley (2005: 161) notes that "majority of Rwandan women are disad-vantaged vis-à-vis men with regard to education, legal rights, health, and access to resources" despite the achievements made by women in the par-liament since 1996. Rwanda also continues to be significantly underdevel-oped in spite of its increased women's representation.

The implication of the above arguments shows the negative and posi-tive relationship between numbers and impact in Africa. While countries such as Tanzania have to an extent felt the impact of female MPs on gender-sensitive policies, other countries such as Botswana and Rwanda only ensure symbolic representation of women. The preliminary submis-sion from this section is that the relationship between numbers and impact in Africa is not an absolute positive as certain factors often impede the effectiveness of female MPs to influence the policy process on behalf of women. This is further interrogated in the subsequent chapters on analysis of findings.

Conclusion

This chapter interrogated the value for quotas beyond numbers into ensuring impact for women's political representation. Quotas have been successful in ensuring increased number of women in politics; however, the question is whether they can work towards protecting women's inter-ests. The chapter found that by debuting women into political positions, quotas create diversity which is further reflected in the kinds of policies passed. They also change the composition of legislative bodies by ensuring that women have fair access to positions of power, further enabling equal-ity. A major aspect of the discussion on substantive representation is the debate around critical mass and critical acts. Critical mass supposes that a sizeable number of women is needed in politics for women's interests to be protected, and while critical acts contend that numbers are not impor-tant as critical acts by specific individuals are what is important. The divi-sion between critical mass and critical acts does not allow for proper identification of the specific measures needed to ensure the substantive representative of women as this debate often invalidates each other's effort. This chapter therefore argued that rather than choosing sides between critical mass and critical acts, it is necessary to look at converging both of them towards protecting women's interests as there is need for women to be descriptively represented in political positions to create a critical mass. By constituting this critical mass, we can begin to identify specific female politicians that will advance women's interests to ensure the introduction of women-friendly policies. Without the numbers, women will continue to remain a minority in political bodies; hence, a merger between numbers and acts is the best way to ensure the substantive representation of women. The chapter also delved into the number versus impact debate in African politics by examining how quotas have translated to symbolic, and in some cases substantive, benefits for African women. It noted that while certain cases can be used to contextualise the relationship between numbers and impact in Africa, there is need for more investigation into the relationship that exists between the two.

REFERENCES

Abou-Zeid, G. 2004. Introducing quotas in Africa: Discourses in Egypt. In *The implementation of quotas: African experiences*, ed. J. Ballington. Stockholm: International Institute for Democracy and Electoral Assistance.

Alexander, A.C. 2012. Change in women's descriptive representation and the belief in women's ability to govern: A virtuous cycle. *Politics & Gender* 8 (4): 437–464.

Baldez, L. 2006. The pros and cons of gender quota laws: What happens when you kick men out and let women in? *Politics & Gender* 2 (1): 102–109.

Barnes, T.D., and M.R. Holman. 2020. Gender quotas, women's representation and legislative diversity. *The Journal of Politics* 82 (4): 1–16.

Bauer, G. 2012. Let there be a balance: Women in African parliaments. *Political Studies Review* 10 (3): 370–384.

Bauer, G. 2016. 'What is wrong with a woman being chief?' Women chiefs and symbolic and substantive representation in Botswana. *Journal of Asian and African Studies* 51 (2): 222–237.

Bauer, G., and H.E. Britton, eds. 2006. *Women in African parliaments*. Boulder: Lynne Rienner.

Beckwith, K. 2002. *The substantive representation of women: Newness, numbers, and models of political representation*. Paper presented at the Annual Meeting of the American Political Science Association, Boston, MA.

———. 2007. Numbers and newness: The descriptive and substantive representation of women. *Canadian Journal of Political Science* 40 (1): 27–49.

Beckwith, K., and K. Cowell-Meyers. 2003. *Sheer numbers.* Paper prepared for the Annual Meeting of the American Political Science Association, Philadelphia, August 28–31.

———. 2007. Sheer numbers: Critical representation thresholds and women's political representation. *Perspectives on Politics* 5 (3): 555–567.

Bratton, K.A. 2005. Critical mass theory revisited: The behavior and success of token women in state legislatures. *Politics & Gender* 1 (1): 97–125.

Bratton, K., and L. Ray. 2002. Descriptive representation, policy outcomes, and municipal day-care coverage in Norway. *American Journal of Political Science* 46 (2): 428–437.

Burnet, J. 2011. Women have found respect: Gender quotas, symbolic representation, and female empowerment in Rwanda. *Politics & Gender* 7 (3): 303–334.

Catt, H. 2003. *Frail success? The New Zealand experience of electing women.* Paper presented at the European Consortium for Political Research, Joint Sessions of Workshops, Edinburgh, Scotland, March 28–April 2.

Celis, K. 2008. Studying women's substantive representation in legislatures: When representative acts, contexts and women's interests become important. *Journal of Representative Democracy* 44 (2): 111–124.

———. 2014. Constituting women's interests through representative claims. *Politics & Gender* 10 (2): 149–174.

Celis, K., S. Childs, J. Kantola, and M.L. Krook. 2008. Rethinking women's substantive representation. *Representation* 44 (2): 99–110.

Childs, S. 2004. *New labour women MPs: Women representing women.* London: Routledge.

Childs, S., and M.L. Krook. 2006. Should feminists give up on critical mass? A contingent 'yes'. *Politics and Gender* 2 (4): 522–530.

———. 2009. Analysing women's substantive representation: From critical mass to critical actors. *Government and Opposition* 44 (2): 125–145.

———. 2012. Labels and mandates in the United Kingdom. In *The impact of gender quotas*, ed. S. Franceschet, M.L. Krook, and J.M. Piscopo, 89–102. New York: Oxford University Press.

Childs, S., and J. Withey. 2006. The substantive representation of women: The case of the reduction of VAT on sanitary products. *Parliamentary Affairs* 59 (1): 10–23.

Clayton, A. 2015. Women's political engagement under quota-mandated female representation: Evidence from a randomized policy experiment. *Comparative Political Studies* 48 (3): 333–369.

Creevey, L. 2006. Senegal: Contending with religious constraints. In *Women in African parliaments*, ed. G. Bauer and H. Britton. Boulder, CO: Lynne Reiner.

Dahlerup, D. 1988. From a small to a large minority: Women in Scandinavian politics. *Scandinavian Political Studies* 11 (4): 275–298.

———. 2006. The story of the theory of critical mass. *Politics & Gender* 2 (4): 511–521.

Devlin, C., and R. Elgie. 2008. The effect of increased women's participation in parliament: The case of Rwanda. *Parliamentary Affairs* 61 (2): 237–254.

Franceschet, S. 2011. Gendered institutions and women's substantive representation: Female legislators in Argentina and Chile. In *Gender, politics, and institutions: Towards a feminist institutionalism*, ed. M.L. Krook and F. Mackay, 58–78. New York: Palgrave Macmillan.

Gender and Media. 2006. Gender and media in Southern Africa. http://www.gemsa.org.za

Goetz, A.M., and S. Hassim. 2003. In and against the party: Women's representation and constituency building in Uganda and South Africa. In *Gender justice, development and rights*, ed. M. Molyneux and S. Razavi. Oxford: Oxford University Press.

Grey, S. 2002. Does size matter? Critical mass and New Zealand's women MPs. *Parliamentary Affairs* 55 (1): 19–29.

———. 2006. Numbers and beyond: The relevance of critical mass in gender research. *Politics & Gender* 2 (4): 492–502.

Hacker, H.M. 1951. Women as a minority group. *Social Forces* 30: 60–69.

Hassim, S. 2002. A conspiracy of women: The women's movements in South Africa's transition to democracy. *Social Research* 69 (3): 693–732.

Hawkesworth, M. 2003. Congressional enactments of race-gender: Toward a theory of race-gendered institutions. *American Political Science Review* 97 (4): 529–550.

Inhetveen, K. 2009. Can gender equality be institutionalized? The role of launching values in institutional innovation. *International Sociology* 14 (4): 403–422.

Kanter, R.M. 1977. *Men and women of the corporation*. New York: Basic Books.

Kathlene, L. 1995. Alternative views of crime: Legislative policymaking in gendered terms. *Journal of Politics* 57 (3): 696–723.

Kaur, R. 2015. *Milk and Honey*. Missouri: Andrew McMeel Publishing.

Krook, M.L. 2006. Reforming representation: The diffusion of candidate gender quotas worldwide. *Politics & Gender* 2: 303–327.

Longwe, S.H. 2000. Towards realistic strategies for women's political empowerment in Africa. *Gender and Development* 8 (3): 24–30.

Lovenduski, J. 2001. Women and politics: Minority representation or critical mass? *Parliamentary Affairs* 54 (4): 743–758.

Lovenduski, J., and P. Norris. 2003. Westminster women: The politics of presence. *Political Studies* 51 (1): 84–102.

Mackay, F. 2008. Thick conceptions of substantive representation: Women, gender, and political institutions. *Representation* 44 (2): 125–139.

Mansbridge, J. 1999. Should Blacks represent Blacks and women represent women? A contingent 'Yes'. *The Journal of Politics* 61 (3): 628–657.

Matemba, Y. 2005. A chief called "Woman": Historical perspectives on the changing face of *bogosi* (chieftainship) in Botswana, 1834–2004. JENDA: *Journal of Culture and African Women Studies* 7: 1–22.

Mateo-Diaz, M.M. 2005. *Representing women? Female legislators in West European parliaments*. Essex: ECPR Monographs.

Meena, R. 2004. The politics of quotas in Tanzania. In *The implementation of quotas: African experiences*, ed. J. Ballington, 82–86. Stockholm: International Institute for Democracy and Electoral Assistance.

Meier, P. 2000. The evidence of being present: Guarantees of representation and the Belgian example. *Acta Politica: International Journal of Political Science* 35: 64–85.

Muriaas, L., and V. Wang. 2012. Executive dominance and the politics of quota representation in Uganda. *The Journal of Modern African Studies* 50 (2): 309–338.

Murray, R. 2010. Second among unequals? A study of whether France's 'Quota Women' are up to the job. *Politics & Gender* 6 (1): 643–669.

Ndlovu, S., and B. Mutale. 2013. Emerging trends in women's participation in politics in Africa. *American Journal of Contemporary Research* 3 (11): 72–79.

Nugent, M.K., and M.L. Krook. 2016. All-women shortlists: Myths and realities. *Parliamentary Affairs* 69 (1): 115–135.

Olaitan, Z.M., and C.A. Isike. 2024. Quotas as a mechanism for engendering Political Transformation in Africa. *The African Review*, 1–21.

Phillips, A. 1995. *The politics of presence*. Oxford: Oxford University Press.

Piscopo, J. 2011. Rethinking descriptive representation: Rendering women in legislative debates. *Parliamentary Affairs* 11 (3): 1–25.

Pitkin, H.F. 1967. *The concept of representation*. Berkeley, CA: University of California Press.

Pottier, J. 2006. Land reform for peace? Rwanda's 2005 Land Law in context. *Journal of Agrarian Change* 6 (4): 509–537.

Powley, E. 2005. Rwanda: Women hold up half the parliament. In *Women in parliament: Beyond numbers*, ed. J. Ballington and A. Karam, 2nd ed., 154–163. Stockholm: International IDEA.

Rwanda Initiative for Sustainable Development. 2013. Securing land rights project. In *A working paper on land tenure regularization in Rwanda*, ed. A. Kairaba and S. Shearer. Kigali: Rwanda Initiative for Sustainable Development.

Sawer, M. 2000. Parliamentary representation of women: From discourses of justice to strategies of accountability. *International Political Science Review* 21 (4): 361–380.

Sgier, L. 2003. *Political representation and gender quotas*. Paper presented at the Joint Session of Workshops of the European Consortium for Political Research, Edinburgh, 28 March–2 April.

Shim, J. 2022. Substantive representation of women and policy-vote tradeoffs: Does supporting women's issue bills decrease a legislator's chance of reelection? *The Journal of legislative Studies* 28 (4): 533–553.

Studlar, D.T., and I. McAllister. 2002. Does a critical mass exist? A comparative analysis of women's representation since 1950. *European Journal of Political Research* 41: 233–253.

Swain, C. 1993. *Black faces, Black interests: The representation of African Americans in Congress*. Cambridge: Harvard University Press.

Tamale, S. 1999. *When hens begin to crow: Gender and parliamentary politics in Uganda*. Boulder: Westview Press.

Tamerius, K.L. 1995. Sex, gender, and leadership in the representation of women. In *Gender power, leadership, and governance*, ed. G. Duerst-Lahti and R.M. Kelly, 93–112. Ann Arbor: University of Michigan Press.

Thomas, S. 1994. *How women legislate*. New York: Oxford University Press.

Tremblay, M. 2006. The substantive representation of women and PR. *Politics & Gender* 2 (4): 502–511.

United Nations Economic and Social Council. 2004. *Review of economic and social council agreed conclusions 1997/2 on mainstreaming the gender perspectives into all policies and programmes in the United Nations system*. ECOSOC Resolution 2004/4. https://www.un.org/en/ecosoc/docs/2004/resolution%20 2004-4.pdf

Verge, T., and S. Claveria. 2016. Gendered political resources: The case of party office. *Party Politics* 24 (5): 536–548.

Weldon, L.S. 2002. Beyond bodies: Institutional sources of representation for women in democratic policymaking. *Journal of Politics* 64 (4): 1153–1174.

Young, I.M. 1994. Gender as seriality: Thinking about women as a social collective. *Signs* 19 (3): 713–738.

———. 2000. *Inclusion and democracy*. Oxford: Oxford University Press.

CHAPTER 6

Women's Political Representation in South Africa and Botswana

We are African women when we live here in Africa and even when we live elsewhere, our focus is on the lives of African women on the continent. Our feminist identity is not qualified with 'Ifs', 'Buts', or 'Howevers'. We are Feminists. Full stop.

—*Excerpt from the African Feminists Charter (2006)*

INTRODUCTION

Chapter 3 of this book provided a global context to the discourse on women's political representation and the forms of representation. To better contextualise the subject of women's representation in Africa, this chapter provides country-specific discussion on women's political participation, gender quotas, and the relationship between numbers and impact in Botswana and South Africa. The country-specific discussion enables the chapter interrogate the value of quotas beyond numbers in Africa. The chapter starts by providing a brief overview of the two countries, it highlights efforts taken by government and women's movements to increase women's political participation in these countries, and it identifies the types of quota systems in place and the effect of the quotas adopted. Specifically, it traces the history of quota adoption in the cases and how and if they have been able to engender descriptive women's representation. The chapter evaluates the role of political parties and the electoral system in aiding the increased numeric representation of women in African

Z. M. Olaitan, *Women's Representation in African Politics*, African Histories and Modernities, https://doi.org/10.1007/978-3-031-76051-8_6

politics. Based on this background, this chapter will analyse whether gender quotas have been effective in mainstreaming women in African politics. This chapter establishes a background to address the first objective of the book which is to understand the kind of relationship that exists between women's participation in politics and the protection of women's interests in Africa.

BOTSWANA

Overview of Women's Representation in Botswana's Politics

Botswana has maintained one of the highest rates of economic growth in the world since 1966. It is categorised as a middle-income country with a per capita income of US$ 15,471 (at purchasing power parity) in 2020 (World Bank 2020). Samatar (1999) calls Botswana an 'African miracle' as it is one of Africa's unquestioned top performers in many governance indicators, faring highly in terms of political and economic development, and one of the oldest democracies. Examples include the country being recognised as the least corrupt in Africa, upholding the rule of law, becoming a middle-income nation, ensuring regular elections and the protection of fundamental human rights and freedoms, and upholding a system of checks and balances among its three branches of government. The Constitution of Botswana establishes a unicameral legislature in the Westminster style and members are elected every five years using either a constituency-based FPTP or simple majority electoral system (Molomo 2005). As a parliamentary republic, it has a unicameral national assembly made up of 57 directly elected representatives, six specially elected representatives, and two ex officio representatives. The number of constituencies expanded from 31 to 57, and this increase occurs with each subsequent population census (Parliament of Botswana 2022). A House of Chiefs (renamed *Ntlo ya Dikgosi* and expanded in 2005) with 35 members acts only in "advisory capacity to the National Assembly, on any matters related to provisions of the constitution and powers of chiefs, sub-chiefs or headmen, customary courts, customary law, or tribal organisation or property" (Parliament of Botswana 2022: 1). Since independence, the number and composition of political parties have mostly remained the same, and the largest political parties over the past 10 years have been the BDP, which is the governing party, the BNF, which separated from the BDP in 1998, and the BCP (Somolekae 2005).

Despite making up the majority of the population in the country, women are underrepresented in decision-making bodies. Following the most recent elections in 2019, only 11% of MPs and 18% of councillors in Botswana are female, which is considerably below the target for gender parity and among the lowest percentages in Southern Africa (Gender Links 2019). This means that in the SADC region, Botswana has the lowest rate of female political participation. Women's representation in the parliament has been steadily declining over time, falling from 18% in 1999 to 7% in 2009. In 2009, only four of the 61 (7%) MPs were female; two of these were elected in an open election and the other two were introduced as special nominees. In 2014, women occupied 10% of parliamentary seats in the National Assembly. Although the proportion of women in the parliament reached an all-time high of 18% in 1999, women have consistently made up between 9% and 13% of parliamentarians in every other election since 1974.

One of the major contributing factors to the low rates of women in politics is the absence of gender equality provisions in Botswana's constitution, which restricts the extent to which political actors can successfully pursue policies that advance women's equality (Scribner and Lambert 2010: 39). Neither the law nor the Constitution of Botswana includes provisions for quotas or affirmative action programmes to increase or guarantee the representation of women in the national parliament. The lack of practical measures to actualise the SADC Protocol on Gender and Development by Botswana's government has been regarded as a sign of the country's lack of support for women's rights and political involvement.

The representation of women in the parliament is also badly affected by the current electoral system. Since the inception of its electoral democracy, Botswana has used the FPTP electoral system. This system, which grants the seat to the candidate who receives a simple majority in a ward or constituency, has been criticised for favouring men over women. Scholars argue that Botswana's FPTP electoral system 'does not work' because it seriously affects the country's effort to increase women's presence in the parliament and disadvantages the country's political opposition (Maundeni et al. 2007; Molomo 2008; Molutsi 2005). For instance, the BDP only received 53% of the popular vote but won 79% of the seats in the parliament in 2009; this has been the trend for at least two decades (Independent Electoral Commission 2009; Maundeni et al. 2007: 23). The government's inability to increase the representation of women in the parliament, women's lack of resources, culture, societal attitudes, and the lack of legal

Table 6.1   Trend of women's representation in the parliament in 1994–2019

	1994	1999	2004	2009	2014	2019
Botswana	10%	18%	13%	11%	10%	11%

Source: Gender Links (2019)

requirements for political parties to field female candidates make the FPTP for Botswana particularly ineffective. Opposition party leaders and the independent media consistently advocate for electoral system reform in Botswana because of the detrimental effect the FPTP has on opposition parties as well as on women's representation. In addition to these factors, there is a growing lack of trust in the ability of women to lead as well as disagreement about the adoption of a national quota system. A survey carried out in Botswana showed that more than 75% of both men and women said they would support a female candidate in their district, and the percentage among women was greater (88%) than among men (76%). Likewise, in response to the question of whether political parties ought to establish a quota system to increase the representation of women in the parliament, more women (65.7%) agreed compared to men (52.5%). Ntseane and Sentsho (2005: 201) explain that "this survey implies a widespread underestimation of women's ability to contest for political office and, in particular, men's lack of trust in women as candidates for public office". This is despite initiatives by CSOs like Emang Basadi and the Botswana Caucus for Women in Politics to inform and sensitise the general public about the importance of women in politics (Table 6.1).

Efforts Taken to Increase Women's Political Participation in Botswana

To encourage and guarantee women's participation in decision-making processes, the government of Botswana signed a number of international and regional treaties and has ratified the updated SADC agreement on gender and development, which demands for countries to adopt specific measures to ensure women are equally and effectively represented in positions of power (Global Database of Quotas for Women 2006; Sebudubudu and Osei-Hwedie 2005: 22). Some of these instruments are CEDAW, the BPfA, the SADC Declaration on Gender and Development, the Commonwealth Plan of Action on Gender and Development, the Nairobi

Forward Looking Strategy, and the African Charter on Human and People's Rights of Women in Africa, which is known as the Maputo Protocol. Ntseane and Sentsho (2005: 193) explain that these instruments mandate member states to mainstream gender into their legislations, policies, projects, and programmes by ensuring the equal participation of women and men in positions of power and decision-making structures. Particularly, the SADC Declaration advanced further by expressly urging SADC heads of state to commit to having at least 30% of women in political and decision-making organisations by the year 2005.

To complement these international conventions, a number of national policies were implemented by the government to facilitate increased participation of women in politics. These policies, which sought to ensure equal rights for men and women at all socio-economic and political levels, often serve as framework for elections in Botswana. Some of these policies are the National Policy on Women and Development, the National Gender Programme, and Vision 2016. Ntseane and Sentsho (2005: 194) explain that these policies sought to recognise the crucial role played by men and women and prioritise power-sharing between men and women as one of the six critical areas of concern. They note further that "Vision 2016 calls on the government and other stakeholders to take proactive steps to ensure that women are fully represented in positions of power, leadership, and decision-making at all levels of society by the year 2016". Other practical steps taken include the appointment of women to executive cabinet and senior positions in civil service and the creation of a dedicated department for women issues, the Department of Women's Affairs, within the ministry of labour and home affairs. The Department of Women's Affairs is in charge of coordinating the implementation of government policy on gender. Despite all these efforts towards ensuring increased women's political participation, there have been no significant changes in Botswana as the percentage of women in the parliament is still below 20%.

Lack of a Vibrant Women's Movement

Prior to the late 1980s, there was an absence of a vibrant women's wing in the two major political parties in Botswana. A quasi-non-governmental women's group called the Botswana Council of Women, which was largely influenced by the BDP, initially took on this role. However, it was not effective in pushing for women's issues as it was heavily influenced by the governing party (Madisa 1990: 22). The late formation of the women's wing in these parties affected the ability to advocate for the increased participation of women in politics. Ntseane (2005: 224) notes that the women's wing of the BDP was formed in 1977 and that of the BNF was formed in 1987. Selolwane (2000: 84–85) claims that when women's wings were first established, neither they nor their members expressed the concerns of female voters or urged women to vote; instead, they were "social clubs for the wives of male politicians, with their political engagement limited mostly to fundraising and canvassing for the men as well as providing entertainment during political rallies". It is important not to conflate the presence of women's wings with the fact that women hold leadership positions in these parties. Mosojane (1993: 44) attests that most political parties had women's wing that were "led by a male prefect who is their political mentor". Bauer (2011) argues that while most of these women caucus peddle the notion that women make up the majority of Botswana's political parties, they have been unable to point to any specific actions that the women's wings or parties are taking to encourage more women to hold leadership positions or run for office other than to note that they are making a lot of effort to inform women about their rights and roles in politics. The most evident and noticeable impact of a diminishing women's movement has been seen in the rapidly decreasing representation of women in the parliament since 1999. In the 1990s, when Emang Basadi ('rise up, women') was active with its political education initiative and in the wake of the SADC Gender Declaration, there was a strong mobilisation around electoral quotas; however, the establishment of a gender quota in elections has received fewer demands in recent times, especially within the governing party.

Quota System in Botswana

There is no legislated quota system dedicated to increasing the representation of women in the national parliament of Botswana. However, there are voluntary party quotas adopted by the BNF and the BCP. These parties voluntarily included a 30% quota in both their party constitutions and election manifestos. The BDP, which is the governing party, does not have a quota, but to enhance the representation of women, it encourages women to run for office in the party's structures, in the legislature, and in local government. Botswana makes provision for specially elected MPs, which women benefit from, but it was not exclusively created for women, and hence, it cannot be regarded as a gender quota. This makes Botswana a voluntary party quota country (30%) with provision for quasi-reserved seats for women using the specially elected MPs system.

Specially Elected MPs System in Botswana

There are 57 directly elected parliamentary seats in the National Assembly of Botswana. In addition to the 57 MPs that are directly elected, there are six specially elected seats in Botswana's National Assembly. Although they are typically referred to as being 'appointed' by the president, the constitution (1966 section 58(2)(b)) specifies that candidates for these seats are nominated by the president and chosen by the National Assembly. According to Maundeni (1998: 128), the seats were initially established to provide representation for groups who were "otherwise unrepresented". Over the years, they have been employed to elect one to three women to the National Assembly against the backdrop of low rate of women elected at the polls. There was a motion to change the Botswana constitution to raise the number of specially elected members from four to eight by a female MP (Botlhogile Tshireletso) in 2009. Tshireletso's motion, however, did not specify how many of the eight specially elected seats would be reserved for women. The motion received harsh criticism for two main reasons: It adopted a piecemeal strategy to address the issue of women's underrepresentation in the parliament in Botswana rather than a comprehensive one, and it was perceived as an effort by the BDP to increase its majority in the parliament (Bauer 2011).

Voluntary Quotas

In the absence of constitutional measures to ensure better representation of women in elective bodies, voluntary quotas imposed by parties on their candidates provide the best prospect for gains to be made. The BNF and the BCP, the two opposition parties, agreed on 30% quotas for election candidates in 1999 (Global Database of Quotas for Women 2006; Kethusegile-Juru 2004: 8). Somolekae (2005: 31) explains that the necessity to increase the representation of women in the BNF and the BCP prompted the development of mechanisms to do so at all levels of the party leadership structures.

The BNF is the main opposition party in the country. Its constitution mandates that 30% of the Central Committee members must be women, which is a strong indicator of the party's dedication to attaining gender equality. There are six women (33.3%) out of the 18 members on the BNF Central Committee. This satisfies the constitutional requirement of 30%. However, the party has not always translated this commitment into fielding women candidates for election. As discussed in the previous chapter, the lack of conscious efforts to nominate women for political positions using this quota is a major shortcoming. While the BNF's 2009 General Elections Manifesto page 7 declares support for the "emancipation of women", its central committee is not required to have a set percentage of women. In the parties' regulations governing primary elections, the BNF promises to implement affirmative action through a 30% quota in favour of women where possible in order to meet the 30% party quota for women's representation in the parliament and councils.

The BCP is the second most popular opposition party and the fastest growing party after the BNF. It was formed as a faction of the BNF. On issues of gender equality, the BCP is committed to the following:

> The renaissance of women's roles in social, economic, cultural and political arenas through strengthening legal instruments to protect women by the abolition of customary and modern laws that discriminate against women; facilitating economic participation of women and devising mechanisms that would record and reorganise the work that women do; strengthening health services for women; making education and training more accessible to women and promoting the political participation of women. (BCP Manifesto 2004 cited in Somolekae 2005)

It is the only of the three major political parties that explicitly mentions quotas in either its election manifesto or constitution. The BCP promises to strive "towards an anti-sexist society" in its Manifesto: 2009–2014 (p. 29). The party's current constitution mandates that 30% of the central committee members must be female, and its 2004 manifesto went as far as to promise the implementation of "a quota system to ensure a fair representation of women at both local and national level, i.e., through transformation of the electoral system". The BCP, for example, changed its structures to ensure women are represented at party congresses and that they are allowed to be nominated for leadership positions from the floor in 2005, but it is unclear whether these actions were sufficient to improve the situation in the party (Somolekae 2005: 31).

The BDP has no provisions for candidate quotas because of strong resistance to the idea of electoral quotas or any kind of affirmative action for women in politics within the party. Except among female activists and candidates, there is little recognition that the 'playing field' for female candidates is not level, which should be the primary justification for the adoption of affirmative action policies like quotas. As in the case of the BDP, there is a growing distrust towards the adoption of gender quotas in Botswana. For instance, Molutsi (1989: 125) notes that over 80% of cabinet ministers and MPs said that nothing needed to be done to increase women's political participation. In one way or another, they claimed that the prerequisites for women to have an equal opportunity with men in politics already exist. In 2009, Mmegi newspaper reported that many male MPs did not like the comment about the unfavourable political environment for women in an article about debate in the parliament. They claimed that if women want their voices to be heard, they must compete with males for all positions. In fact, it is often claimed that gender quotas would unjustly favour women and give them seats in the parliament "on a silver platter" (Mmegi 2009 cited in Bauer 2016). It is also frequently asserted that gender quotas for the parliament would merely result in many seats being occupied by unqualified, elite women. This distrust for quotas among male MPs citing reasons such as discrimination against men and the need to ensure merit is one of the major reasons why women's political representation is low in the country. Coupled with this is the inability of the governing party to adopt quotas for its party platform, which will significantly increase the number of women in the parliament.

Effect of Quotas on Women's Political Participation in Botswana

The fact that two of the three major political parties set quotas calling for 30% female leadership has not translated into significant effect for increased women's political participation. This is despite the fact that parties acknowledge that women are the foundation of their respective parties, carrying out the majority of the necessary duties to keep them running (organising and preparing food for party rallies, providing entertainment for party events, canvassing, and raising money for local campaigns and party offices, etc.). In 2009, there were no female members in the BDP executive committee; just three female members among the 18 members of the BNF Central Committee, six female members among the 20 members of the BCP central committee, and only two female members among the seven members of the BCP executive committee. This low presence of women within party structures and political positions are a consequence of lack of conscious efforts and instruments to increase women's representation. It is interesting to note that the BDP, which did not commit itself to any quotas, performed better in 2004 in terms of nomination of women candidates and ensuring their election than the two opposition parties that had committed themselves in this way (Sebudubudu and Osei-Hwedie 2005: 31; Somolekae 2005: 31). Despite the fact that its 2008 constitution does not include a provision for a certain number of women on the central committee, the BDP's 2009–2014 manifesto declares that the party "continues to promote the entry of women into prominent positions in the public and private sector".

SOUTH AFRICA

Overview of Women's Representation in South African Politics

South Africa is a model country for understanding women's political participation due to its significant percentage of women in politics. Following the end of apartheid in 1994, the South African government initiated a number of reforms aimed at fostering increased women's participation in politics and in the new democratic state. This effort included signing and ratifying several international and regional conventions that were created to remove barriers, abuse, and discrimination faced by women. South Africa is a parliamentary PR, with a bicameral legislature (the national parliament and the national council of provinces; the latter is less notable for legislative duties) (Parliament of South Africa 2022). Prior to 1994 when the ANC adopted gender quotas for the first democratic elections, women's representation in the parliament was extremely low because the then apartheid government employed a racist and sexist franchise to choose the members of South Africa's parliament. Following South Africa's first democratic election in 1994, women made up 27.75% of the National Assembly members; this number increased to 30% in 1999, 32.75% in 2004, and 43% in 2009. Similar trends were seen in provincial legislatures where women were represented by 24% in 1994, 27% in 1999, 32.3% in 2004, and 41% in 2009 (Hendricks 2005: 81; Morna et al. 2009: 17). These increases can be attributed to agitations from women's movements to ensure gender parity in political parties, and the voluntary adoption of quotas by parties like the ANC, Economic Freedom Fighters (EFF), and Inkatha Freedom Party (IFP) (Table 6.2).

Table 6.2 Trend of women's representation in the parliament in 1994–2024[a]

	1994	1999	2004	2009	2014	2019	2024
South Africa	27.8%	30%	32.8%	43%	44.1%	46.5%	45.04%

Source: Gender Links (2019); IPU (2024)

[a]Although South Africa conducted an election in 2024 which would establish a new percentage for women in its national parliament, the book adopts the 2019 election percentage. This is because the percentage of female MPs in the new parliament cannot be used to measure the effectiveness of quotas as it is yet to commence its parliamentary proceedings resulting in legislative and policy outcomes as at the writing of this book. Hence, the book maintains the scope of 2010–2022 indicated in Chap. 1

Efforts Taken to Increase Women's Political Participation in South Africa

The 1996 Constitution's Bill of Rights, which requires the government to ensure women's involvement and representation in decision-making, enshrines South Africa's commitment to gender equality. This was the first time that the rights of women were enshrined in the constitution, regardless of race (Constitution of the Republic of South Africa 1996). Section 19(3) of the 1996 Constitution provides that "every adult citizen has the right to stand for public office, and if elected, to hold office". The 1996 Constitution, in particular, enshrines the right to equality and prohibits discrimination on any basis, including race, gender, sex, age, disability, marital status, ethnic or social origin, colour, culture, language, and place of birth. This Constitution aided in the adoption of a number of national legislations promoting gender equality as well as the creation of comprehensive national institutions for its advancement, such as the Commission for Gender Equality and the National Gender Machinery. Their mission is to safeguard and advance gender equality in South Africa. A number of specific pieces of legislation were also important for ensuring women's participation and representation in decision-making processes and for promoting quotas, such as the Electoral Act (No. 73 of 1998), which enjoins every registered party to uphold the rights of women. This mandates political parties to follow the Act's requirement to guarantee that female candidates can interact freely with parties and other candidates and engage fully and equally with their male counterparts. Additionally, it calls on political parties to ensure women have unrestricted access to all public gatherings, marches, protests, rallies, and other public events and to take all reasonable measures to protect their right to participate freely in political activities.

From the 1990s, ANC Women's League mobilisation was central in ensuring women's participation in party and broader negotiation processes. This aided in the increased percentage of women in senior leadership roles inside party organisations, which further aided in securing women's political participation (Hendricks 2005). Their mobilisation led to the establishment of a framework for gender equality in party policy papers, including the constitution. In essence, the ANC was able to adopt a number of strategies for developing into a more responsive and inclusive political party. For example, the Preamble of the ANC Constitution states that "the fundamental goal of the ANC is to build a united, non-racial, non-sexist, democratic and prosperous society in South Africa" (ANC 2017: 2). Within the party's internal institutions, the ANC Women's League has always been at the forefront of persistently bringing up the topic of gender equality. Their campaigning efforts were always focused on the question of a gender quota. Although the purpose of using a quota system was to enhance the presence of women in the executive committees and political party structures, they were able to extend it to the larger political system. There was initial opposition to the use of quotas within the ANC, and criticism revolved around the fact that quotas had not been sufficiently addressed by the women in their organisations and that it would somehow call into doubt the qualifications of the female candidates. However, women in the ANC Women's League advocated for and obtained a quota system to ensure that at least 30% of candidates on their lists were female before the first general elections in 1994. The 30% quota was applied during the elections from 1994 to 2004 and increased to a 50% quota at the Polokwane Conference in 2007, which took effect during the 2009 elections (Morna et al. 2009). The ANC was able to pioneer quota policies and corresponding gender equality policies to ensure women's participation and representation in South African politics as a result of efforts by women activists to advance women inside the party structures.

Quota System in South Africa's Politics: Voluntary Quota

To increase the representation of women at all levels of governance, the ANC, EFF, and IFP adopted voluntary quota systems for their party lists. The ANC, which is the governing party, has a gender parity quota system for women, the EFF uses the zebra stripe approach wherein men and women are alternated on the party lists, and the IFP has a 40% gender quota. So far, the ANC has reached gender parity using the voluntary quota system, and the EFF is one percent short of meeting the 50% mark. On the other hand, the official opposition party, the Democratic Alliance (DA), opposes all forms of quotas.

In order to promote women's inclusion at all levels of the party, the ANC set internal quotas for each organisational structure. In 1994, the ANC committed itself to a 30% quota for women's representation in elective bodies. It was common practice to ensure that at least every third candidate on party lists for the National Assembly and provincial legislatures was a woman, achieving at least a 33.3% representation of women (Kethusegile-Juru 2004). According to Rule 14.1 of the ANC Constitution 1997, a quota of at least one-third (1/3) in all its structures to enable such effective participation was necessary to increase women's representation. As a result, the National Assembly met the 30% UN target, with a record of women's representation of 35.7% in 1994, 1999, and 37.3% in 2004 (Hendricks 2005: 82). By 2007, the ANC modified its quota provision by adopting the principle of parity in gender representation at its conference in Polokwane. At the congress, the 30% provision was revised to enhance the quota to parity (Zuma 2007). Consequently, it pledged in its 2009 election manifesto to "increase women representation in the parliament and government to 50%"; a goal that has been met in the National Assembly, where 49.2% of ANC members were women (ANC 2009; Morna et al. 2009: 11). Consequently, 50% of the individuals elected to the National Executive Committee and 50% of the National Working Committee at the congress were women. Women have been well represented in the national parliament due to the ANC's overwhelming dominance in the National Assembly and its dedication to women's representation. On a provincial level in 2009, 48.3% of the ANC seats in the provincial legislatures were occupied by women (Morna et al. 2009: 16). The diffusion factor also applies here, and because of the ANC adopting a gender quota, other parties were forced to consider gender representation in their party lists. The percentage of female candidate nominated by opposition parties increased and in 1994, it was 14.2%, 18.7% in 1999, 22.3% in 2004, and in 2009 it reached 30.9%.

While the ANC, EFF, and IFP use gender quotas for their electoral list, other opposition parties such as the DA, African Christian Democratic Party (ACDP), and Freedom Front Plus do not commit themselves to quotas for women's representation. The DA asserts that no special mechanism is required to include women because they presume that socio-economic disadvantages and not the electoral system or political institutions are to blame for women's underrepresentation, and that these conditions will only improve once women are adequately empowered (Albertyn et al. 2002: 36). During the 2019 general elections, the DA received a lot of criticism for its lack of woman representation. Mmusi Maimane, the former leader of the DA, justified the party's lack of gender equality on its list of prospective province premiers. Despite only two women making the cut, Maimane argued as follows: "Ideally I would want more women, but I'm not going to set a quota for women because I don't believe in quotas" (Ndenze 2019: 1). This implies that DA candidates were mostly selected without the use of gender quotas. This assertion may indicate that Maimane has deeply ingrained patriarchal attitudes toward women, which continue to downplay the substantial role that women may play in society and their ability to hold positions of authority on equal level with men. It is important to remember that the DA did have a female leader for eight years. One woman was among the DA's top 5 candidates, and eight women were among the top 25. However, irrespective of its use of quotas, the DA has seen a steady increase in the proportion of its women's representatives from 14.3% in 1994 to 29.9% in 2009 (Hendricks 2005: 81; Morna et al. 2009: 11).

Effect of Quotas on Women's Political Participation in South Africa

At 45.04%, South Africa is among the top five African countries with increased women's political representation (International IDEA 2022). Overall, South Africa has advanced significantly, and its parliament, which ranks third in Africa and tenth globally, is undoubtedly one of the most gender diverse in the world (IDEA 2022). South Africa's 2015 report to the African Commission on the achievement of Article 9 of the Maputo Protocol notes that the country has made significant progress in ensuring women's participation in political and decision-making processes. The ANC quota system substantially and single-handedly improved the representation of women in the National Assembly because the ANC gender parity quota has been consistent in supporting the need for affirmative action to advance gender equality (Sonke Gender Justice 2019). Due to this, women's participation in terms of seats held by women in the National Assembly has significantly been on the rise following the 1994 general elections. The Dullah Omar Institute (2019) notes that the ANC appears to have achieved their 25-year goal to boost women's seniority and leadership. Political parties such as the EFF implemented progressive strategies to increase women's political participation because they have been influenced by the strategy of the governing party (the diffusion effect) in advancing women's representation.

Williams (2006: 36) argues that the ANC, which is in power, committed itself to a quota system to ensure increased participation of women at different levels of governance. Letsholo (2006: 12) adds that this commitment included their pledge to achieve gender parity in the run-up to the local government elections in 2006. Mottiar (2006: 43) argues that this commitment turned out to be idealistic in terms of practical implementation as it sparked opposition within the party as several members of the party, particularly the men, expressed concern that the parity target would disenfranchise them. Despite this opposition to the policy, a quota system was adopted, and some provinces exceeded expectations with an average rate of 46%, while other provinces fell short of expectations (Mbeki 2006). Collaborative efforts between the governing party's adoption of a quota system, the directive by the Local Government Municipal Structures Act (No. 117 of 1998) and a national advocacy to increase women's political participation motivated other parties to be gender conscious when compiling their list. In light of this, Chikulo and Mbao (2006: 54) affirm that political parties appear to have complied with the 2005 national campaign on 50/50-Get the Balance Right organised by the local government association to ensure increased participation of women at the local government level. This effort has yielded the desired result with South Africa experiencing increased women's presence in politics.

Overall changes and improvements are noted at the national and provincial level, but disparities continue within parties. For instance, parties like the DA, ACDP, and Freedom Front Plus remain gender-blind and do not see the need for gender quotas. This means all these parties still have a substantial share of men in positions of power. Therefore, it is important to give women's leadership in senior positions within parties more attention. However, there has been progress toward achieving the 50% representation of women in political leadership that has been envisioned by the ANC, as well as the transformation of previously male-dominated, patriarchal structures. Sonke Gender Justice (2019: 2) notes that despite what one might anticipate, "gender currency did not run along the ANC manifesto as strongly as one might expect from a party with such a long history". This demonstrates how decisions in these parties are still largely made by men. Important questions remain regarding the impact of women's representation in these structures due to ongoing obstacles to their full and equal participation.

CONCLUSION

This chapter provided in-depth background on women's political presentation and gender quotas in South Africa and Botswana. It started by discussing women's political representation in the case studies and the need for a quota system. In Botswana, the underrepresentation of women persists in the face of several international and regional treaties that have been signed by the government. However, the lack of a dedicated gender equality provision in the constitution has hampered these efforts. It further noted that save for the 30% voluntary quota by the BNF and BCP, the governing party does not make provision for any gender quotas. The effect of this is the relatively low presence of women in the parliament, even though women are often appointed as part of the specially elected MPs. The lack of an active women's group that can mobilise for the adoption of gender quota either in the constitution or by the governing party is also responsible for the low participation of women. The chapter moved on to discuss women's political representation in South Africa, which provides for a starkly different scenario from Botswana. It noted that following the end of apartheid, the ANC put in place an initial 30% gender quota, which it modified to 50% in 2007. This singular effort has been credited for South Africa's increased women's political participation. Although other parties such as the EFF and the IFP employ the zebra approach and 40% gender quotas respectively, the significance of the ANC's effort cannot be overstated. Opposition parties, such as the DA and other smaller parties, however, do not see the need for a gender quota as they argue that the empowerment of women is what is needed rather than gender quotas. A further investigation showed the central role that the ANC Women's League played in advocating for quotas to advance women's participation within the party structures and in the larger political system.

REFERENCES

African National Congress (ANC). 2009. Manifesto: Working together we can do more. https://www.anc1912.org.za/wp-content/uploads/2021/05/Election-Manifesto-Policy-Framework-2009.pdf

———. 2017. African National Congress Constitution. https://www.anc1912. org.za/wp-content/uploads/2021/01/ANC-Constitution-2017.pdf

Albertyn, C.H., S. Hassim, and S. Meintjies. 2002. Making a difference? Women's struggles for participation and representation. In *One woman one vote, the gender politics of elections in South Africa*, ed. G. Fick, S. Meintjies, and S. Simon, 24–52. Johannesburg: Electoral Institute of Southern Africa.

Bauer, G. 2011. Update on the women's movement in Botswana: Have women stopped talking? *African Studies Review* 54 (2): 23–46.

———. 2016. 'What is wrong with a woman being chief?' Women chiefs and symbolic and substantive representation in Botswana. *Journal of Asian and Africa Studies* 51 (2): 222–237.

Charter of Feminist Principles for African Feminists. 2006. Available at; https://awdf.org/wp-content/uploads/2016/12/AFF-Feminist-Charter-Digital-AcA_A_-English.pdf

Chikulo, B., and M. Mbao. 2006. Northwest: Gender. In *Electoral Institute of Southern Africa Election Update* 2006, 1.

Constitution of the Republic of South Africa 1996. No. 108 of 1996.

Dullah Omar Institute. 2019. The ANC—More of the same: Lip service to womxn. https://dullahomarinstitute.org.za/women-and-democracy/submissions/anc-key-points-2019-1.pdf

Electoral Act. 1998. (No. 73 of 1998) [South Africa].

Gender Links. 2019. Botswana: Gender and Elections. https://genderlinks.org.za/what-we-do/sadc-gender-protocol/advocacy-50-50/botswana-gender-and-elections/

Global Database of Quotas for Women. 2006. *Gender quotas.* International IDEA and Stockholm University. http://www.quotaproject.org.

Hendricks, C. (2005). Women and party Representation. In *South Africa's 2004 election: The quest for democratic consolidation*, ed. L. Piper. EISA Research Report 12.

Independent Electoral Commission. 2009. Results of the 2009 general election. www.iec.bw

International Institute for Democracy and Electoral Assistance. 2022. *Global database of quotas for women.* Stockholm University and the Inter-Parliamentary Union. https://www.idea.int/data-tools/data/gender-quotas.

Inter-Parliamentary Union (IPU). 2024. South Africa. https://www.ipu.org/parliament/ZA

Kethusegile-Juru, M. 2004. Quota systems in Africa: An overview. In *The implementation of quotas: African experiences*, ed. J. Ballington. Stockholm: International Institute for Democracy and Electoral Assistance.

Letsholo, S. 2006. *Democratic local government elections in South Africa: A critical review.* EISA Occasional Paper No 42. https://www.eisa.org/pdf/OP42.pdf

Madisa, M. 1990. Women and politics: Few women participate in the political process. *Southern African Political and Economic Monthly* 3 (7): 22–23.

Maundeni, Z. 1998. The struggle for political freedom and independence. In *Botswana politics and society*, ed. W.A. Edge and M.H. Lekorwe. Van Schaik Publishers.

Maundeni, Z., D. Mpabanga, A. Mfundisi, and D. Sebudubudu. 2007. *Consolidating democratic governance in Southern Africa: Botswana*. EISA Research Report No. 31. Johannesburg: EISA.

Mbeki, T. 2006. ANC women councillors at the command post! *ANC Today* 6 (9): 10–16.

Molomo, M. 2005. Electoral systems and democracy in Botswana. In *40 years of democracy in Botswana*, ed. Z. Maundeni. Gaborone: Mmegi Publishing House.

———. 2008. Political parties. In *Transparency, accountability and corruption in Botswana*, ed. Z. Maundeni. Made Plain Communication.

Molutsi, P. 1989. The ruling class and democracy in Botswana. In *Democracy in Botswana*, ed. J.D. Holm and P.P. Molutsi. Ohio University Press.

———. 2005. Botswana's democracy in a Southern African regional perspective: Progress or decline? In *40 years of democracy in Botswana*, ed. Z. Maundeni. Gaborone: Mmegi Publishing House.

Morna, C.L., K. Rama, and L. Mtonga. 2009. *Gender in the 2009 South African elections*. Gender Links, 11 May. http://www.genderlinks.org.za/attachment_view.php?pa_id=1056

Mottiar, S. 2006. KwaZulu-Natal: Gender representation. In *EISA election update: South Africa*. https://www.eisa.org/pdf/eusa200603.pdf

Ndenze, B. 2019. Maimaine not concerned about gender quota for now. *Eyewitness News*, 23 April. https://ewn.co.za/2019/04/23/maimane-not-concerned-about-gender-quota-for-now

Ntseane, D. 2005. Women in party politics. In *40 years of democracy in Botswana*, ed. Z. Maundeni. Gaborone: Mmegi Publishing House.

Ntseane, D., and J. Sentsho. 2005. Women's representation in parliament and council: A comparative analysis. In *40 years of democracy in Botswana*, ed. Z. Maundeni. Gaborone: Mmegi Publishing House.

Parliament of Botswana. 2022. History of parliament. https://www.parliament.gov.bw/index.php/about-parliament/history

Parliament of South Africa. 2022. About Parliament. https://www.parliament.gov.za/about-parliament

Samatar, A.I. 1999. *An African miracle: State and class leadership and colonial legacy in Botswana development*. Portsmouth, NH: Heinemann.

Scribner, D., and P. Lambert. 2010. Constitutionalizing difference: A case study analysis of gender provisions in Botswana and South Africa. *Politics & Gender* 6 (1): 37–61.

Sebudubudu, D., and B. Osei-Hwedie. 2005. *Democratic consolidation in SADC: Botswana's 2004 election*. EISA Research Report No. 11. Johannesburg: EISA.

Selolwane, O. 2000. Civil society, citizenship and Women's right in Botswana. In *International perspectives on gender and democratisation*, ed. S.M. Rai. London: Palgrave Macmillan.

Somolekac, G. 2005. *Political parties in Botswana*. EISA Research Report No. 27. Johannesburg: EISA.

Sonke Gender Justice. 2019. A gender and migration analysis of 2019 election manifestos.   https://genderjustice.org.za/publication/a-gender-and-migration-analysis-of-2019-election-manifestos/

Williams, J. 2006. *Western Cape: Gender issues*. EISA Election Update: South Africa. https://www.eisa.org/pdf/eusa200601.pdf

World Bank. 2020. GDP Per Capita, PPP (Current International $)—Botswana. https://data.worldbank.org/indicator/NY.GDP.PCAP.PP.CD?locations=BW

Zuma, J. 2007. Statement by the President of the African National Congress, Cde Jacob Zuma, to the closing of the 52nd National Congress of the ANC, Polokwane, Limpopo Province 20 December. https://www.sahistory.org.za/archive/closing-speech-anc-president-jacob-zuma-anc-20-december-2007-52nd-national-conference.

CHAPTER 7

Gender-Based Violence and Femicide as Substantive Women's Representation

Discrimination against women violates the principles of equality of rights and respect for human dignity, is an obstacle to the participation of women, on equal terms with men, in the political, social, economic and cultural life of their countries"

—Convention on the Elimination of All Forms of Discrimination Against Women (1979)

INTRODUCTION

A major issue around the concept of the substantive representation of women is the contention of what women's interests means. The contestation on defining women's interests led feminist political theorists to advocate for a shared perspective among women as a group to consolidate calls for more engagement between women politicians and women populace. Feminist scholars and gender theorists note that collaborative procedures of interest articulation, rather than just the perspective of one legislator, are the best ways to define 'women's interests' (Lovenduski 2005; Childs 2004; Dahlerup 2006). There are too many issues affecting women to assume on a centralised and universal notion of "women's interests". This does not mean that they are no common areas that women can agree upon, for instance, violence against women, menstrual hygiene, and gender pay gap are some of the very many issues that can be categorised as women issues. Gender-based violence and femicide remains one of the prevalent problems that women in Africa face (Olaitan 2024). The

Z. M. Olaitan, *Women's Representation in African Politics*, African Histories and Modernities, https://doi.org/10.1007/978-3-031-76051-8_7

prevalence and severity of GBVF cases across Africa makes it an important issue that affect women all over the continent, and thus, it is necessary to understand if numbers translate to impact in the broader discussion on women's political representation. Thus, the reduction of GBVF is used as an index to measure the substantive representation of women in both countries and the extent to which legislations/policy can help address it.

This chapter delves into the prevalence of gender-based violence and femicide in both cases as a precursor to operationalising it as an index to measure impact. It starts by conceptualising gender-based violence due to its multiplex nature, the book adopts the 1993 definition of violence against women provided by the United Nations as it better captures the multiplex nature of the concept. This chapter highlights the drivers of gender-based violence and femicide to better understand its prevalence in Africa. Drawing from this, it establishes the extent to which GBVF has eaten deep into both cases showing relevant statistics. Secondly, this chapter identifies different legislations and policies on GBVF that have been passed in Botswana and South Africa. It presents legislative outcomes and policy efforts that have been passed on GBVF in South Africa and Botswana from 2010 to 2022. It explains the aim of the identified legislations with overview on what they sought to do and how they address GBVF. The overview on legislations/policies enables the book to confirm the data findings on whether the presence of women in parliament translates to increased legislations/policies that address GBVF.

Conceptualising Gender-Based Violence

GBVF is a multiplex concept that covers various forms of violence meted out on the basis of gender. It is the general term used to capture violence that takes place within the framework of a particular society as a result of the uneven power relationships between the two genders and the normative role expectations connected with each of them (Bloom 2008: 14). It can be physical, emotional, sexual, verbal, psychological, economic, or cultural. Though GBVF is largely perceived as violence against women, it can affect all people, including men, and gay, lesbian, bisexual, transgender, queer, and intersex persons. Simply put, it is violence against another person because of their gender. Because women are often the most affected when issues of GBVF arise (Saferspaces 2020), there is a substitution of GBVF with violence against women and girls.

To understand violence against women, the most widely adopted definition is found in the UN Declaration on the Elimination of Violence against Women of 1993. It defines GBVF as "any act of violence that results in, or is likely to result in, physical, sexual, or psychological harm or suffering to women, including threats of such acts, coercion, or arbitrary deprivations of liberty, whether occurring in public or private life" (UN 1993: 2). Drawing from this definition, violence against women is spotlighted to symbolise GBV due to the prevalence of the former all over the world. The definition further asserts the following:

> Violence against women shall be understood to encompass, but not be limited to the following: physical, sexual and psychological violence occurring in the family and in the community, including battery, sexual abuse of female children, dowry related violence, marital rape, female genital mutilation and other traditional practices harmful to women, non-spousal violence and violence related to exploitation, sexual harassment and intimidation at work, in educational institutions and elsewhere, trafficking in women and forced prostitution and violence perpetrated or condoned by the state. (UN 1993: 2)

It is interesting to note that the above definitions are relevant and also apply to the selected case studies. Therefore, for the purpose of this research, GBVF is defined as "any act of violence that results in, or is likely to result in, physical, sexual, or psychological harm or suffering to women, including threats of such acts, coercion, or arbitrary deprivations of liberty, whether occurring in public or private life" (UN 1993: 2). This definition focuses on violence against women and girls because of the high rate of such cases in South Africa and Botswana over the years.

Drivers of Gender-Based Violence and Femicide

Saferspaces (2020) opines that GBVF is structural and deeply ingrained in institutions, cultures, and traditions, making it a serious and pervasive issue that affects practically every facet of daily life. Jewkes and Morell (2018) argue that patriarchy in most societies provides justification for situations that perpetuate harmful societal norms that leads to continuing violence against women and girls. Mshweshwe (2020: 1) highlights that it starts by prescribing numerous patriarchal attributes "that are tied directly to masculine social identities which are often enforced by men, the result being violence against women and girls". This type of violence takes many forms and is rooted in women's political, economic, and social subordination. It is crucial to understand that women's experiences with this violence vary widely since they are influenced not only by patriarchal institutions and practices but also by other types of inequality and discrimination (UN 1993). Violence against women is a derivative of the unequal power relations between genders in our society (Olaitan 2020). Bloom (2008: 13) argues that gender norms that govern expectations of the roles that women and men are expected to play in the family, community, and society at large propagate violence as a means of restricting and limiting women's autonomy and sexual activity. She further argues that these gender norms delineate the boundaries of acceptable behaviour for men and women in the family, community, and society within a given culture.

The vast majority of violence suffered by women and girls is often perpetrated by men and boys, whether as individuals or as a part of male-dominated institutions, despite the fact that not all men are violent (Gender Links 2012). However, the biological composition of being a man is not an adequate explanation for male violence against women because there are differences in prevalence, patterns, and individuality between men in any setting. Moolman (2017) opines that this is the reason the social construction of masculinity is identified as the culprit when it comes to men's perpetration of GBVF. Though there are differences based on race and tribe, the dominant messages about what a 'real man' is emphasise the superiority of masculinity over femininity and the authority of men over women (Jewkes et al. 2015: 98). Ideas about feminine weakness/vulnerability and masculine strength/protection expose girls and women to more violence and reinforce the belief in masculine superiority, which is central to patriarchy. Violence is often used to coerce women into obedience and uphold the hegemony of the men over the women, and it is also used by men to keep women in their position of having less economic, political, and social power (Gender Matters 2017). When women try to assert their claims to such power, for example, when they are involved in protests over economic and political rights, they are often verbally and physically attacked. Thus, Jewkes and Morell (2018) note that GBVF is maintained by ideas about the practices of hegemonic masculinity. By investigating the links between men's use of violence and social construct of masculinity, we discover that men are accorded more privilege than women, symbolising that masculinity is given priority over femininity (McVittie et al. 2017). Violence against women is thus born out of the privilege that manifest from this unequal relation. Drawing from this, men feel entitled to use violence against those who are less than them because they fear the loss of such privilege or feel unable to live up to the expectations associated with being the dominant gender (Bassey and Bubu 2019). Stromquist (2014) argues that in most African societies, men are raised to be men, they are socialised into learning that violence is a way to demonstrate their masculinity and control women, often at great cost not only to the women and girls in their lives but also to themselves. Violence against women and girls constitutes a key manner of such control that prevents women from asserting their roles as individuals with rights (Gender Matters 2017). Kapur (2013) asserts that GBVF is an important tool that consolidates the functionality of patriarchy as it ensures that women are only seen in relation to men, which means their status as wives, mothers, or daughters deprives them of their individual agency.

Prevalence of Gender-Based Violence in Selected Case Studies

South Africa was ranked fourth (the highest in Africa) in the 2012 Social Institutions and Gender Index of the Organisation for Economic Cooperation and Development for progress made in promoting gender equality and women's rights, and Botswana is often regarded as a developmental state because of its increasing economic growth. However, despite this progress made by these two countries, GBVF remains unacceptably high because cultural, religious, social, and economic factors play a role in driving GBVF. The prevalence and severity of GBVF is demonstrated in the fact that at least one in three women worldwide has experienced one form of abuse (UN 1993). According to Abrahams and Gevers (2017: 1), the South African Police Service reported that a total of 62 649 sexual offence complaints were recorded between 2013 and 2014. They further note that 34.6% of rape was committed by victims' relatives or close friends, 26.1% by random acquaintances, and 24.4% of victims had no relationship with their abusers. Statistics South Africa (2016) reports that one in five (21%) partnered women has experienced physical violence by a partner. The report goes further to state that one in five women in South Africa has been sexually abused and will experience sexual abuse in their lifetime. It notes that two in five have experienced physical abuse by their intimate partner, making their homes or surroundings unsafe for them.

South Africa as a patriarchal society exposes women to violence perpetrated by men and the assumption that women are sub-ordinate to men. In such communities, women are rendered defenceless, helpless, and disadvantaged, which inevitably increases their vulnerability to violence meted out on them. Rape is characterised by Gqola (2015) as a manifestation of male power and female vulnerability, which is consistent with the idea that GBVF results from an ongoing systemic power dynamic that maintains the objectification and stereotyping of women. Given the significance of rape kits in gathering evidence when a rape crime occurs, it is concerning that 76% of police stations in South Africa did not have rape kits in 2019 (Whitfield 2019). Enaifoghe et al. (2021) report that 75% of men in the Gauteng province of South Africa reported having committed GBVF at least once in their lifetime, compared to 51% of all the women in the sample who had experienced any type of violence. During the first week of the lockdown in 2020, gender-based violence (GBV) figures rose to 2 320 complaints. According to South African Minister of Police Bheki Cele, this statistic is 37% higher than the weekly average of domestic violence cases reported to the police in 2019 (Commission for Gender Equality 2022).

Nduna and Nene (2014) argue that while there is a lack of up-to-date statistics that tracks GBVF cases, women in South Africa are subjected to a prevalent rate of this violence. The National Institute for Crime Prevention and Rehabilitation claims that only one in 20 rape cases are reported to the South African Police Services, and human rights organisations estimate that only one in nine cases of sexual violence are. The Medical Research Council and Gender Links assert that only one in 20 women reported rape to the police, and 0.3% report domestic violence. Between 2018 and 2019, the South African Police Services documented almost 330 000 assault cases involving women (cited in Enaifoghe et al. 2021). High rates of sexual assault, rape, and femicide continue to occur in South Africa despite numerous campaigns and interventions conducted by the government groups and CSOs surrounding GBVF (South African Human Rights Commission 2018). Statistics South Africa (2016) indicate that 6% of women over the age of 18 have suffered sexual abuse in a relationship, and 21% of women over the age of 18 have experienced physical violence by a boyfriend. The inability of the criminal justice system to hold offenders accountable show that patriarchy and gender imbalance continue to operate and sustain gender hierarchies through essentialised ideas of gender and physical and/or sexual violence in South Africa (Rape Crisis

Cape Town Trust Prevalence 2017). As a result, this led to further perpetration of violence as the lack of punishment echoes the notion that it is not a grievous offence. The low rate of prosecution and conviction of GBVF offenders convey that perpetrators of such acts are not held accountable, thereby endangering the lives of women (Commission for Gender Equality 2022).

Botswana has a higher gender development index than some other African countries, but it is disturbing that the effects of GBVF continue to hamper the country's efforts to advance gender equality. Recent national data puts the GBVF rate in Botswana at 67%, with most women saying they have suffered at least one form of violence (Gender Links 2012). GBVF happens because men and women hold different levels of authority, and like the other SADC countries, Botswana has a long history of patriarchy because men continue to dominate major structures in the society. The killing of women by intimate partners, often known as intimate partner violence or passion killing, in which the perpetrator typically kills his spouse and then dies by suicide is one of the major GBVF-related issues that is now on the social and political agenda in Botswana. In many Batswana households, GBVF is widespread, and it is frequently used interchangeably with the term 'domestic violence' because it typically happens in a household setting. This type of violence affects all women, transcending social class, educational qualification, and religion.

Two surveys were conducted in 1999 by the Botswana Police Service and the Women Affairs Department to gauge the rate of GBVF. The Botswana Police Service survey found that there was an 18% increase in cases of rape reported in the country, rape of girls below age 16 increased by 65%, 58% of rape victims were aged 16 and 30 years; and 27% of rape victims were aged below 16 years. The report found that men between the ages of 18 and 32 make up most of the perpetrators of this act, and they are often known to their victims. The Women Affairs Department survey on the other hand sought to understand the types, degree, and consequences of GBVF in the country. It found that 60% (three in five women) of women have been victims of one form of violence. It sub-divided violence against women into different categories, namely sexual harassment, emotional abuse, physical abuse, sexual assault, verbal abuse, severe beatings, murder, etc. Intimate partner violence is the most prevalent type of violence, signifying that GBVF happens mostly in the domestic space.

The UN office in Botswana conducted a GBVF situation analysis in 2007 and discovered that the number of femicide cases doubled between in the period 2004–2007, and that physical violence against women by their partners is a recurring problem that usually ends with the murder of the woman. As a result of this, the report noted that 101 women were victims of intimate partner violence and femicide. Due to increased awareness on GBVF, the police service reported that there was a significant increase in the reporting of GBVF cases between 2003 and 2007. Of the GBVF cases reported between this period, rape occupies over 70%, 67% of women interviewed indicated that they had suffered from some form of violence, and 44% of men interviewed indicated that they had perpetrated some form of violence against women. The report notes that intimate partner violence is the most prevalent, often manifesting in emotional abuse followed by sexual and physical violence. Of the women interviewed, 11% indicated that they had experienced rape, 11% of men said they had engaged in it; 16% of the women said they had been a victim of attempted rape, and 2.2% of the men admitted to attempted rape; 24% of pregnant women said they had been exposed to abuse during the course of their pregnancy; and 23% of the women indicated that they had been victims of sexual harassment in different spaces. Women often do not seek medical attention for physical abuse suffered during intimate partner violence, and only 4.75% agreed that they sought medical attention and only 7.1% admitted that they reported it to the police. One out of every nine women who were raped did not call the police, and one in seven women told a doctor about being raped.

In 2012, Gender Links in conjunction with the department of women affairs commissioned another survey to investigate GBVF rate in Botswana. This study provides the most cited statistics as it is the most national and comprehensive survey on GBVF. It notes that 62% of women in a relationship had experienced some form of intimate partner violence, and 48% of men indicated that they had abused their partners. After intimate partner violence, sexual harassment is the most prevalent with 23% women indicating that they had been victims (Gender Links 2012). The study found that women often do not report cases of GBVF, consolidating the findings from 1999 and 2007. Kang'ethe (2014) notes that in spite of the prevalence of GBVF in the country, only 1.2% of women reported to the police, which shows that reporting was 24% less than the percentage of GBVF cases in the country. The lack of reporting on GBVF by women is due to societal attitudes towards such cases where it is assumed that violence such as marital rape and domestic violence are a non-matter because the man is the head of the household and can therefore treat his partner as he wishes. Kang'ethe (2014) argues that this manifests in traditional courts or traditional chiefs/courts not recognising GBV cases stemming from their demeanour of not encouraging women to report. Olaitan and Isike (2019) add that patriarchy legitimises such violence meted out under the guise of acceptable cultural norms. Gender Links (2012) notes that a woman reporting GBVF case to the traditional court or the police is seen as an embarrassment to the community, especially in cases of intimate partner violence. In 2018, a National Relationship Study was done to update the 2012 national statistics on violence against women. The study found that one in three women have experienced violence, and it notes that 37% women have experienced GBVF as well intimate partner violence (Chiramba et al. 2018). This puts the figure for Botswana in the same rank as the GBVF numbers reported for South Africa.

In 2020, the Botswana Police Service reported that 2 789 GBVF cases were reported during the period of the lockdown, compared to 2 265 cases for the whole of 2019 (Kuhlmann 2022). This demonstrates a significant spike in the rate of GBVF in the country during the Covid-19 lockdown, which is similar to South Africa. The tracing of GBVF cases across different time periods in the two case studies shows the consistent prevalence of GBVF, the types, and the degree to which women are exposed to it.

Legislative and Policy Outcomes on Gender-Based Violence and Femicide in Botswana and South Africa

Legislative and Policy Outcomes on Gender-Based Violence and Femicide in South Africa from 2010 to 2022

Prior to 2010, various legislative and policy outcomes have been formulated to address the prevalence of GBVF in South Africa. They include the following: Magistrates' Courts Act (No. 32 of 1944); Criminal Procedure Act (1977); Criminal Law Amendment Act (No. 107 of 1997); Domestic Violence Act (No. 116 of 1998); Maintenance Act (No. 99 of 1998); and Criminal Law (Sexual Offences and Related Matters) Amendment Act (No. 32 of 2007). However, the focus was limited to 2010–2022 to adhere to the scope delimited in the book.

1. The Protection from Harassment Act (No. 17 of 2011).
2. The Criminal Law (Sexual Offences and Related Matters) Amendment Act (No. 6 of 2012) (Sonke Gender Justice 2018).
3. In 2013, the president assented to the Commission on Gender Equality Amendment Act (No 17 of 2013). The act was amended to align with the constitution of the country. The preamble for the act was amended to represent women as important target group, and it states that "the object of the commission on gender equality shall be to promote gender equality, to advice and to make recommendations to Parliament or any other legislature with regard to any laws or proposed legislation which affects gender equality and the status of women".
4. Formation of the National Council on Gender-Based Violence in 2014, which was created for the purpose of drafting and implementing the National Strategic Plan for Gender-Based Violence and Femicide (2020).
5. Development of the National Strategic Plan for Gender-Based Violence and Femicide (2020), which was adopted by the president in 2020.
6. The president expressed the government's commitment to addressing the pandemic of GBVF by announcing the Emergency Response Plan, which included the applicable legislative framework in September 2019 (ERAP 2019).
7. In 2022, the government announced that three bills were signed into law to strengthen efforts to end GBV with a victims-centred focus (South African Government 2022). These approved legislations are a product of the National Strategic Plan for Gender-Based Violence and Femicide (2020). The National Assembly undertook the task of developing three bills as part of legislative measures to strengthen South Africa's response to GBVF. The bills are listed next:

The Criminal and Related Matters Amendment Act (No. 12 of 2021);
The Criminal Law (Sexual Offences and Related Matters) Amendment Act (No. 13 of 2021); and
The Domestic Violence Amendment Act (No. 14 of 2021).
The Criminal and Related Matters Amendment Act is an act that amends the Magistrates' Courts Act (No. 32 of 1944). It seeks to do the following:

- To amend the Superior Courts Act (No. 10 of 2013) to provide for the appointment of intermediaries and the giving of evidence through intermediaries in proceedings other than criminal proceedings; the oath and competency of intermediaries; and the giving of evidence through audio-visual link in proceedings other than criminal proceedings;
- To amend the Criminal Procedure Act (No. 51 of 1977) to further regulate the granting and cancellation of bail; the giving of evidence by means of closed-circuit television or similar electronic media; and the giving of evidence by a witness with physical, psychological, or mental disability;
- To amend the appointment, oath, and competency of intermediaries; and the right of a complainant in a domestic related offence to participate in parole proceedings; and
- To amend the Criminal Law Amendment Act (No. 107 of 1997) to regulate sentences in respect of offences that have been committed against vulnerable persons; and
- To address gendered violence and offences committed against vulnerable persons; and provide for additional procedures to reduce secondary victimisation of vulnerable persons in court proceedings. The Act expands the circumstances in which a complainant can give evidence through an intermediary and provides for evidence to be given through audio-visual links in proceedings other than criminal proceedings. This legislation tightens bail and minimum sentencing provisions in the context of GBVF.

The Criminal Law (Sexual Offences and Related Matters) Amendment Act (No. 13 of 2021) amends the Criminal Law (Sexual Offences and Related Matters) Amendment Act (No. 32 of 2007) to do the following:

- Extend the ambit of the offence of incest; introduce a new offence of sexual intimidation; substitute the phrase 'a person who is mentally disabled' or 'persons who are mentally disabled' wherever the phrase appears with the phrase 'a person with a mental disability' or 'persons with mental disabilities';
- Regulate the inclusion of particulars of persons in the National Register for Sex Offenders;
- Extend the list of persons who are to be protected in terms of Chapter 6 of the Act;

- Extend the list of persons who are entitled to submit applications to the Registrar of the National Register for Sex Offenders; regulate the removal of particulars of persons from the National Register for Sex Offenders; and regulate the reporting duty of persons who are aware that sexual offences have been committed against persons who are vulnerable; and,
- The legislation expands the scope of the National Register for Sex Offenders to include the particulars of all sex offenders and not only offences against children but also persons with mentally disabilities. It aims to improve the country's prevention of sex crimes, particularly of paedophilia, by expanding on the crime of incest and introducing a new offence of sexual intimidation.

Finally, the Domestic Violence Amendment Act (No. 14 of 2021) amends the Domestic Violence Act (No. 116 of 1998) to amend and insert certain definitions:

- To further provide for the manner in which acts of domestic violence and matters related thereto must be dealt with;
- To further regulate protection orders in response to acts of domestic violence; amend provisions of certain laws; and provide for matters connected therewith. It sought to address practical challenges, gaps and anomalies that have manifested since it came into operation in December 1999; and,
- In particular, the amended legislation includes new definitions of violence such as controlling behaviour and coercive behaviour and expands existing definitions of domestic violence to include spiritual abuse, elder abuse, coercive behaviour, controlling behaviour, and/ or exposing subjecting children to certain listed behaviours. It introduces online applications for protection order against acts of domestic violence and imposes obligations on functionaries in the appropriate departments to provide certain services to victims of domestic violence (South African Government 2022).

Overview of Previous Legislations and Policy on Gender-based Violence and/or Protecting the Rights of Women in Botswana

There are broad legislative outcomes that protect the rights of women in Botswana. The following laws were passed prior to the stated scope of this research: the Deeds Registry (Amendment) Act (No. 10 of 1996), the Criminal Procedure and Evidence (Amendment) Act (No. 7 of 1997), the Penal Code (Amendment) Act (No. 5 of 1998), the Affiliation Proceedings (Amendment) Act (No. 8 of 1999), and the Public Service (Amendment) Act (No. 5 of 2000).

Notably, Domestic Violence Act (No. 10 of 2008) is an important legislation with regards to GBVF in Botswana. This Act was sponsored by a female MP in 2007, which is the only time a bill has been sponsored by a private member in parliament. The government passed this law to protect women who are in a domestic relationship and provide protection to survivors of domestic violence. The Act deals with the jurisdiction of the courts and describes how a person who alleges to have been subjected to an act of domestic violence can submit an application for an order by the court. It explains how documents are served to the alleged perpetrators, and also identify the nature of proceedings in a domestic violence case. Specifically, it empowers the courts, including customary courts to pass an order. Section 7 of the Act prescribes orders available to applicants, such as restraining orders and interim orders. Section 9(2)(b)(i) proscribes that the order shall direct a member of the police to prohibit the perpetrator from committing an act of domestic violence.

Legislative Outcomes and Policies on Gender-based Violence and Femicide in Botswana from 2010 to 2022

1. National Gender-Based Violence Strategy 2015–2020: This is a multi-prolonged and multi-sectorial approach to prevent and eliminate GBVF. The strategy recognises men as critical partners in the fight against GBVF and led to the establishment of a men's sector under the ministry responsible for gender.
2. In December 2020, the Sexual Offenders Registry Act (No. 7 of 2021) was passed by the national parliament to make provision for

the establishment of a sexual offenders register and a sexual offenders inter-sectorial council. It includes provisions for the supervision of sexual offenders, their monitoring and psychological counselling. It further provides for the court to declare a person a dangerous sexual offender and create a report on sexual offenders by an authorised officer. It makes provision for those who have been declared dangerous offenders who do not comply with supervision or do not disclose their status as sexual offenders to be found guilty of an offence or liable to pay a fine and/or prison term (The Botswana Gazette 2020). Sections 4 and 5 of the Act provides for the definition of sexual offence and sexual offender, respectively. Section 3(1) (a–c) outlines the guiding principles, which are that the best interest of the survivor of the sexual offence is paramount, the privacy of survivor is protected, and the need to raise awareness of sexual abuse, sexual offenders, and emerging forms of sexual offences.

3. In November 2021, the parliament of Botswana enacted an amendment to the Penal Code to provide a new definition for rape and to enhance penalties for sexual offences. Section 141 of the Penal Code (Amendment) Act (No. 42 of 2021) was amended by substituting it for a new section that provides a new definition of rape. The new section states the following:

> any person who has unlawful carnal knowledge of another person or who causes the penetration of a sexual organ or instrument of whatever nature into the person of another, or who causes the penetration of another person's sexual organ, into his or her person without the consent of such other person or with such person's consent if the consent is obtained by force or means of threats or intimidation of any kind, by fear of bodily harm, or by means of false pretence as to the nature of the act, or in the case of married person by personating that person's spouse is guilty of the offence termed rape.

Section 142 introduced stricter, tougher penalties for the crime of rape, and provides the following:

> any person charged with the offence of rape upon conviction will be sentenced to minimum of 20 years in imprisonment, where the act of rape is tended to harm the victim it will be minimum of 25 years, where the perpetrator is unaware of their HIV status 25 years, where they are aware minimum of 30 years to life imprisonment, where the

perpetrator is a parent, guardian, repeat offender, or where the victim is below age of 14 years or persons with disability, the person will be sentenced to minimum of 30 years to life imprisonment.

In addition to this, Section 143 of the Act increases the punishment for attempted rape from five years to 15 years.

This list shows that between the period of 2010–2022, South Africa and Botswana enacted new legislation and policies that address the prevalence of GBVF and rape. These efforts include amendments to previous legislations to provide new definitions, tougher penalties for sexual and gender crimes, developing and consolidating sexual offenders registers, improving court proceedings on sexual offences, and protecting women. The findings confirm the claim made by female MPs in both case studies that new pieces of legislations have been passed on GBVF. The passing of multiple legislations relating to GBVF within the selected period also attests to their claim that the presence of women in parliament influences the kind of legislations that are passed, which often end up being gender sensitive.

Conclusion

This chapter examined gender-based violence and femicide as the selected indices to measure substantive women's representation in Africa. It noted that GBVF is a prevalent issue in both case studies as women are mostly affected by this violence. The high rate of GBVF in both case studies made it a suitable problem to represent women's interests given the contestation regarding the latter that was identified in Chap. 5. This chapter establishes that GBVF affects women irrespective of their race, social class or sexuality although these identities can affect the degree to which women are susceptible to it. This chapter notes that GBVF is a worrying concern considering its high prevalence in both cases. The second part of this chapter identified legislative and policy outcomes on GBVF or closely related instruments from 2010 to 2022. Thematic analysis was used to organise the different legislations that have been passed on GBVF. In generating themes from these legislations/policies, document review method was used to identify GBVF-targeted measures. The chapter finds that the identified legislations were passed to amend previous laws on domestic violence, sexual offences, and other related acts that constitute GBVF. The legislations identified mostly provide new definitions for sexual offences, introduced sexual offenders registers, and ensure stricter penalties for GBVF-related offences. The data findings on legislative and policy outcomes were presented to identify and briefly discuss what each selected outcome aims to achieve and how it addresses GBVF.

REFERENCES

Abrahams, N., and A. Gevers. 2017. A rapid appraisal of the status of mental health support in post-rape care services in the Western Cape. *South African Journal of Psychiatry* 23 (1): 1–8.

Affiliation Proceedings (Amendment) Act. 1999. No. 8 of 1999 [Botswana].

Bassey, S., and G. Bubu. 2019. Gender inequality in Africa: A re-examination of cultural values. *Cogito; Bucharest* 11 (3): 21–36.

Bloom, S. 2008. *Violence against women and girls: A compendium of monitoring and evaluation indicators.* Chapel Hill, NC: Measure Evaluation.

Childs, S. 2004. *New labour women MPs: Women representing women.* London: Routledge.

Chiramba, K., L. Musariri, and G. Rasesigo. 2018. *Botswana national relationship study.* Gaborone: Ministry of Nationality, Immigration and Gender Affairs.

Commission for Gender Equality. 2022. Submission to the UN special rapporteur on violence against women. Increase of gender-based violence against women and domestic violence in the context of the COVID-19 pandemic. https://www.ohchr.org/sites/default/files/2022-01/south-afri-commission-gender.pdf

Commission on Gender Equality Amendment Act. 2013. No. 17 of 2013 [South Africa].

Convention on the Elimination of All Forms of Discrimination Against Women 1979.

Criminal and Related Matters Amendment Act. 2021. No. 12 of 2021 [South Africa].

Criminal Law (Sexual Offences and Related Matters) Amendment Act. 2007. No. 32 of 2007 [South Africa].

———. 2012. No. 6 of 2012 [South Africa].

———. 2021. No. 13 of 2021 [South Africa].

Criminal Law Amendment Act. 1997. No. 107 of 1997 [South Africa].

Criminal Procedure Act. 1977. No. 51 of 1977 [South Africa].

Criminal Procedure and Evidence (Amendment) Act. 1997. No. 7 of 1997.

Dahlerup, D. 2006. The story of the theory of critical mass. *Politics & Gender* 2 (4): 511–521.

Deeds Registry (Amendment) Act. 1996. No. 10 of 1996.

Domestic Violence Act. 1998. No. 116 of 1998 [South Africa].

———. 2008. No. 10 of 2008 [Botswana].

Domestic Violence Amendment Act. 2021. No. 14 of 2021 [South Africa].

Enaifoghe, A., M. Dlelana, and A.A. Durokifa. 2021. The prevalence of gender-based violence against women in South Africa: A call for action. *African Journal of Gender, Society and Development* 10 (1): 121–150.

ERAP [Emergency Response Action Plan]. 2019. Emergency response plan on gender-based violence and femicide in South Africa. https://www.nda.org.za/assets/download/Tenders/Background_Document_Victim_Empowerment_Programme.pdf

Gender Links. 2012. *The gender-based violence indicators study.* Joint Report by Botswana Women's Affairs Department and Gender Links. http://genderlinks.org.za/wp-content/uploads/imported/articles/attachments/15554_gbv_indicators_executivesummary.pdf

Gender Matters. 2017. Manual on addressing gender-based violence affecting young people. https://rm.coe.int/chapter-1-gender-identity-gender-based-violence-and-human-rights-gende/16809e1595

Gqola, P.D. 2015. *Rape: A South African nightmare.* Johannesburg: MF Books.

Jewkes, R., and R. Morell. 2018. Hegemonic masculinity, violence and gender equality: Using latent class analysis to investigate the origins and correlates of differences between men. *Men Masculinities* 21 (1): 547–571.

Jewkes, R., R. Morell, E. Lundgvist, D. Blackbeard, G. Lindegger, M. Quayle, Y. Sikweyiya, and L. Gottzen. 2015. Hegemonic masculinity; Combining theory and practice in gender interventions. *Culture, Health, and Sexuality* 17 (2): 96–111.

Kang'ethe, S.M. 2014. The perfidy and ramifications of gender-based violence meted against women and the girl-child in Botswana. A literature review. *Mediterranean Journal of Social Sciences* 5 (23): 1563–1567.

Kapur, R. 2013. *Violence against women in South Asia and the limits of law. Background paper for current report.* Washington, DC: World Bank.

Kuhlmann, M. 2022. How gender-based violence became Botswana's parallel pandemic. *Sunday Standard*, 7 February. https://www.sundaystandard.info/how-gender-based-violence-became-botswanas-parallel-pandemic/

Lovenduski, J., ed. 2005. *State feminism and political representation.* Cambridge: Cambridge University Press.

Magistrates Courts Act. 1944. No. 32 of 1944 [South Africa].

Maintenance Act. 1998. No. 99 of 1998 [South Africa].

McVittie, C., J. Hepworth, and K. Goodall. 2017. Masculinities and health: Whose identities. In *whose constructions? In The psychology of gender and health: Conceptual and applied global concerns,* ed. M.P. Sanchez-Lopz and R.M. Liminana-Gras, 119–141. Cambridge, MA: Academic Press Elsevier.

Moolman, B. 2017. Negotiating masculinities and authority through intersecting discourses of tradition and modernity in South Africa. *Norma* 12 (1): 38–47.

Mshweshwe, L. 2020. Understanding domestic violence: Masculinity, culture, tra-ditions. *Heliyon* 6 (10): 1–5.

National Strategic Plan for Gender-Based Violence and Femicide. 2020. Available at: https://www.justice.gov.za/vg/gbv/NSPGBVFFINAL-DOC-04-05.pdf

Nduna, M., and N. Nene. 2014. *Review and analysis of South Africa's implementa-tion of 365 days National Action Plan.* Johannesburg: Department of Psychology, University of Witwatersrand and Ifalezwe Learning Express.

Olaitan, Z.M. 2020. *Analysis of women's participation in peacebuilding in West Africa: The case of Sierra Leone.* Masters Dissertation, University of Pretoria.

———. 2024. Using digital technology to address gender-based violence in South Africa. In *African women in the fourth industrial revolution*, ed. T.A. Ojo and B. Ndzendze. London: Routledge.

Olaitan, Z.M., and C.A. Isike. 2019. The role of African Union in Fostering Women's Representation in formal peacebuilding: A case study of Sierra Leone. *Journal of African Union Studies* 8 (2): 135–154.

Penal Code (Amendment) Act. 1998. No. 5 of 1998 [Botswana].

———. 2021. No. 42 of 2021 [Botswana].

Protection from Harassment Act. 2011. No. 17 of 2011 [South Africa].

Public Service (Amendment) Act. 2000. No. 5 of 2000 [Botswana].

Rape Crisis Cape Town Trust Prevalence. 2017. Gender-based violence in South Africa. https://rapecrisis.org.za/

Saferspaces. 2020. Gender-based violence in South Africa. https://www.safer-spaces.org.za/understand/entry/gender-based-violence-in-south-africa

Sexual Offenders Registry Act. 2021. No. 7 of 2021 [Botswana].

Sonke Gender Justice. 2018. *Stop gender-based violence: A national campaign.* Available at: https://genderjustice.org.za/project/policy-development-advocacy/stop-gender-violence-national-campaign

South African Human Rights Commission. 2018. *Unpacking the gaps and chal-lenges in addressing gender-based violence.* Research brief April. https://www.sahrc.org.za/home/21/files/SAHRC%20GBV%20Research%20Brief%20Publication.pdf

South African Government. 2022. *President Ramaphosa assents to laws that strengthen the fight against gender-based violence.* Available at: https://www.gov.za/speeches/president-cyrilramaphosa-assents-laws-strengthen-fight-against-gender-basedviolence-28

Statistics South Africa. 2016. *Crimes against women in South Africa: An analysis of the phenomenon of GBV and femicide: An overview of the prevalence of crimes against women in the country and the conditions that exacerbate GBV leading to femicide.* https://www.parliament.gov.za/storage/app/media/1_Stock/Events_Institutional/2020/womens_charter_2020/docs/30-07-2020/A_Statistical_Overview_R_Maluleke.pdf

Stromquist, N. 2014. *Women in the third world: An encyclopedia of contemporary issues.* New York: Garland Publishers.

Superior Courts Act (No. 10 of 2013) [South Africa].

The Botswana Gazette. 2020. *Draft sexual offenders bill opened to public input.* November 5. Available at: https://www.thegazette.news/news/draft-sexual-offenders-registry-bill-opened-to-publicinput/#

United Nations (UN). 1993. *Declaration on the elimination of violence against women.* Proclaimed by General Assembly resolution 48/104 of 20 December 1993. https://www.ohchr.org/sites/default/files/eliminationvaw.pdf

Whitfield, A. 2019. National rape kit crisis: 76% of SA police stations have no rape kits in stock for victims. *Democratic Alliance*, 11 August. https://www.da.org.za/2019/08/national-rape-kit-crisis-76-of-sa-police-stations-have-no-rape-kits-in-stock-for-victims

Impact of Gender Quotas on Substantive Women's Representation: Perspectives from Botswana and South Africa

we all move forward when
we recognise how resilient
and striking the women
around us are

–Rupi Kaur (2020)

INTRODUCTION

The assumption that women's participation in politics enables the substantive representation of women is one that has been peddled for a long time, and the notion is titling towards affirming that women's presence can ensure the protection of women as a collective group. Hence, this book's rationale focuses on interrogating whether there is a relationship between the numbers of women participating in politics and protecting women's interests, and more importantly, how the participation of women in politics impacts the reduction of the rate of GBVF in South Africa and Botswana. It further aims to recommend alternative pathways to ensure the substantive representation of women to reduce the dependence on female political leaders as advocates for women issues as the over-reliance on them may not yield positive results for representing women's interests in Africa. This chapter is central achieving that objective as it uses data findings to understand the impact of women's representation in politics beyond numbers.

Z. M. Olaitan, *Women's Representation in African Politics*, African Histories and Modernities, https://doi.org/10.1007/978-3-031-76051-8_8

This chapter is divided into two parts: the first part analyses the responses of participants in line with the research objectives according to participant groups (female MPs in South Africa, female MPs in Botswana, and women working in CSOs). The section presents the research findings to address the objectives; the objectives were to investigate whether there is a relationship between numbers and impact; to re-examine the relevance of quotas beyond being a pathway for mainstreaming women into politics; to measure the effectiveness of gender quotas in enabling women's substantive representation using GBVF; and to recommend alternative pathways to ensure substantive women's representation. Based on the findings, 10 themes were drawn that form the framework for this section, they are; relevance of gender quotas, women's political participation benefits women, critical mass necessary for impact, gender-based violence and femicide, effectiveness of legislative outcomes on GBVF, impact of the presence of female MPs on legislative outcomes on GBVF, self-evaluation of impact of female MPs, impact of female MPs on addressing GBVF, improving the quality of women's political representation and recommendations to reduce the rate of GBVF. These themes help us to understand the significance of women's representation in politics beyond numbers into how it enables qualitative well-being of African women.

The second part discusses and analyses the data findings to address the research questions. It examines how the research process has addressed the research questions with reference points to literature on women's representation in politics, and the data findings. The section answers these questions: What is the relationship between numbers and impact in terms of women's political representation in Africa? Do gender quotas have relevance beyond being a pathway for mainstreaming women into politics? How do gender quotas impact policy and legislative outcomes in GBVF in Botswana and South Africa? What alternative pathways are there to ensure the substantive representation of women in African politics? The questions were answered on a country basis for female MPs as their perspective is crucial to the research, and women in CSOs is done as a collective group. This highlights the responses of participants to allow for country-specific answering of the research questions. This section also uses the findings from the legislative and policy outcomes to confirm the impact female MPs have made on GBVF. A brief comparison between South Africa and Botswana is made to identify the differences and similarities in how gender quotas impact on policy and legislative outcomes on GBVF.

As previously mentioned in Chap. 1, 43 interviews were conducted with female MPs in South Africa, female MPs in Botswana, and women working in CSOs in Botswana and South Africa. The first group of participants were numbered Participants 1–36, the second group; Participants 39–41, and the last group were numbered Participants 37 and 38 for South Africa and Participants 42 and 43 for Botswana. Additionally, an overview of legislative and policy outcomes that have been passed on GBVF from 2010 to 2022 in both countries is provided to consolidate the analysis of the questions.

Relevance of Gender Quotas in Mainstreaming Women

This theme addresses the objective on examining the relevance of quotas as a mechanism beyond increasing the number of women in politics into fostering substantive women's representation. Considering that quotas have been adjudged to be a 'fast-track' mechanism to ensure women's political participation (Dahlerup 2006a), it is important to explore how the numbers created by quotas can ensure the representation of women's interests. This is in acknowledgement that the impact of gender quotas needs to move beyond the numbers of women in politics to the representation of their interests. The corresponding research question to this theme is 'do gender quotas have relevance beyond being a pathway to mainstreaming women in politics?' All three participant groups contributed to this theme, and they were asked whether gender quotas are necessary to ensure women's political participation.

Perspectives of Female Members of Parliament in South Africa on Relevance of Gender Quotas

Thirty-six participants, female MPs in South Africa, were asked whether they think gender quotas are necessary to ensure women are represented in the political system. Data findings showed that 25 participants believed that quotas are necessary to ensure women's political representation, while 11 did not agree that quotas are necessary. This demonstrates that gender quotas are not unanimously seen as a necessary instrument for women's political participation. However, considering that 69% of the participants believed in the necessity of quotas for women to participate in politics, we

Fig. 8.1   Illustration of participants' responses on relevance of quotas. (Source: Olaitan 2023)

can deduce that quotas are relevant for women's representation in politics (Fig. 8.1).

The 25 participants who agreed noted themes such as inclusion, representation of women, and equality. The significance of these sub-themes is that the participants did not only see quotas as ensuring women can participate in politics, but they also saw it as an instrument that works for women as a collective group. The participants explained that quotas ensure women are included in politics because of long-standing exclusion, which is often the result of the patriarchal system, which limits their participation. They noted that it can help correct the gender imbalance that exists in society and also make space for women in the decision-making sphere. This depicts that quotas can be used to ensure the inclusion of women in the political system and in other spheres of society at large. Most of the participants saw quotas as a levelling tool that allows women to be on equal footing with men in society. Importantly, the participants noted that while quotas ensure women's participation in politics, the participation of these women can lead to better representation of women issues. Participant 29 argued that "quotas ensure that women take space, we need to represent ourselves, we have issues that we as women need to take decision on in making sure they are being implemented and they suit our needs" (P29 29 April 2022). This means that female MPs do not just see quotas as an end in itself, they also see it as a mechanism that ensure women's issues can be represented in decision-making spheres. This posits that quotas have relevance beyond ensuring numbers via women's political participation. It is a means to ensure women can be included in society, are put on equal footing with men, and are able to represent issues that are specific to them.

Perspectives of Female Members of Parliament in Botswana on Relevance of Gender Quotas

Unlike South Africa where the governing party uses quotas to mainstream women into political positions, the governing party in Botswana does not use quotas. However, there is a provision for specially elected MPs who are appointed by the president. It is through this appointment that a certain number of women are selected. To understand the position of female MPs in Botswana as a separate group from their counterparts in South Africa, they were asked whether quotas are necessary. All participants agreed that gender quotas are necessary to ensure women's political representation in Botswana, even though Participant 39 did not personally believe in it. The three interviewed participants noted that quotas are necessary to mainstream women into politics. Similar to their South African counterparts, they explained that quotas help ensure the equality of women, inclusion of women, and representation of women issues. Participant 39 noted that quotas ensure that women are included. She stated:

> I am not one for quotas because I'm one for motivating women to compete at the same level with men. But unfortunately, our world is not like that because we belong to a very chauvinistic, patriarchal society. We are then forced to consider things like quotas as they make way for women in politics. (P39 9 February 2022)

Participant 40 stated that "to ensure proper representation of the issues that women face, it is important that women participate in politics, which quotas help ensure" (P40 16 April 2022). The general notion from this is that quotas are an important instrument for ensuring that women who understand the problems of women and the interests of women are able to participate in politics to make sure that those interests and issues receive attention. The prevalence of gender stereotypes due to patriarchal culture and norms has limited the extent to which women's voices can be heard in society. This affects how women's issues are addressed or how their interests are protected. The adoption of gender quotas thus helps ensure women participate in politics, which invariably means that the selected women will champion and represent women's issues in parliament and decision-making spheres. This is made possible by ensuring women's voices are heard through the women that were selected and elected to political positions. The above perceptions indicate that female MPs in Botswana agreed that quotas have relevance beyond mainstreaming women into politics as they are able to ensure the substantive representation of women.

Perspectives of Women in Civil Society Organisations on Relevance of Gender Quotas

The third participant group were women working in CSOs that deal with GBVF. Their contribution was important as it ensured balance and differing perspectives from that of female MPs. This was critical as it represented the other side of the coin, that is, what the average woman who is not a parliamentarian thinks about the relevance of gender quotas. All four participants in this group agreed that quotas are necessary to ensure women's participation in politics. They believe that quotas can ensure the protection of women's interest, inclusion of women, and transformation of the system. This is somewhat similar to what female MPs in Botswana and South Africa stated about the relevance of quotas beyond ensuring numbers of women in politics.

Perspectives from all participant groups on re-examining the relevance of gender quotas beyond mainstreaming women into politics indicate that there was consensus among female MPs in South Africa, female MPs in Botswana, and women working in CSOs in South Africa and Botswana that the relevance of gender quotas goes beyond the participation of women in politics. By virtue of quotas mainstreaming women into politics, their political participation ensures inclusion of women in society, representation of women issues in decision-making spheres, and the equality of women and men in society. This creates a new lens with which to understand the relevance of gender quotas within the discourse of women's political representation.

Women's Political Participation Benefits Women

Having established that gender quotas are useful mechanisms to ensure women's political participation in politics, it was important to establish whether and how the participation of women in politics benefits women. This theme consolidates the first objective that sought to understand the relationship between numbers and impact in Africa. Participants were asked if the participation of women in politics benefits the general women populace? All participant groups were asked whether they agreed that women's political participation can ensure substantive representation of women. Their answers lent credence to the link between descriptive women's representation and substantive representation of women within the African context. While studies have been done on the link between the two in other regions of the world, an extensive study on Africa has not been done, which was a major objective of this research.

Perspectives of Female Members of Parliament in South Africa on Whether Women's Political Participation Benefits Women

All participants in this group agreed that women's political participation benefits women, thereby confirming that there is a relationship between the number of women in politics and the impact on women as a whole. Further consolidating the relationship, participants discussed how numbers create benefits, which are discussed under corresponding sub-themes in the following subsections.

- Represent women issues

Participants believed that their participation in parliament enables them to represent women issues, protect women's interests, and cater for women's needs. Participant 17 confirmed that "the participation of women in politics allows for issues of women to be escalated to the high echelon of power" (P17 22 March 2022). To support this notion, Participant 27 argued that "because women are represented within decision-making structures, it is easier for female voices to speak on behalf of women than a male voice would" (P27 24 April 2022). Participant 2 noted that "their participation benefits women because they get different ideas and ways of thinking to deal with issues that affect women while working to provide solutions to them" (P2 18 February 2022). The numbers that women build with their participation allow them to echo and represent the issues that affect women as a collective in parliament. They are able to serve as the medium through which the problems that affect women are dealt with in parliament.

- Influence legislations and policy

Participants noted that their participation in politics enables them to influence policy and legislations on women issues. Participant 17 explained that "when women get to decision-making sphere, they influence policies that deal with women issues" (P17 22 March 2022). Participant 11 confirmed that "as women we are able to influence legislations pertaining to women and women's rights, we are the voice of women on the ground" (P11 7 March 2022). Participants saw themselves as lobby groups for women because they believed their participation in politics allows them to contribute to the kinds of legislations that are passed to ensure a gender-conscious parliament. Participant 35 better encapsulated the link between their participation and representation of women's interest that translates to legislations as follows:

> Because women are able to advance issues that affect women, they speak to issues and translate them to legislation into a bill that protects women. And that only women participating in politics can adequately speak for women … if women do not voice out, we would have no one that speaks for women that are being violated. (P35 12 May 2022)

This aligns with the literature that argues that women MPs see themselves as representatives of women in parliament and are likely to table women's issues to ensure the protection of their interests (Mansbridge 2005; Williams 2000).

- Challenge gender stereotypes and serve as role models to young girls;

Participants believed that their participation is symbolic as it challenges gender stereotypes that seek to limit the extent of women's capability. They explained that being able to participate in politics sends a message to other women that women are not inferior beings and deserve to be included in positions of power. Participant 18 stated that "the participation of women in politics allows for women to take over careers that are dominated by men. We are getting the same respect as men because society is starting to recognise that women are not inferior to men" (P18 25 March 2022). Furthermore, they believed their participation inspires young girls and ensures they have role models to look up to. To support the role model point, Participant 6 stated:

> I was chosen by my party to give a speech at SONA. I posted it for my community to watch it because they were the one that sent me to parliament. My pastor's wife said she watched it with her daughters because she wanted them to see a woman using her voice for change. Yes, my participation allows for those girls to have female MPs they can emulate. (P6 24 February 2022)

Perspectives of Female Members of Parliament in Botswana on Whether Women's Political Participation Benefits Women

To establish the relationship between women's political participation and its benefit for women in Botswana, MPs in Botswana were also asked the corresponding question. Unlike South Africa that had a collective agreement to the question, Participant 39 in Botswana gave a slightly different answer to the question by stating that "I would not describe the relationship as 'benefit' but as a sort of responsibility" (P39 9 February 2022). Participants 40 and 41 did not disagree with the semantics of the relationship between numbers and impact. Apart from the semantics divergence, female MPs in Botswana had similar views to their South African counterparts. They believed that the participation of women in politics enables them to advocate for women issues, represent women issues, and be role models to younger women. Participant 41 explained that "having women in political positions is a motivation to younger women. We are used to seeing men all over so seeing women in power empowers young females that they can get there too" (P41 14 April 2022). Participant 39 echoed that women in politics are the voice of other women, and she noted that "women in politics are there to be the voice of the other as they are able to advocate for issues that affect women as a whole" (P39 9 February 2022). About representing women's issues, Participant 40 explained that "women in political positions are able to cater for the needs of women. If it is just men at the table, there will be no one to bring up the struggle that women have because men will overlook or side-line it. So, the participation of women allows for such issues to be brought it up because they know what it feels like" (P40 16 April 2022).

Perspectives from female MPs in South Africa and Botswana confirmed that the participation of women in politics benefits women. Hence, there is a link between the descriptive representation of women and the substantive representation of women because their participation means women's issues can be better represented, they can influence legislations and policies for the benefit of women, they serve as role models for other women, and their presence challenges gender stereotypes that limit women in society.

Perspectives of Women in Civil Society Organisations on Whether Women's Political Participation Benefits Women

To provide a different perspective to the relationship between numbers and impact, women in civil society were asked whether they believed the participation of women in politics is necessary to advance women's interests, that is, whether numbers are necessary to ensure impact. While all participants agreed that ideally women's participation in politics should be able to advance women's interests, there was lack of a consensus about the existence of this relationship within their given context. They noted that the mere participation of women in politics does not automatically translate to benefits for women as other factors determine these result. For instance, Participant 43 from Botswana expressed doubt about the possibility of the participation of female MPs yielding benefits for women in Botswana by arguing that the lack of a critical mass of women makes it difficult for them to be able to protect women's interest. She noted that "because women are few in the parliament of Botswana, they are unable to work as collective lobby group that advocates and advances women's issues. Also because of the minute number that they occupy they tend to get swallowed up by the voices of men, who are significantly more than them" (P43 11 February 2022). This supports the critical mass argument for enabling substantive representation of women: Women must occupy a considerable percentage before they can influence the system. This is a relevant argument considering that the representation of women in the Botswana parliament stands at 11.11%, which is 19% lower than the prescribed 30% critical mass needed to protect women's interests.

Participant 38 from South Africa raised a fundamental point:

It is not about their participation of women in parliament, but how these women see themselves. Do they see themselves as women who are representing the interests of women or as parliamentarians who are there to advance their party mandate? ... MPs often advance their party's mandate and not all of them talk about advancing women issues. (P38 13 April 2022)

The perspectives from this participant group showed a divergence from that of the female MPs on the relationship between numbers and impact in Africa. While they all agreed that ideally the participation of women is necessary to protect women's interests, they differed on the reality of the participation of women in their respective national parliament. They noted that female MPs face different obstacles which goes on to affect such a relationship. This highlights that beyond establishing the linear relationship between numbers and impact in Africa, there are factors to consider when trying to understand why such a linear relationship might not exist. Additionally, the assumption that female MPs automatically champion and prioritise women issues when they get to parliament was challenged by women in civil society. While the first opposition was due to lack of critical mass, the other was due to the fact that female MPs advance party mandates over women issues.

CRITICAL MASS NECESSARY FOR IMPACT

To understand the relationship between numbers and impact, participants were asked whether a considerable number is needed to ensure the substantive representation of women. Participants were asked the following question: To protect the interest of women, do you think it is necessary to have a certain percentage of women participating in politics? This question also draws from the sub-theme where one of the participants argued that critical mass is needed before impact can be made.

Perspectives of Female Members of Parliament in South Africa on Whether Critical Mass Is Necessary to Create Impact

Out of 36 participants, twenty-nine participants (81%) indicated a percentage and agreed that there is a need for a critical mass to ensure the protection of women's interests. On the other hand, seven participants (19.4%) stated that numbers do not matter at all and did not suggest any

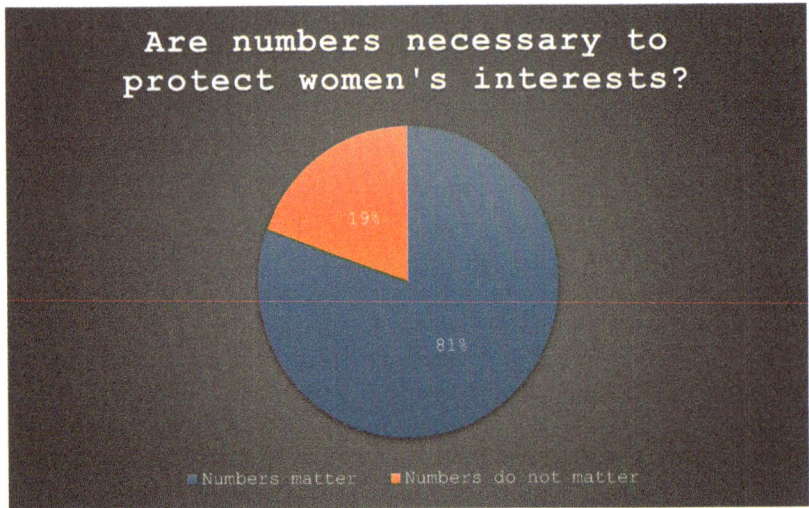

Fig. 8.2 Participants' responses on necessity of numbers for impact. (Source: Olaitan 2023)

percentage, depicting that they did not agree that a critical mass is needed to create an impact (Fig. 8.2).

Of the 29 that agreed with numbers, 25 registered 50% and above as the ideal critical mass needed to protect women's interest (Fig. 8.3).

Participant 29 commented that "to undo the past injustice women have suffered, women should occupy 60–70% of space in politics so that they are in a position to implement policies that speak directly to women's issues" (P29 19 April 2022). Among the participants that disagreed with critical mass, the argument for critical actors emerged. For instance, Participant 3 stated that "it does not matter the percentage of women, as long as they get the job done" (P3 19 February 2022). This signifies that a certain number of women in politics is not needed to protect women's interests. Participant 9 explained that "we don't need any numbers, what is needed are competent women who can lead by example. I do not think we need a set percentage to do that, even one woman can make a difference" (P9 4 March 2022). This further consolidated the critical actors' analysis that a critical mass of women is not needed to ensure the substantive representation of women as long as there are women who can be critical actors (Childs and Krook 2009).

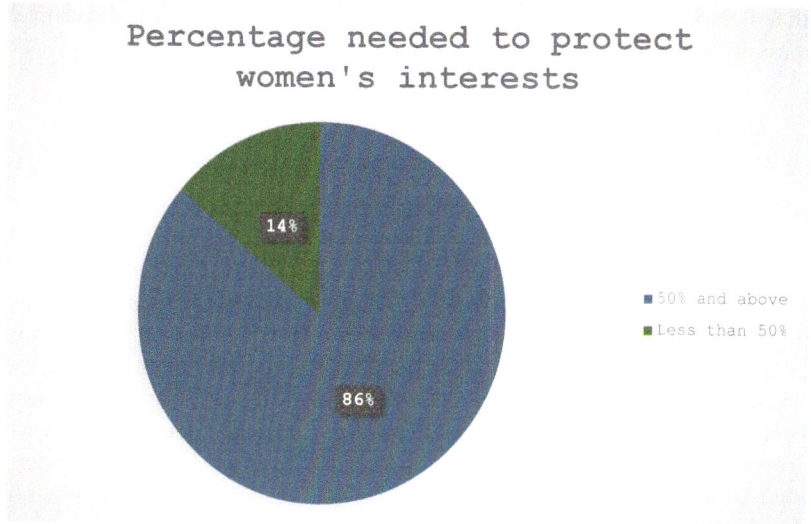

Fig. 8.3 Participants' responses on percentage needed to protect women's interests. (Source: Olaitan 2023)

Perspectives of Female Members of Parliament in Botswana on Whether Critical Mass Is Necessary to Create Impact

Participants 40 and 41 suggested a set percentage needed to ensure the protection of women's interests, agreeing with the need for a critical mass. They indicated 40% and 50%, respectively, as the preferred critical mass needed to ensure the protection of women's interests. However, Participant 39 argued that it is not so much about numbers. She stated, "I think given our environment to me, it depends not so much the number but the quality of women that put in positions. You can have one woman with great impact equals that of 10 women. So, it's not a question of number but that of representation" (P39 11 February 2022). This perfectly embodies the critical actors' argument that numbers do not matter as along as the quality of women ensures the adequate representation of women's interests. You only need certain individuals to act for women rather than having a set percentage to act for women. It further indicates that there is no conclusion concerning the best way to ensure substantive representation of women; however, given that two-thirds of MPs in Botswana believed that a critical mass is needed, it shows majority alignment with the critical mass argument.

Perspectives of Women in Civil Society Organisations on Whether Critical Mass Is Necessary to Create Impact

All participants belonging to this group agreed that a critical mass of women is needed to protect the interest of women, and they all suggested a set percentage. They all suggested 50% and above as the minimum percentage of women needed to form a critical mass to protect women's interests. The percentages suggested were similar across all participant groups, and most suggested 50%. This shows an increase from the universal 30% suggested by the BPfA in 1995. Literature focus on critical mass needed to ensure substantive representation of women starts at 30%; however, participants in this research noted that 30% is not enough considering that women are half of the population in their respective countries and the critical mass should reflect that. To support the critical actors' argument echoed by a few participants in the previous group, Participant 42 voted for both critical mass and critical actors, and she stated that "even with numbers, we will still have women who do not represent women's interests. It's not just a numbers game. It is about having the right women representative so just having 50% does not necessarily guarantee a fairer or feminist outlook" (P42 11 February 2022).

Perspectives on this theme indicated that most participants recognised the importance of numbers (critical mass) for there to be impact. This supports the critical mass argument on how best to ensure women's interests are better protected. A minority recognised the necessity for critical actors as critical mass does not translate to automatic impact. This aligns with the submission made in Chap. 2 that suggested a combination of critical mass and critical actors. This complementarity was also suggested by Participant 42, who noted that while numbers are important, women parliamentarians need to work as critical actors to consolidate efforts on how to protect interests that directly affect women. Merely reaching critical mass might not create the needed impact if these women do not work conscientiously to advocate and represent women issues.

Gender-Based Violence and Femicide

This theme interrogates GBVF as a very important problem that women in Africa face. This was done to legitimise its selection as an index to measure the substantive representation of women. All participants across the three groups decried the prevalent rate of GBVF, specifically pointing out that it is a menace and pandemic that affects women as group. Hence, the selection of GBVF as an index to represent the substantive representation of women is well within acceptable based on the perspectives from the participants. Secondly, this theme was used to resolve the contestation concerning what constitutes women's interests, because of the disagreement prevalent in literature. GBVF poses a central interest that affects women in both case studies, permeating the nuances that exist within the group.

Effectiveness of Legislative Outcomes on Gender-Based Violence and Femicide

To delimit a specific medium by which the effectiveness and impact of female MPs on GBVF could be understood, legislative and policy outcomes were used. To enable the operationalisation of impact as legislative and policy outcomes that have been passed on GBVF, participants were asked whether legislations and policies can be used by female MPs to address the rate of GBV in the given context. Most participants agreed that legislations and policies can be used if they are effectively implemented.

Perspectives of Female Members of Parliament in South Africa on the Effectiveness of Legislative/Policy Outcomes on GBVF

Out of 36 female MPs, 28 participants (78%) agreed that legislation and policies can be used by female MPs to reduce the rate of GBVF, and eight participants (22%) agreed with certain reservations. This supports the notion that legislations and policies are powerful tools towards reducing the rate of GBVF, allowing for the impact of female MPs to be measured by this instrument. Participant 18 explained that "the law can be used to protect women because women in South Africa are mostly disadvantaged. Most of the women are poor, heading households alone and some of them are not active, so the policies/legislations we pass are measures that can be used to protect such women" (P18 25 March 2022). The eight participants that expressed reservations cited issues such as lack of support, lack of proper implementation, and laws being too top-down as factors that might hinder the effectiveness of legislations towards the stated goal.

Perspectives of Female Members of Parliament in Botswana on the Effectiveness of Legislative/Policy Outcomes on GBVF

Unlike South Africa where most participants agreed that legislations and policies can be used to protect the interest of women and in extension reduce GBVF, participants in Botswana expressed divided affirmation. They all agreed that the law can be used to address the rate of GBVF; however, they noted that factors such as inadequate resources, lack of support, and the small number of women in parliament hinder this possibility in the current terrain in which they find themselves.

Perspectives from female MPs in South Africa suggested that the law can be used to protect the interests of women while that of Botswana indicated that the legislations and policies are only as effective as the implementation and resources dedicated to it, which is a sentiment to which a minority of participants in South Africa agreed.

Perspectives of Women in Civil Society Organisations on the Effectiveness of Legislative/Policy Outcomes on GBVF

All participants in this group agreed that legislations are an important mechanism in addressing GBVF; however, just like the reservations noted in the previous participant group, they believed legislations are not enough. Participant 37 noted that "legislation is just a first step. It does not translate to anything on the ground if there is no proper implementation" (8 February 2022). Participant 42 supported this notion by stating that "Botswana has laws that addresses violence against women but implementing it is very difficult" (P42 11 February 2022). Participant 38 gave a different reason the laws might not work and explained that the "law has its limitations. We write legislations, but if there is no education or training, it will not yield the needed result" (P38 13 April 2022). This submission adds awareness and training as important factors for any law to work along with the proper implementation echoed by all participant groups.

Perspectives across all groups indicated that they all agreed that legislations can be used to address GBVF; however, certain factors can hinder it.

Given the majority affirmation on the possibility of legislative and policy outcomes being used to reduce the rate of GBVF, this supports the selection of legislations as the instrument with which to measure the impact of female MPs on GBVF.

Impact of the Presence of Female MPs on Legislative Outcomes on Gender-Based Violence and Femicide

This theme addresses the third research objective, which was understanding how gender quotas impact policy and legislative outcomes on GBVF. Having established that gender quotas ensure the presence of women in politics, the following question was asked: How does the presence of women in parliament impact on legislative and policy outcomes on GBVF? As indicated in the previous theme, legislative and policy outcomes are effective instruments that can be used to protect women's interests and reduce the rate of GBVF. The convergence between gender quotas and legislative and policy outcomes enabled the researcher to understand whether the relationship between numbers and impact is positive. Secondly, it allowed the book to examine how the participation of women in parliament of the selected case studies has led to more legislations and policies to address GBVF. This is important as it situates the numbers and impact dilemma within the two case studies to provide a better illustration of the relationship that exists between having women in the South African and Botswana parliament and legislation and policies that will be used to address the prevalence of GBVF.

Perspectives of Female Members of Parliament in South Africa on Impact of Presence on Legislative/Policy Outcomes on GBVF

All 36 female MPs in South Africa that were interviewed were asked how their presence in parliament impacts legislative and policy outcomes for GBVF. They agreed that their presence in the South African parliament has yielded increased and better legislations and policies to fight GBVF. Participants cited many ways through which they have been able to effect policy and legislations on GBVF, which are discussed in the following subsections.

- Multiparty women's caucus

A major sub-theme that was echoed by all participants was that female MPs in the South African parliament have an umbrella body called the multiparty women's caucus. This platform is for all female MPs across party lines to discuss, deliberate, and advocate for women issues in parliament. They noted that the main task of this caucus is to advocate and speak for women's issues in parliament, and that GBVF occupies a major position in it. They explained that this caucus is where they all come together to deliberate on women's issues and the position to take as a collective before presenting it to the larger floor. Participant 23 explained it as follows:

> There is a multiparty women's caucus where as women we go there and deal with women issues. If there are any challenges that women face, we all come together to speak to those issues. It does not matter whether you are ANC, EFF or DA member, these issues affect us all as women so us women come together in one room and deliberate on the issues and come up with solutions or responses to say, for instance, how do we fight this issue of GBVF. (P23 13 April 2022)

Participant 22 stated that "in our multiparty women's caucus, the president of the committee said in 2019 that there must be a document called the national strategic plan to fight against the pandemic of GBVF" (P22 5 April 2022). Participant 4 noted that "the women's parliament has representation across the board, and they meet regularly. All parties are represented even in the senior positions in the committee. It is good because it cuts across all parties" (P4 20 February 2022).

- Awareness on gender-based violence issues

Participants explained that by virtue of the fact that women constitute a sizeable number in parliament, they are able to collectively raise the issue of GBVF as a priority to the rest of the house through the multiparty women's caucus. They all agreed that their presence in parliament means that the issue of GBVF gets escalated as a national crisis that needs the collaborative efforts of all MPs. Participant 10 explained that "female MPs often lead motions and debate on GBVF. They raise issues on behalf of women, thereby bringing much needed attention to GBVF" (P10 4 March 2022). Participant 34 noted the following:

> The fact that is out there, that we are talking about it, is a good first step. If you can go back some of the thing happening now were happening before, but because of the patriarchal system, they were hidden and not talked about. Let us appreciate the fact that we have female MPs speaking out and bringing it out in the open, and that is because we have women participating in the politics and in parliament. When politics was dominated by men, that was not discussed. There was no topic that touched on GBV, but because we have women in parliament now who are discussing it, everyone wants to participate. (P34 12 May 2022)

This is a succinct way to demonstrate how the participation of women in the parliament has enabled issues such as GBVF to be discussed in society and in decision-making spheres.

- Advocacy on gender-based violence

Another major sub-theme is that female MPs act as advocates for women issues. They are vocal about GBVF, they demand better accountability from responsible ministries, and they champion GBVF issues. Participant 18 noted that "women MPs are vocal about the issue of GBV. There was a time when they called the president and forced him to do something about it" (P18 25 March 2022). Participant 5 attested to this notion by stating the following:

> Because female MPs have various experiences of GBVF issues, they are able to speak for women and in terms of keeping the heat on departments, on our colleagues within the caucuses to get our bills through, I think we have been successful ... We have made our plight on GBVF known. We have created that awareness, sensitised our colleagues in terms of the way we talk about GBV to rid of stigma. We have managed to keep those discussions going. We often discuss ways of protesting, a sit-in, to force the president to deal with it. (P5 24 February 2022)

Participant 4 stated the following:

> I find that a lot of MPs from other parties are coming out strong, and I have seen that when issue of GBV are raised or discussed, women in parliament

in all parties come out very strong and that is an advantage. We need to strengthen that. It can be very powerful, assist and contribute to doing more and showing more progress. (P4 20 February 2022)

- Legislations on gender-based violence and femicide

A major result of the presence of female MPs is the passing of three new legislations on GBVF in South Africa. All participants confirmed that because of their collective effort as female MPs, through the multiparty women's caucus serving as a unified platform, they were able to speedily call for and garner support for better legislations, which translated into new laws on GBVF. The new laws on GBVF are the Criminal and Related Sexual Matters Amendment Act (No. 12 of 2021), Criminal Law (Sexual Offences and Related Matters) Amendment Act (No. 13 of 2021), as well as the Domestic Violence Amendment Act (No. 14 of 2021). All these laws were passed in 2021 as confirmed by the female MPs. Participant 22 explained it as follows:

We female MPs are the lawmakers. We develop legislations, recently there were three bills on GBV which are the domestic act, sexual offence act. I can't remember the third one. We as women in parliament have a structure called the multiparty women's caucus where all women parliamentarians sit and discuss issues of legislations that impact on women. These legislations are presented, and we give input as female MPs. After all members of the caucus agree with the legislation and the amendment of the bills, we take it to the larger floor where it will be debated on. (P22 5 April 2022)

Participant 3 also noted the following:

The large presence of women and the consensus among women MPs was a major catalyst for the three new bills to be passed into law ... We work, as our job is to make legislations. It takes 6–7 years to get a bill passed. There is a process, and it is an extremely long one. However, because of the constant push by female MPs and with the help of the president, we managed to pass the bills quickly. (P3 19 February 2022)

In support of this notion, Participant 24 noted the following:

If we were not so many women in parliament, I don't think we will be able to have these new laws. To change the policy in parliament takes up to 5–10 years, but I think we as female MPs were very serious and close with the president on GBVF. If not, it would have taken 10–12 years to change those legislations on GBV, but we were able to change it within this term. It didn't exceed the 6th parliament. (P24 19 April 2022)

Consolidating on the consensus of female MPs, Participant 2 noted that "these three bills that were passed had little to no opposition because everybody voted for the same reason, and that is to ensure that we have legislation that protects women" (P2 18 February 2022). To better encapsulate how the participation of women in the parliament enabled the development of these legislations, Participant 36 explained that "we as South African female MPs enter the political arena with a strong activist and mobilisation background and have worked at the grassroot level. The activism and mobilisation experience informs our drive for new legislations" (P36 12 May 2022). The use of gender quotas enables these women with vast activist experience to participate in politics, thereby allowing them to influence legislations for women. Participant 36 further noted that "having more women with the requisite skills and experience entering the parliament through quotas allows for the development of a conducive environment where legislative and policy outcomes with regards to GBVF can thrive, like we have seen with the recent passing of the three bills on GBVF" (P36 12 May 2022).

- Programmes and support initiatives for women

Another emergent theme is that apart from speaking out on GBVF issues or influencing legislations on GBVF, female MPs go the extra mile to ensure that the implementation of policies on GBVF are appropriately done. They support survivors of GBVF and advocate for better resources to be directed to Thuthuzela Centres across the country. Participant 35 noted that "if you are found to have a case of GBV, MPs who are responsible for those areas, they go out and support other NGOs to make sure that they support victims of GBV. Now it's not just a legislation issue, it becomes an action-oriented work for us" (P35 12 May 2022). Participant 26 stated the following:

I can tell you that when GBV was prevalent, we went through parliamentary offices. We have a programme going on every Friday that deals with GBV. We go to communities, talk to them; go to courts, magistrate courts, we check the progress of GBV cases, where the perpetrators are held and how they are assisting in protecting women. We are able to assist those women who are victims through counselling, social services and have social workers provide psycho-social therapy. MPs who are women do have several programmes on GBV, and I speak for my party as I am one of those women MPs who are on the ground. (P26 20 April 2022)

Perspectives from this theme indicates that the presence of women in the South African parliament has produced positive results for legislative and policy outcomes on GBVF. Their presence has not only ensured that new laws and policies are formulated to address the prevalence of GBVF but also that female MPs act as advocates and lobby groups that constantly place GBVF issues at the top of parliamentary business. It is important to recognise the role of the multiparty women's caucus in this: Due to their sizeable number in parliament, they were able to form a collective caucus that deals with women issues, which is then able to influence policies further translating to three new bills on GBVF.

Perspectives of Female Members of Parliament in Botswana on Impact of Presence on Legislative/Policy Outcomes on GBVF

All three female MPs in Botswana that were interviewed were asked how their presence in parliament has impacted on legislative and policy outcomes for GBVF. All participants agreed that their presence in the parliament of Botswana has yielded increased and better legislations and policies to fight GBVF. The participants cited many ways in which they have been able to effect policy and legislations on GBVF, which are discussed in the following:

• Awareness of gender-based violence and femicide issues

Similar to what female MPs in South Africa claimed, female MPs in Botswana noted that their presence in parliament allows for GBVF issues to be vocalised and spoken about. Participant 41 explained that "the presence of female MPs helps because we are there to speak and raise awareness on these issues. We are saying something about it bringing awareness to the matter. We are playing a huge role in keeping the conversation alive" (P41 14 April 2022). Participant 40 stated that "because we female MPs see things differently, we are able to bring about a new shift in discussions that happen on GBV in parliament" (P40 16 April 2022).

- Advocate for better legislations and policies

Participant 39 explained that through the women's caucus in parliament they are able to influence policies, which enabled the introduction of policies with tougher penalties for perpetrators. She noted that "what we have done is try and put a task team together, a parliamentary team, look at the issues. We have introduced legislations with tougher penalties" (P39 9 February 2022). New legislations such as the Penal Code (Amendment) Act (No. 42 of 2021) and the Sexual Offenders Registry Act (No. 7 of 2021) were passed to address the prevalent rate of GBVF cases in Botswana.

- Demand for more resources

Participants also indicated that their presence in parliament enables them to demand better funding for the implementation of GBVF policies. Participant 39 stated that "right now we are asking in parliament with the Minister of Finance to tell us what is in the box for us. Because of that the amount of funding that has gone into GBV issues has doubled since COVID-19" (P39 9 February 2022). This indicates that beyond influencing the development of new legislations on GBVF, they were able to act as a lobby group to demand better resources towards the reduction of the rate of GBVF.

Perspectives from female MPs in Botswana regarding the impact of presence on women on policy and legislative outcomes is similar to that of female MPs in South Africa. They indicated that the participation of women in parliament ensures more awareness is raised on GBVF; enables them to advocate for better policies, thereby leading to the introduction of new legislations on GBVF; enables them to demand better funding to be directed to the implementation of policies on GBVF, which were granted.

Self-evaluation of Impact Made on Legislative and Policy Outcomes on Gender-Based Violence and Femicide

To consolidate how the presence in parliament has impacted addressing the rate of GBVF in their respective countries, female MPs were asked the following: Can you say female MPs in the South Africa or Botswana parliament have made an impact with regards to addressing GBVF?

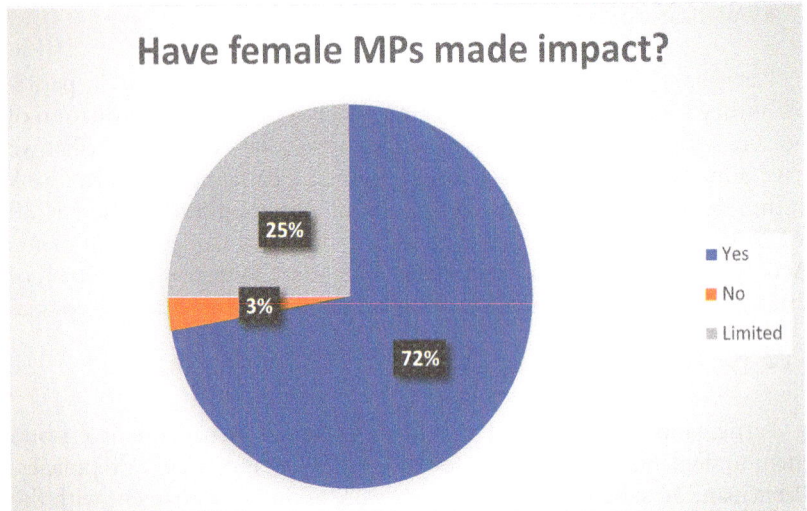

Fig. 8.4 SA female MPs responses on if they have made an impact. (Source: Olaitan 2023)

Perspectives of Female Members of Parliament in South Africa

Out of 36 participants, 26 participants (72.2%) agreed that female MPs have made an impact with regards to addressing the prevalence of GBVF. Nine participants (25%) responded that an impact has been made to an extent, signifying limited impact, and one participant (2.8%) did not think any impact has been made (Fig. 8.4).

Perspectives of Female Members of Parliament in Botswana

All participants agreed that they have made an impact with regards to addressing the prevalence of GBVF. However, Participants 40 and 41 further highlighted that the impact is limited and depends on the adequacy of implementation of the approved legislative and policy outcomes.

The perspectives from the female MPs group indicated that most female MPs in South Africa and Botswana believed that their presence in parliament impacted their ability to influence policy and legislative outcomes on GBVF, advocate for GBVF issues, raise awareness, demand more resources to be directed at GBVF issues, and pose effective solutions for the reduction of GBVF. All participants stressed the importance of implementation to consolidate this impact, stating that legislations and policies must be effectively executed to ensure GBVF is properly tackled.

IMPACT OF FEMALE MEMBERS OF PARLIAMENT ON ADDRESSING THE RATE OF GENDER-BASED VIOLENCE AND FEMICIDE

To provide an alternative perspective on how the presence of women in parliament in Botswana and South Africa impacted GBVF, women in civil society were asked a different question to provide an outsider evaluation of the effectiveness of the impact that female MPs have had on GBVF. They were asked the following question: Has there been considerable change in the fight against GBVF with the inclusion of women in parliament in South Africa/Botswana?

Perspectives of Women in Civil Society Organisations in South Africa

Participant 37 explained it as follows:

> Speaking from the South African perspective, you would see the president has been talking a lot against GBVF, but this is pressure coming from civil society organisations. I am trying to think of a female member of parliament, apart from the concerned Minister of Women. You do not have anyone else speaking on the issue. You have personalities, you have CSOs, president and Minister of Women, Youths and Persons with Disabilities speaking on it. So, I would say it's more of the civil society that is pushing the agenda against GBV. CSOs have been creating awareness, raising sensitisation, organising marches. (P37 8 February 2022)

Participant 38 stated the following:

> It is a question of mutual inclusivity. I do think female MPs have played a big role within their own spaces to make people unlearn horrible traditional views about subjugation of women and make certain change in the fight against GBV. But the question is, is that big enough to sort out the issue of GBV? I think the stats will say no. So, it's like even when they get into positions of power, the power is limited that they cannot eradicate the issue of GBV ... Their impact is limited looking at the composition of our parlia-

ment. How many females do we have that are deployed to different corners of the country? Having just one female MP in a community does not assist in terms of ensuring that they have in their power to make change. (P38 13 April 2022)

Explaining why female MPs only have limited impact in addressing GBVF, Participant 38 argued the following:

The people that should be working on addressing GBV are the male MPs. When they are seeking vote from us, they do not segregate voters. They don't say I want only male voters. Everybody votes for them. When you are serving and protecting your constituency, you must ensure that everyone has the right to be protected. This is important because female MPs cannot do it alone. (P38 13 April 2022)

Perspectives of Women in Civil Society Organisations in Botswana

Participant 42 responded as follows to the question:

This is a hard one. It's hard because we have changes. The government during COVID-19 opened a hotline with police services, which was toll-free for GBV survivors. There has been a GBV enquiry that has been conducted though the office of the president. But these efforts have not come from our female MPs, they have come from male alliance and CSOs, so I will say no. (P42 11 February 2022)

Participant 43 firmly asserted the following:

There has not been considerable change in the fight against gender-based violence with the inclusion of women in parliament. There isn't. They just talk, but there is no action on the ground … the day action is taken is the day men will fear raping a woman, hitting a woman, committing marital rape, saying I have paid for the sex, I have paid lobola and married you, therefore I must have sex with you whenever I want. When those laws are repealed and people understand that a women's body is hers and it's not for anybody, regardless of whether they are married or whatever relationship they are in, a woman's body is hers. (P43 11 February 2022)

The perspectives from women in civil society on the theme indicated two things: Firstly, the impact female MPs have had in addressing GBVF is not significant enough to make considerable change in the fight against

GBVF; and secondly, most of the efforts to reduce the rate of GBVF come from CSOs. The first point was strongly supported by Participant 38, and the second point was echoed by Participants 37 and 38. What this means for individual countries is that women in CSOs in South Africa believed that female MPs are not able to make a considerable impact because there is a need for holistic interventions and there is a need for male MPs to collaborate with them. Secondly, most efforts on GBVF have been the products of individual efforts rather than from female MPs as a collective. The women working in CSOs in Botswana believed that the inclusion of female MPs in the parliament had not yielded any considerable change in the fight against GBVF, and similar to South Africa, they believed most efforts have come from CSOs and male alliances, the latter which poses a different angle to the women as critical actors for women issues. This section created a major contradiction with regards to how female MPs believed they have made impact with regards to addressing GBVF. While women in CSOs do not believe that considerable change has been made with the inclusion of women in parliament with regards to addressing GBVF.

Improving the Quality of Women's Political Representation

This section addresses the fourth research objective, which was to suggest alternative pathways for the substantive representation of women in Botswana and South Africa. The assumption that the presence of women in politics ensures women's interests are protected creates a sort of segregation with regards to how policy makers address issues and how citizens demand accountability from the government. The burden to address women issues and protect women's interest is often wholly placed on women politicians, or more specifically female MPs. The implication of this is that women issues are not considered as part of the larger policy needs of the people. Like Participant 38 argued in the previous theme, when contesting for election, male MPs do not discriminate among voters because both men and women vote for them. So why does the burden of protecting women's interest only fall on female MPs when they get into office? This section provides recommendations of alternative pathways to ensure the substantive representation of women, and hence, participants were asked the following question: Besides quotas, which measures can you recommend to improve the quality of women's political representation?

Perspectives of Female Members of Parliament in South Africa on How to Improve Quality of Women's Political Representation

Each participant provided multiple suggestions on the stated themes as they argued that improving the quality of women's political representation is a necessary step to protecting women's interests as a whole. Participants gave different opinions on how to improve women's political representation, and these are discussed in the following subsections.

- Education

Participants believed in the importance of educating the society on equality between men and women, which, according to them, is a foundational step to other measures. Participant 3 stated the following:

> We need to get women to be in politics. We need to do upliftment and education for them like a political school where women can enrol, but we know schools are expensive. Politics require a bottom-up approach. If we start on top, we miss a lot of things. We find interested women who have the abilities, they should get involved with parties. It increases their knowledge of politics." (P3 19 February 2022)

Participant 25 suggested that "we need to develop women coming after us. Push them to go to school. We need women with advanced educational qualifications because there are some departmental positions for women, and you find that there is no one that is qualified to be in that department" (P25 20 April 2022). Participant 29 noted the following:

> It starts with our education system. If our children get to be exposed in politics at a very young age so that we create skills in terms of economic development so that as they grow, they understand their space, they are able to come out. Many of our female counterparts are scared to be in the same space as men, scared to speak out because of patriarchy. So, if this gets instilled at a young age, our families would be comfortable in talking about issues of abuse, inequality, economic challenges and social ills that we are faced with. Number one is education. We need to fix our education system so that our people can open up their minds and do not have to learn politics

at old age, which is hard because you do not have much insight on what is happening around you. (P29 29 April 2022)

Participants believed that education plays a fundamental role in building a better society.

- Transform the system

Under this sub-theme, most participants argued for dismantling patriarchal and societal norms that limit women's self-actualisation in society. Participant 17 stated that "issues of tradition and culture that has become a problem in our society. These two things need to adjust to the material conditions of society today. We ought to speak to it. We cannot have young women in cases of arranged marriage. We need to say such practice does not assist in building a better society" (P17 22 March 2022). Participant 7 explained it as follows:

> If we try and transform cultural attitudes. These attitudes exist across all spectrums of society. Attitudes towards women are prejudicial and very little progress has been made to change people's ingrained mindset. I think we need to start with changing the cultural perspective. Women have to start demanding equal respect for being women without having to pretend to be men. We have to start raising our boys same way we raise our girl. We have to start actively demanding that our specific needs are catered for. For instance, there is no maternity leave for the Western Cape provincial legislature at the time, until one of the MPLs pushed for it because she had a baby. These are subtleties that we as women understand. We are not going to encourage women's participation in political spaces until we can create environment where they are able to thrive and given the assistance that they need as the primary caregivers. Women are socialised to be nurturers, gentle. There are few young white English-speaking women. The African culture is deeply patriarchal, so it is important to confront these prejudices. (P7 25 February 2022)

Participant 36 noted that "there is need to undertake comprehensive reforms to eliminate laws, policies, and regulations that discriminate against women" (P36 12 May 2022).

- Supporting other women and women empowerment

All participants noted that it is important for women to come together and support one another and ensure the empowerment of women as a collective group. Participant 9 suggested that "we should look at the empowerment programme. We should look at the socio-economic status of girl-children. Many girls miss out in school if they have their periods because they cannot afford sanitary pads. We should look at empowering our girls" (P9 4 March 2022). Participant 14 recommended that "we need to empower women. At the crux we need to create spaces of empowering women to know that they too can occupy these spaces. I do not think women can't be in these spaces. It is about creating these spaces that women are empowered to be in and building that confidence" (P14 14 March 2022). Participant 22 stated that "we need to support women so that women are more in structures where decisions are taken for the betterment of our people" (P22 5 April 2022).

- Mentorship of young women and girls into political positions

The participants suggested that it is necessary to mentor and engage young girls and women to be politically active. Participant 5 stated the following:

> It starts with strong female examples. Start with current female MPs setting an example, leading by example. I believe we should pay it forwards. We need to play a more active role in our communities as female political leaders to make sure that girls are taught and have positive examples. We need to encourage girls to be more, to encourage them to do what they want, be it debate, sports, traditionally male sports, to push the boundaries. (P5 24 February 2022).

Participant 10 supported this suggestion by asserting that "training is always important, as well as providing on the job support. We need female leaders who have been part of the political establishment for many years to commit to training and mentoring young women" (P10 4 March 2022). Participant 4 stressed that "we need young people to be involved. We as MPs need to engage more with young women on what we in parliament. We need to invite them to spend time with us physically in committees, plenaries in whichever form so they get inspired enough to want to get involved in the political landscape of the country" (P4 20 February 2022).

Perspectives of Female Members of Parliament in Botswana on How to Improve Quality of Women's Political Representation

- Change patriarchal attitudes

Similar to what MPs in South Africa suggested, MPs in Botswana believed that it is necessary to change the patriarchal attitudes that are prevalent in society.

- Education

They also agreed that education is important. Participant 41 suggested that "people need to start studying towards political leadership. Starting from the education sector, government affect everyone. Teaching young people about the effect government has on everyone and the institutions of government will help" (P41 14 April 2022).

- Advocate for inclusion

Participant 39 explained the need for women political leaders to champion for the better inclusion of women. She stated the following:

We are mobilising women for training on political matters. There are so many brilliant women who are afraid to join politics. That is not a challenge. Even though we want large representation, they can't afford firstly because they are poor and can't afford the expense. However, with mobilisation, training and empowerment we believe we can have more of them, which is what we as female MPs are doing. (P39 9 February 2022)

Perspectives of Women in Civil Society Organisations on How to Improve Quality of Women's Political Representation

In relation to the theme, participants in this group were asked whether removing obstacles to women's political participation is a better alternative to quotas when it comes to increasing women's political participation. All participants argued for a collaborative effort between using quotas and addressing the obstacles that hinder women's political participation.

- Complementarity between quotas and resolving obstacles

Participants 37 noted the following:

Quota system and addressing obstacles to women's political participation should work hand in hand. You might be raising awareness on why women's political participation is important, but the laws or political leaders do not want to appoint you in their political party. You will not go anywhere. I always believe in the holistic approach to problems. You cannot be like this is what we are going to do and then we are done, you can't just do one intervention. I have been working in the area of women's rights since 2014, and I feel like I haven't done much because everything you do is a small legal block, and you are building something big. So, I feel like you are just contributing your legal block, and it will take years to get where we want to be. (P37 8 February 2022)

Participant 42 stated that" they have to work hand in hand. There are clear impediments. Even if you remove those impediments, it does not mean that you will suddenly have a rise in female politicians. You also still have to have a quota system" (P42 11 February 2022).

- Political education and understanding the importance of human rights;

Participant 43 recommended political education and understanding of human rights. She explained it as follows:

That should go with a lot of education because you find that politics and human rights do not necessarily go hand in hand. We have politicians who have no idea about human rights or who feel human rights is just a waste of time. So, we must elect these women and give them direct entry into politics, but they will have no idea on what is happening to the other parts of the community. What is happening to women, children because they are not in touch with the realities of women and girls. So, there will be a lot of education needed before we elect them to offices so that they really up to speed and have the interest of the community at heart because not all politicians have the interest of the community at heart. Some go there to enrich themselves or look for opportunities to enrich themselves and not what is necessary for the community. So, there is a lot to be done before we directly elect women to positions of power. Education for the community because they are responsible for choosing these leaders. So, they must know what qualities to look out for that can truly move our interest forwards. (P43 11 February 2022)

Recommendations to Reduce the Rate of Gender-Based Violence and Femicide

To further consolidate on recommendations for alternative pathways to ensure the substantive representation of women, participants were asked to suggest measures that can help reduce the rate of GBVF. They were asked the following question: Which measures can you recommend to address the rate of GBVF?

Perspectives of female members of parliament in South Africa on how to reduce the rate of GBVF

- Political and institutional measures

In suggesting measures to address GBVF in South Africa, all participants stressed the need for political will to ensure the proper implementation of policies that have been passed on GBVF. Participant 36 stated that "within the parliamentary arena, political will for change and commitment towards ending GBVF is imperative" (P36 12 May 2022). Participants suggested the need for better awareness on legislations that have been passed on GBVF. Participant 15 suggested that "we need to educate the society on every legislation passed on GBV to say how does it help them and how they can work with together to help society at large. If we can deal with GBVF as we dealt with COVID-19, we can win as institutions, government, and society at large" (P15 19 March 2022). Participant 7 suggested the following:

> We need treasury to direct the necessary resources to the security apparatus, for example SAPS [South African Police Services], forensics so that Domestic Violence unit, special offences court, children's court. This comes from budget. We need resources to be allocated to agencies that are responsible for investigating/prosecuting gender-based related matters. From a social development perspective, we need more resources dedicated to shelters for women, and we need Chapter 9 institutions like the Commission for Gender Equality to be adequately resourced so that they are able to oversight functions effectively. Then the Commission for Gender Equality report that

comes to parliament needs to be very strong binding resolutions taken by the committee that process those report in parliament, so that parliament can adopt binding resolution that adhere and respond to the research and agenda outlined by Commission for Gender Equality in terms of addressing the rights and concerns of women specifically in South Africa with regards to GBV, which has been a big focus of the Commission for Gender Equality. Essentially, it requires political will. So, we need the right people to sit on those finance portfolios in the ministry, etc. We need the right legislation. Twenty-six years into democracy we have the right legislation in place, but the resources don't follow the right legislation, and if we cannot change the culture of the police service, which is quite an inherently patriarchal organisation. You know how women are treated when they try to report their case. So, we need more women in law enforcement and GBV unit that when women are victimised, they receive the help that they need whether resources exist. (P7 25 February 2022)

- Cultural and societal efforts

Participants advocated for a holistic approach to solving GBVF, which can be reached through cultural changes as well as society-wide collaboration. Participant 18 suggested the following:

"We must start with the family structures. They need to be empowered. We need to have more awareness on the equality of family. We must encourage the old ones to make sure that they let go of old system of thinking. Also, the education curriculum must have empowerment of mindset that there are no gender specific jobs" (P18 25 March 2022).

Participant 26 recommended a change in societal norms and stated the following:

We need to get society involved. I am not happy about it. As society we need one that is really involved in the social compact. You are part of a society such that you do not tolerate any form of violence perpetuated around women and children. GBV goes deeper to children, and they get so affected in schools. We have cases of younger women who are raped but still go to school. We need the communities to speak out loud. We need them to have the community policing forum. What we have in the security cluster and safety that ensure that is not happening. GBV needs community. The more we need to have awareness, volunteers within the communities. We need have mothers and father to get involved who will pledge themselves to be part of the society to make it better. A collective responsibility to protect young women. The environment we are in, we need to change the culture and tradition. Important to educate ourselves, inform our communities and ensure that everybody understands their rights. We all have right to equal justice, right to choose for ourselves, right to sexuality. (P26 20 April 2022)

Participant 31 suggested a society-wide effort as follows:

I believe in us fighting GBV. We need to come together as society. GBV should not just be a matter of government, should be a matter of our churches, society, chiefs, amakhosi. In some parts amakhosi are still practicing forced marriages, which for them it's something they think is right, which for us is wrong. So, we need to come up with some policies that are going to fight all these things. Young girls should be in schools not in forced marriages because that's when these things lead to GBV. These young girls end up growing and understanding that they are independent people from there. The man will not allow that. We need to fight GBV together as society and be one. In that way, we will come to end of it, as it stands now. It's happening every time. If we go to the Vuvuzela centres, the kids that are there, the women are women that were raped by families. Hence, I am saying GBV is an issue we need to deal with as a society. (P31 8 May 2022)

- Reform policing and justice system;

Most participants advocated for strengthening the justice system as well as reforming the police apparatus. Participant 23 noted the following:

There is no other way than courts because you cannot take law into your hands. So, it is only the judiciary we need make sure that we strengthen our judiciary when it comes to court so that people that are perpetuating violence against women are put in jail and behind bars for their wrongdoing. We need to make sure as women in these caucuses or whatever forum that we have to make sure that legislations are implemented in our courts. Each and every place where we are to follow up to ensure strict compliance to what the law says. If we do that, our courts will be very strong so that cases of GBV will be handled better and taken seriously, but right now we have got backlog of cases in our courts. (P23 13 April 2022)

Participant 27 suggested that "we should have specialised courts that deal with GBV. Specialised courts should be established so that the law takes action so that perpetrators understand the consequences of their actions that the law will deal with them harshly" (P27 24 April 2022).

- Better resources and programmes

Participant 16 stated that "our Thuthuzela Centres are not well resourced. I do not think we have in every town. We need to have more of those. Partner with non-governmental organisations [NGOs] that are dealing with GBV, provide them with resources and encourage them to stay operational. If they do not have resources, they cannot operate. We need to make sure we have the right resources to address GBV" (P16 19 March 2022).

Participant 3 recommended the following:

> There should be proper shelters for women. Programmes to help the women and their children and for them not to go back to the abusive home. The police do something where they bring couples together to solve the problem. The government should ensure there are less expensive counselling centres for victims. It is a society thing. We need to raise awareness on it. (P3 19 February 2022)

- Support among women and collaboration with men

Participant 5 explained that it is necessary for women to work together with men to address GBVF. She suggests the following:

> We as females need to start talking, supporting females. Even though we have different parties, female MPs need to support each other. We should break stereotypes. We should not be the ones that negatively re-enforce negative stereotypes. We can't want equal rights. We can't say we want to end GBV but go ahead to say all men are trash. We need to work with men (P5 24 February 2022)

Participant 3 suggested,

> When we speak of GBV, there is an attack on men, so we need to communicate our message better without attacking men. We need programmes for men where we can assist them. Let's not forget GBV is a problem of poverty and unemployment. We need to go to schools. The socialisation of our boys/girls, we need a programme for them too. How to deal with attitudes and bodily changes. How to treat women. Workshops for the policewomen should work with them. A man can work with a woman if he can treat her

with respect. A woman does not ask for it. She does not play a role in her own abuse. (P3 19 February 2022)

• Women empowerment and creating safe spaces

Participant 14 recommended empowering women by stating the following:

We have spoken about policy changes, talk to the challenge that women face. I think our organisations structures and procedure need to change. There are cases of women being victimised, but they are not comfortable of speaking out in the workplace. If you do speak out, you are stigmatised or criticised. We need to change thing structurally, not just policy because policy needs a conducive environment to be implemented in. We can influence policies and can get them right, but if we do not have the conducive environment for policies that allows us to speak out, allows us to report incidences where GBV rears its head, then we are working backwards. We need more than just policies. We need support structures in workplace or political space. We need to create safe spaces for women to speak up against men when they are violated. We need to talk about it more. I feel like incidents happen, but people do not talk about it. We do not realise the power of sharing our experiences. Also, that speaks to safe spaces, how safe we feel in supporting one another. In some instances, women perpetuate GBV. With questions like why was she wearing that suit to work? We need to get beyond that even us as women. Creating safe spaces for people to speak out, creating safe spaces for GBV to be dealt with without victimisation. (P14 14 March 2022)

Perspectives of Female Members of Parliament in Botswana on How to Reduce the Rate of GBVF

• Women empowerment

Participant 39 advocated for the economic empowerment of women so they can be independent beings, by stating the following:

We have to empower women economically because as long as women are not economically empowered, they cannot be politically and socially empowered. Because if you are dependent on your concubine or husband, your brother for survival, you will be their subject. So, you have to be independent. And the other thing is you find that we have female headed household.

Females whether married or single are basically head of households. They've got kids without father, and they have this heavy burden that they carry but they don't have the means, they are less paid in their jobs compared to men. So, until such time that we empower women to stand for themselves and be independent, it's going to take a long time. It is then we can say the quota system will assist them. (P39 9 February 2022)

- Socialisation

Participant 40 stressed the need for better socialisation processes for children. She explained the following:

We need to look at the raising of human beings. We could consider number of factor that contribute to GBV, like childhood trauma, which speaks to raising of young children which might relate to perpetration of violence later on. That should be worked on by government. What could government do because when we consider these issues, they are so personal, and they are not something government can have a direct authority or make a direct decision about. It is in our homes. Most rape cases happen in our homes and often perpetrated by family members. We need to heal. Government can advocate, make a case for, and raise awareness. The responsible government person needs to be cognizance of such issue and aware of the root causes in order to propose sustainable solutions. Interrogating how we raise children and the influence of parenthood on a child's upbringing, which speaks to holistic well-being of a person that will be impacted by a lot of things. (P40 16 April 2022)

- Strengthen institutions

Participant 41 advocated for the following:

There needs to be programmes that protect women in danger, for instance, when a woman goes to report a case of GBV, they have to go back to the same house where their abuser lives, or they have to be in the same neighbourhood, meaning the perpetrator still has access to them. The country does not do restraining order. They need to be efficient with this. I am aware of a case where a lady reported her husband and had to go back home, but they made the man leave the house. But that is not enough because he can come back when the woman is alone and vulnerable. She put in a request for restraining order. She had to wait for 3 months to get it, which is a long time. A day is enough for a perpetrator to kill their victims. There needs to be more effectiveness with protective measures when someone reports GBV. (P41 14 April 2022)

Perspectives of Women in Civil Society Organisations on How to Reduce the Rate of GBVF

- Education and awareness

Participant 37 suggested that "educating people about the law and that what are you doing is gender-based violence. In many instances people don't know that their actions constitute GBV, like a husband hitting his wife at home, for him its entitlement. Awareness raising which goes hand in hand with education" (P37 8 February 2022). Participant 42 stated the following:

> The other thing that has to happen is education on the grassroots' level because we vote for politicians, we keep them in power. Unless us as community and nation understand what, we need to put on the table demand what we will like politicians will have their way. We will not have the right representative to represent us. We are also not going to know how to keep our parliament in check and how to monitor. (P42 11 February 2022)

Participants also noted the importance of legislative education. They argued that society should be trained on the legislations that have been passed on GBVF and to advocate for their right to make these legislations and policies work for them. Participant 38 noted that "we need to review our curriculum to teach about GBV for children to understand that looking after each other is human right. If my rights are violated, I must speak out. There needs to be education so that we all understand what we mean on GBV" (P38 13 April 2022).

- Collaborative efforts

Participant 37 recommended that "working with traditional and religious leaders, non-locals championing the cause of GBV is a must. People listen to church leaders, community leaders, chiefs, so involving them in the fight is very important. You will go nowhere without them because you can be talking at high level, but it doesn't trickle down" (P37 8 February 2022). Participant 38 supported this notion by stating that "the president speaking about GBV is a good thing because it brings it into focus, and everyone listens to him. Working together with experts on culture is very important. We can come from one perspective and say this particular culture is affecting women and its perpetrates GBV" (P42 11 February 2022).

- Transformation of society

Participant 42 noted the following:

There has to be sensitisation and education, and also the removal of these bad apples. We need to remove perpetrators from leadership positions before we can do anything, otherwise it's going to be a brick wall. You are going to move for change, and perpetrators will stop that move. No perpetrators will advance women's rights in parliament where there are perpetrators. (P42 11 February 2022)

Participant 38 explained that "our society needs to be transformed to ensure that both men/women are partners in household, community and there is not contestation that women are the one doing the most work on GBV" (P38 13 April 2022).

- National database and reporting system

Participant 43 provided the following detailed recommendation on a national database:

If we look at the GBV report as a country, we don't have a national database that monitors the type and when violence is happening in the country; for instance, you check where does physical violence happen, who does it happen to, is there sexual violence, which part of the country does it happen, and we will be tracking the numbers and demography of who is affected, the areas its happening. But now we only rely on police cases. The police numbers are the only statistics that are used to give an indication of where we are as a country and we all know to go and report a case of domestic violence in Botswana, it must have happened to you numerous times, 10, 20 times before one can report. This is because of the silence of the community. The expectations that you have to silent about what is happening in your marriage, relationship. You are tarnishing someone's image. You must have done something to provoke that. The victim is blamed. So only a tiny number goes to report to police. A study in 2020 shows that only one in nine rape cases are reported. That tells us that 90% of cases go unreported. The police numbers does not represent what happen in Botswana. So, until we have a database where GBV is captured at every point, whether you go to the police, hospital, social worker, chief, there should be a link because we all have a national identity number. That number can be used to track one's movement so we can have true figures of what is happening in the country. My organisation and myself feel we are underreporting what is happening in Botswana with regards to GBV, so we cannot really measure impact because we do not know what is out there. (P43 11 February 2022)

Perspectives on this theme indicated that all participant groups agreed that it is necessary to ensure education, awareness, and sensitisation of GBVF. There is a need for a more societal and collaborative effort, to empower women and to strengthen institutions such as the police and the judiciary.

Discussion and Analysis

The section links the analysis of the themes in the previous section with the research questions. In answering the research questions, the researcher mostly refers to data gathered from participants, and uses findings from legislations as well as analysis from literature and theories. This allows for synergy between the data gathered, literature, and theories to answer the research questions. The overview of the data gathered from interview and legislative outcomes in South Africa emphasises that gender quotas have been effective in mainstreaming women into political positions because women occupy 45% of the seats in the South African national parliament. Due to the number of women in parliament, they were able to advocate and influence policy making, which led to the passing of new legislations on GBVF. It is noted that addressing the prevalent rate of GBVF in South Africa needs more than just legislations as government, society, and other relevant stakeholders need to be involved. For Botswana, the lack of a specific gender quota by the governing party, which is different from the specially elected MPs system, has not allowed women to occupy a considerable number of seats in the national parliament, and there are only seven women out of 63 MPs, amounting to 11%. Though they were able to influence the legislative process, the lack of a critical mass has impacted the capacity of MPs to use their presence to enable notable impact on addressing GBVF. The summary of recommendations notes that the education and transformation of society are very important measures to address GBVF in South Africa and Botswana.

What is the relationship between the numbers and impact in terms of women's political representation in Africa?

The literature on critical mass postulates that a sizeable number of women are needed in the parliament to ensure the substantive representation of women (Dahlerup 2006b). Female MPs in Botswana and South Africa confirmed that the participation of women in the political system yields benefit for the general women populace. This affirmation provides ground to argue that there is a positive relationship between numbers and impact in the selected case studies. Furthermore, these MPs argued that only women can represent women issues accurately because of the difference in lived experiences. This notion is a major postulation of the relational feminist theory, which states that the fundamental difference between men and women enables women to better represent the intrinsic issues that affect them (Offen 1988). Additionally, while confirming that there is a relationship between the participation of women in politics (numbers) and benefits for women (impact), female MPs cited themes such as representing women issues, influencing legislations, advocating for women, and being role models for younger women as the output of the relationship between numbers and impact. The existence of this relationship was further supported by women in civil society, although this affirmation came with reservation concerning the possibility of current female politicians enabling such a relationship. While the women in civil society doubted the reality, they noted that the participation of women in politics benefits women. This points to the fact that there is a relationship between numbers and impact in Africa but that certain factors must be in place to ensure the positive connotation of that relationship. One of the factors cited is that the current socio-cultural system does not favour women who participate in politics as patriarchy still limits their efforts. This calls for a critical mass of women participating in politics as their numbers can help normalise their participation, which solidifies the thesis that numbers are necessary to make an impact. Another factor affecting this relationship is that some female politicians often advance their party mandate over women issues. This notion was observed across most female MPs while sampling their motivation for taking up political positions. Most of the female MPs did not explicitly identify gender and women issues as their motivation for taking up political positions, and instead gave blanket responses about wanting to create change. The lack of majority feminist thinking in female MPs creates a problem for the numbers and impact dilemma. The fact that they did not accrue their participation in politics to championing women issues shows that it might not be a major concern for them. On the other hand, their lived experience and identity as women can contend with this narrative as they see themselves as women first before parliamentarians, which can influence how they address issues. Moreover, Phillips (1995) argued that women often agree on certain interests that affect them, and these interests can override political mandates. GBVF in this case is a central interest that female MPs in both case studies agreed affects women.

Do gender quotas have relevance beyond being a pathway for mainstreaming women into politics?

Gender quotas are only seen as effective to the extent that they are able to ensure the descriptive representation of women in the political system. All participant groups agreed that quotas are necessary to ensure the participation of women in politics. However, in re-examining the relevance of quotas beyond numbers, all participant groups cited that quotas ensure the representation of women and the inclusion of women and equality in society. In agreeing that quotas help mainstream women into politics, they noted further that by virtue of women participating in politics, they are able to speak for other women, represent women issues in echelons of power, ensure women are included in decision-making spheres, and ensure equality between men and women in society. This highlights that the participation of women in politics is a requirement to challenge the gender stereotypes that limit women from being visible in society. Quotas foster the inclusion of women across decision-making spheres as their participation in politics creates a domino effect that allows the ability of women as important members of society to be acknowledged. By being able to debut into politics via quotas, women are seen in a new light, i.e., equal beings to men in society. A major theme is that it allows for women issues to be spoken for, again highlighting the notion that only women can represent women, this was well-supported by all participant groups. The findings from participants create a new lens through which to view the relevance of quotas as a mechanism for ensuring the representation of women. It contends with major studies that limit quotas to an instrument that only engenders an increase in political participation of women. The implication of this narrative manifests in seeing quotas as a means to an end, which is the participation of women. However, the reconfiguration of what the end is allows for the re-examination of the relevance of quotas, and in this case, the end is the substantive representation of women, which is ensured with the participation of women in politics. This analogy lends credence to the first research question on numbers and impact, i.e., quotas are not an end in themselves but are a means to protect the interests of women as a group (impact). Therefore, to directly answer the research question, quotas are relevant beyond mainstreaming women in politics by ensuring the inclusion of women in the political system. They create the critical mass of women needed to challenge gender stereotypes, represent women issues, and ensure gender equality in the society. These benefits are almost impossible without quotas fostering the increased participation of women in politics.

How do gender quotas impact policy and legislative outcomes on gender-based violence and femicide in Botswana and South Africa?

To measure the impact of gender quotas on the substantive representation of women in Botswana and South Africa, GBVF was used as the index to measure the substantive representation of women and legislative and policy outcomes were used to measure their impact. GBVF is an endemic and systemic problem that affects primarily women. Participants across all groups condemned the high rate of GBVF while expressing concern for women. Related reactions capturing this are pandemic, abysmally high, shocking, alarming, serious challenge, worrying phenomenon, evokes anger, very sad, horrific, and feel pain. These expressions point to the fact that GBVF is an important issue that affects women across the selected case studies. Saferspaces (2020) argued that GBVF is a systemic problem that women face in South Africa. The appropriateness of using legislative and policy outcomes to measure impact was supported by participants who noted the importance of laws and policies to address GBVF. Lack of implementation or adequate resources are some of the limitations that hinder the effectiveness of these outcomes. However, when properly implemented, legislation and policies are very powerful instruments in addressing the high rate of GBVF.

Female MPs in South Africa argued that due to their presence and considerable number in parliament, they are able to form a platform for women's issues (the multiparty women's caucus), create awareness on GBVF issues, advocate for women issues and GBVF, influence policy-making processes, and carry out programmes on GBVF. All these efforts are possible because of their umbrella platform, which is the multiparty women's caucus. This caucus deals with women issues in parliament. The participation of women in parliament is a function of gender quotas, the numbers they have built up in parliament enable them to come together to act as a lobby group for women issues. Their task, which mostly focuses on women issues, allows them to prioritise GBVF, which is a major problem that affects women. They are able to communicate the severity of what women go through due to GBVF while putting pressure on relevant departments to take more practical steps. The most significant impact their presence has had is the introduction of legislations to address GBVF.

The assertion made by female MPs in South Africa is supported by findings from the legislative outcomes from 2010–2022 that demonstrate that there have been numerous legislations and policies developed to address GBVF. In 2022, the South African government announced that three new pieces of legislations were passed to fight against the prevailing rate of GBVF. These legislations are the Criminal and Related Matters Amendment Act (No. 12 of 2021), the Criminal Law (Sexual Offences and Related Matters) Amendment Act (No. 13 of 2021), and the Domestic Violence Amendment Act (No. 14 of 2021). Some prior legislations are the Protection from Harassment Act (No. 17 of 2011); the Criminal Law (Sexual Offences and Related Matters) Amendment Act (No. 6 of 2012), which was further amended as part of the newly introduced legislations; and the Commission on Gender Equality Amendment Act (No. 17 of 2013), which was amended to align with the Constitution of the Republic of South Africa (No. 108 of 1996). A national council on GBVF was formed in 2014 to oversee the development of the National Strategic Plan for Gender Based Violence and Femicide (2020) that was adopted in 2020. The adoption and passing of numerous legislative and policy outcomes is a testament to the notion made by female MPs in South Africa that their presence in parliament has impacted legislative and policy outcomes on GBVF. Participants highlighted that this impact would not have been possible if women did not have the needed critical mass to make it happen.

On the other hand, women working in CSOs that deal with GBVF in South Africa argued that the impact female MPs have made is limited. This divergence in perception of impact can be a function of lack of awareness of the relevant legislations and policies on GBVF. Secondly, it points to the need for more societal and collaborative effort in addressing GBVF. To assign the burden of significantly reducing the rate of GBVF to what female MPs do is an impossible task, which was voiced by all participants. It was noted by all participants that reducing GBVF goes beyond laws and policies: There must be a major transformation in patriarchal attitudes as well as collaboration with male MPs. However, to the extent that female MPs in South Africa have fulfilled their responsibility to develop legislations and policies that addresses GBVF, this book argues that they have been able to make an impact. This is in acknowledgement that their efforts transcend developing legislations as they have also created awareness, advocated for women issues, supported NGOs that work on GBVF, and are overseeing the implementation of policies on GBVF to ensure a holistic approach to addressing GBVF. Moreover, there is only so much they can do, as indicated by all participant groups. It is necessary to dismantle the patriarchal system that perpetuates hegemonic masculinity that manifests in violence against women. Female MPs are also victims of this system, and hence, their numbers in parliament does not mean much, which is why men, faith-based organisations, and traditional leaders must work together to make considerable impact towards reducing the rate of GBVF.

For Botswana, female MPs argued that they have been able to create better awareness on GBVF, advocate for better policies, and demand more resources. These actions have manifested in the introduction of new legislations that provide tougher penalties for perpetrators of GBVF. Participants explained that most of the funding that go to NGOs that work on GBVF are from female MPs who support different initiatives on GBVF. The claim made by participants on new legislations was confirmed by the findings presented on legislative and policy outcomes on GBVF from 2010–2022. These are the National Gender-Based Violence Strategy 2015–2020, which is a multi-prolonged and multi-sectorial approach to the prevention and elimination of GBV; the Sexual Offenders Registry Act (No. 7 of 2021), which was passed by the national parliament to make provision for the establishment of a sexual offenders register and a sexual offenders inter-sectorial council; and an amendment to the Penal Code in November 2021 to provide a new definition of rape and to enhance penalties for sexual offences in Sections 141 and 142. Furthermore, the amount of funding that went into GBVF doubled during the Covid-19 pandemic period. There were also initiatives such as the GBVF hotline introduced during Covid-19 to ease the reporting system, to which women in CSOs attested.

On the other hand, members of CSOs argued that there has not been any considerable change in the fight against GBVF with the inclusion of women in parliament. Just as in South Africa, they did not think female MPs have done enough to address GBVF. The perception of impact between female MPs in Botswana and women in CSOs differ significantly. The first group feels that they have made an impact, but the latter disagrees. The same dilemma found in the case of South Africa applies here where efforts made by female MPs are not known to the public as citizens only see them as a unit of the collective, namely parliament. Secondly, women in CSOs explained that the lack of a critical mass of women in the parliament of Botswana is another reason for their lack of impact on GBVF issues as they are too few to make a considerable difference. Compared to South Africa that has 45% of women in its parliament, Botswana has just 11%, which confirms this challenge. However, similar to South Africa, in the period 2010–2022, there have been new legislations and policies passed to address GBVF, and therefore, it can be argued that female MPs in Botswana have made an impact on addressing GBVF.

As echoed by one of the participants, it is a matter of mutual inclusivity. It can be agreed that female MPs in both case studies have made impact on legislative and policy outcomes while also acknowledging that their efforts may not translate to a significant drop in the rate of GBVF. The lacuna between their efforts and a significant drop in the rate of GBVF is a function of collaborative and much more holistic interventions on GBVF. While legislations and policies are very important mechanisms through which GBVF can be addressed, their existence does not translate to an automatic reduction in the rate of GBVF. Therefore, gender quotas that ensures women participate in parliament have enabled the building of the needed critical mass of female MPs to be critical actors that go on to create awareness, support, advocate, influence, and lobby, thereby translating to several legislative and policy outcomes on GBVF in Botswana and South Africa. This aligns the critical mass and critical acts theses, showing that quotas allowed for sizeable number of women to participate in parliament. These women came together to be critical actors that represent women issues and specifically do something about GBVF. Due to their numbers and actions, they were able to influence the legislative process to ensure the substantive representation of women.

What alternative pathways are there to ensure the substantive political representation of women in African politics?

The expectation that women issues should only be addressed by female politicians places a burden on the latter to be the only representatives for women issues. Women issues must be seen as part of the broader needs of the people. Certain issues affect women uniquely as a group, such as childcare, sexual and reproductive health rights, and pregnancy, thus creating a vacuum that only female politicians can fill. The critical recommendation echoed by participants is the need for education either to improve the quality of women's political representation or to reduce the rate of GBVF. Participants suggested that women must be empowered so they can own their agency as equal members of the society. Transformation of society must happen by changing patriarchal attitudes that limit the participation of women in politics while also engendering the oppression of women. Obstacles that hinder women's political representation must be addressed while embracing quotas to complement such efforts. Government as an institution must foster political education among young girls and women to engage them in politics at an early age.

To reduce the rate of GBVF, participants stressed the need to reform the policing and justice system to enable women to easily report abuse cases and ensure that perpetrators of such violence are adequately dealt with. Participants suggested that there must be awareness raising on GBVF, which can start by fixing the education curriculum to educate society on the ills of GBVF. It is believed that if women are socio-economically empowered, they would not be dependent on their abusers, which is often the case. A community-based approach to GBVF is necessary where both men and women collaborate to better address the prevailing rate of GBVF. Patriarchal stereotypes regarding masculinity must be discarded to avert the perpetuation of violence on women. Government should introduce more programmes and resources to better consolidate existing efforts geared towards addressing GBVF.

Conclusion

The chapter was divided into two sections, and the first section was a presentation of themes according specific objectives to align the perspectives of the three participant groups on each theme. This enabled the research to synergise the sub-themes that emerged in each section while providing clarification on the difference and similarities in views. The themes used to present the findings allow the reader to systematically understand the data findings on how each theme relates to the corresponding research objective.

The second section was a discussion and analysis that answered the research questions with the data gathered from both the interview findings and the legislative outcomes. It employed the interpretative analysis of participants' perspectives on each theme to answer the research questions drawing from the book's objectives. The section showed there is a relationship between numbers and impact in Africa, although certain factors affect the nature of the relationship. It further noted that gender quotas are relevant beyond ensuring descriptive women's representation as they foster inclusion, representation, and equality of women in the selected case studies. The findings from Botswana and South Africa revealed that the increased number of women in parliament enabled them to influence the legislative process translating to policies and legislations on GBVF. An interesting observation made from this section is that the efforts of female MPs on legislation and polices on GBVF are often not known to the women they represent, which creates a disconnect between the impact they have made and how women perceive their impact. Several recommendations were made on how to improve the quality of women's political representation as well as reduce GBVF to provide alternative pathways to ensure the substantive representation of women. The discussion and analysis provided the needed clarity on how the data gathered responded to the research questions.

References

Childs, S., and M.L. Krook. 2009. Analysing women's substantive representation: From critical mass to critical actors. *Government and Opposition* 44 (2): 125–145.

Commission on Gender Equality Amendment Act. 2013. No. 17 of 2013.

Constitution of the Republic of South Africa. 1996. No. 108 of 1996.

Criminal and Related Matters Amendment Act. 2021. No. 12 of 2021.

Criminal Law (Sexual Offences and Related Matters) Amendment Act. 2012. No. 6 of 2012.

———. 2021. No. 13 of 2021.

Dahlerup, D. 2006a. *Women, quotas and politics.* London: Routledge.

———. 2006b. The story of the theory of critical mass. *Politics & Gender* 2 (4): 511–521.

Domestic Violence Amendment Act. 2021. No. 14 of 2021.

Kaur, R. 2020. *Homebody.* Missouri: Andrew McMeel Publishing.

Mansbridge, J. 2005. Quota problems: Combating the dangers of essentialism. *Politics & Gender* 4: 622–638.

National Strategic Plan for Gender Based Violence and Femicide. 2020. National Strategic Plan on gender-based violence & femicide: Human dignity and healing, safety, freedom & equality in our lifetime. https://www.justice.gov.za/vg/gbv/NSP-GBVF-FINAL-DOC-04-05.pdf

Offen, K. 1988. Defining feminism: A comparative historical approach. *Signs* 14 (1): 119–157.

Olaitan, Z.M. 2023. *Gender quotas and the substantive representation of women in African politics: Case studies of Botswana and South Africa.* Doctoral Thesis, University of Pretoria.

Penal Code (Amendment) Act. 2021. No. 42 of 2021.

Phillips, A. 1995. *The politics of presence.* Oxford: Oxford University Press.

Protection from Harassment Act. 2011. No. 17 of 2011.

Saferspaces. 2020. Gender-based violence in South Africa. https://www.saferspaces.org.za/understand/entry/gender-based-violence-in-south-africa

Sexual Offenders Registry Act. 2021. No. 7 of 2021.

United Nations. 1995. *Beijing declaration and platform for action.* https://www.un.org/womenwatch/daw/beijing/platform/

Williams, M. 2000. The uneasy alliance of group representation and deliberative democracy. In *Citizenship in diverse societies*, ed. W. Kymlicka and W. Norman, 124–153. Oxford: Oxford University Press.

CHAPTER 9

General Conclusion

Remember all the women who write for you. all the women like you,
with skin like yours. women who were once enslaved. women who were
once colonized. women who hold languages that when you try to speak
it, it tears your tongue wide open. remember all these women who were
singers, poets, priestesses, artists, healers, whose lives were declared
anonymous, whose paintings hang in foreign museums as "unknown",
whose lives declared unlived. remember them

—Ijeoma Umebinyuo (2016)

Two issues serve as the motivation for this book: (1) the need to understand whether the participation of women in politics benefits women and (2) the need to understand the relevance of gender quotas on the representation of women in African politics beyond numbers. The understanding of these issues would allow us to consolidate efforts to increase women's representation in politics and proffer pathways that foster the qualitative representation of women in Africa. The book established that gender quotas have been effective in ensuring the increased participation of women in politics, thereby fostering descriptive women's representation, particularly in South Africa. In Botswana, the use of specially elected MPs system has also created space for women to be included in parliament, but this is not significant enough. The book argues that the use of voluntary quotas by the governing party in South Africa, the ANC, largely

© The Editor(s) (if applicable) and The Author(s), under exclusive   213
license to Springer Nature Switzerland AG 2024
Z. M. Olaitan, *Women's Representation in African Politics*,
African Histories and Modernities,
https://doi.org/10.1007/978-3-031-76051-8_9

accounts for the increased presence of women in parliament. This increased presence was further solidified by other parties such as the EFF and the IFP, and although the official opposition party does not use quotas, it factors in gender representation in its party list. It further notes that the presence of women in Botswana and South Africa created ground for women to form a critical mass and impetus to act as critical actors that advocated for women's issues. Women's presence, which is a function of gender quotas impacted legislative and policy outcomes on GBVF in both case studies as female MPs were able to use their influence to advocate for the policies and legislation. This aligned the debate on critical mass and critical acts: The former argues that when women form a considerable number in parliament, they are able to better represent women issues; and the latter argues that numbers are not what is needed but rather the specific actions of certain women to speak and act for women. The findings from the research showed that not only did the women use their numbers to form a force, but they also used their position to initiate legislations and policies on GBVF. The book confirmed the thesis of the two theories employed that the presence of women in politics creates impact for women and that because of their lived experiences as women, female politicians are able to represent women issues. As established, women in the two case studies were able to use their presence to create awareness for GBVF, advocate for GBVF issues in parliament, demand better resources towards GBVF, and most importantly, influence policy making and pass new GBVF legislations. The existence of GBVF legislations and policies between 2010 and 2022 confirms this statement, demonstrating that there is indeed a relationship between numbers and impact, that women's political participation benefits women, and that gender quotas can ensure the substantive representation of women.

The book makes new contributions on two levels: firstly, on the in-depth, country-specific analysis of the relationship between numbers and impact in Africa; and secondly on expanding the relevance of gender quotas beyond ensuring descriptive women's representation. However, the findings made in the book do not conclude that GBVF has been significantly reduced because there are several contributing factors that fuel its prevalence. It was able to show that having women participate in parliament can lead to more policies and laws to address GBVF and that these women often supervise the implementations of these laws to ensure their effectiveness. Unfortunately, the problem of GBVF goes beyond laws and policies, as systemic, cultural and societal factors are also responsible.

Therefore, the impact of female MPs on the rate of GBVF is limited as their effort is not significant enough to uproot the system that perpetuates GBVF because they are also victims of this system. The book recommends that to ensure the effectiveness of the efforts of these female MPs, there must be a more holistic intervention to addressing GBVF. This raises calls for collaboration among all sectors of the society because socialisation starts in the family, and hence, GBVF must first be addressed there. Harmful patriarchal attitudes that perpetuate violence must be changed to allow for new attitudes that foster equality between men and women. Institutions such as the police and the courts must play their part to ensure victims are comfortable enough to report cases and get the justice they deserve. Political will on the part of the government to ensure the proper implementation of policies on GBVF is paramount to all these recommendations because laws are only as effective as their implementation, and laws need adequate resources to be effectively implemented. Lastly, it poses an important contribution to the discourse on gender quotas and women's political representation as it established that rather than seeing gender quotas as a means to numbers, it should be seen as a means to impact. The book also devised a new way to ensure substantive representation of women by arguing that rather than an 'either-or' situation between critical mass and critical acts, it should be a case of 'and'. The merging of critical mass and critical acts enables better result for protecting women's interests and quality of representation because it allows for the strength of numbers to be combined with the intentionality of actions to protect women as a collective group.

Recommendations

The book makes broad recommendations on improving women's political representation, drawing from responses from participants, and it proposes strategies for increasing women's numeric participation in politics and also reducing the rate of gender-based violence and femicide in Africa.

The recommendations align with the last research question that focused on alternative pathways for women's substantive representation in African politics. The responsibility of how best to protect and represent women issues is often placed on female politicians without recourse for the role the larger society plays in those problems. The underrepresentation of women in politics and the perpetuation of violence against women are both manifestations of harmful cultural and societal practices that can be traced to patriarchy. The notions that women are inferior to men, that women should be seen and not be heard, and that women are not meant to participate in politics all stem from the inferiority status attached to the female gender. Societal stereotypes that perpetuate the superiority of men create hegemonic or toxic masculinity, which views women as lesser and as objects that can be oppressed. Based on the recommendations discussed in Chap. 8, this section provides an overview of what needs to be done to reduce the prevalent rate of GBVF in Africa.

Gender-Based Violence and Femicide Education

The findings indicate that many perpetrators of GBVF do not understand that their actions constitute such. This lack of awareness is due to the normalisation of abuse against women in the form of normal marital relations. For instance, it is difficult to prove marital rape because of the entitlement of husbands to their wives' body even if consent is not given. The idea that 'I have paid her bride price, and therefore, I have the right to do whatever I want with her' is used to violate women's bodies. This male ego and entitlement often lead to men abusing their wives or inflicting violence on women. Education and awareness on what GBVF is is paramount to addressing the problem. This endeavour should start in schools, and the curriculum system must be reviewed to include education on GBVF and signs of GBVF. This education can also be done in men's forums in different communities, and NGO programmes can sensitise both men and women on it.

Resocialisation

At the root of GBVF lies patriarchy, gender stereotypes, and harmful societal practices, and, therefore, the resocialisation of society is necessary, and it should particularly focus on the male gender. Sociologist Erving Goffman (1961) defined resocialisation as a process of tearing down and rebuilding an individual's role and socially constructed sense of self. It is often a deliberate and intense social process because it revolves around the notion that if something can be learned, it can be unlearned. The resocialisation process of men and boys should focus on unlearning the negative traits of masculinity they have been taught while embracing positive masculinity which will introduce them to their new role as participants for positive change. This entails explaining the negatives of the present socialisation process that contributes to violence against women while re-orienting them on the new traits of masculinity that help them become participants for change.

Collaboration

Significantly reducing GBVF requires collaborative efforts among relevant stakeholders in the society. Female MPs should not be solely tasked with it as male MPs, men, and society at large all have a role to play. For instance, men have a critical role to play as active bystanders in taking action to respond to incidents of GBVF when they witness them. This active bystander approach is especially important in terms of engaging men on efforts to challenge the normalisation of violence against women in public spaces. Organisations such as Men Imbizo and Sonke Gender Justice work with men, and they must tailor their training and orientation to focus on how men can be collaborators towards addressing GBVF. It is necessary to engage with traditional institutions, family, and the community on the need to change the narrative on masculinity. Local chiefs, family units, and community organisations should be partnered with on their role as participants in ending violence against women and girls.

Strengthening Institutions

On the corrective side, the security and justice system must be well resourced and trained to deal with GBVF issues. Firstly, there should be a database of GBVF cases across the country wherein all reports of cases are fed. This will allow the country to keep track of GBVF and to have up-to-date statistics of the GBVF rate in the country. Police officers should be sensitised and trained how to treat GBVF survivors when they come to report, and rather than referring the victim back to the scene of the abuse, they should investigate the problem while contacting social workers and shelter homes to protect the victims. The courts must ensure perpetrators of GBVF are prosecuted and punished based on provision of what the law says, and they should not let culture and patriarchy determine rulings on cases. It is important for the law to protect the victims.

Women Empowerment

The dependence of women, their inability to own their agency, and the oppression of women are some of the factors that contribute to the continuity of GBVF. Women who are abused are scared of reporting their perpetrators because they are also the source of their economic survival. This necessitates organising economic empowerment programmes to engage women and enable them to be financially included. This can be in the form of support grants for those who have businesses, employment for those in need of jobs, or vocational training for those with skills in crafts and other areas. The ability to make a living without depending on a man will give women the ability to leave when they spot signs of GBVF, which is why education and awareness are important. They need to be sensitised to their status as equal beings in the society rather than objects or helpers in relation to men, which can further enable them to assert their rights.

FURTHER RESEARCH

An interrogation into the impact of gender quotas on substantive women's representation in Botswana and South Africa showed a positive relationship between numbers and impact. Additionally, the prioritisation of data from female MPs and women in CSOs enabled the book to explore new grounds on how to understand the numbers and impact dilemma. However, this cannot be generalised for all 54 countries in Africa as certain regional and country-specific factors might produce different results. Hence, I propose that to ensure a continent-wide understanding of this relationship, research should be done on other countries on the continent. More research on how gender quotas and the descriptive representation of women are important for substantive representation on a country basis should be done. The research should employ field data from these contexts to provide a deeper understanding of how factors that are unique to these contexts can impede the relationship between numbers and impact. There is also a need for more research that re-examine the relevance of quotas beyond numbers and impact to expand the scope of quotas. Secondly, an in-depth analysis is needed to understand the gap between efforts of female MPs on gender issues and awareness on the part of women in the society. This can explore how the uniformity of parliament as an institution affects such awareness since female MPs are just part of a whole and are therefore judged as such. The lack of awareness was a major observation of this book, and it was revealed that it impacted the perception of impact by women working in CSOs. This gap often creates contention concerning the effect of descriptive women's representation on substantive women's representation. A deeper study will provide new insight into why women in the society are often unaware of what female parliamentarians do to protect their interests.

References

Umebinyuo, J. 2016. *Questions for Ada*. California: CreateSpace Independent Publishing Platform (CPSIA).

Index[1]

[1] Note: Page numbers followed by 'n' refer to notes.

GPSR Compliance

The European Union's (EU) General Product Safety Regulation (GPSR) is a set of rules that requires consumer products to be safe and our obligations to ensure this.

If you have any concerns about our products, you can contact us on ProductSafety@springernature.com

In case Publisher is established outside the EU, the EU authorized representative is:

Springer Nature Customer Service Center GmbH
Europaplatz 3
69115 Heidelberg, Germany

The manufacturer's authorised representative in the EU is Springer
Nature Customer Service Centre GmbH, Europaplatz 3, 69115 Heidelberg,
Germany. If you have any concerns regarding our products, please
contact ProductSafety@springernature.com

Printed and bound by CPI Group (UK) Ltd, Croydon, CR0 4YY
28/05/2025
01885630-0001